THE INTERNATIONAL

SAKHAROV HEARING

THE INTERNATIONAL SAKHAROV HEARING

Edited by

MARTA HARASOWSKA and OREST OLHOVYCH

SMOLOSKYP PUBLISHERS

Baltimore ● **Toronto**

THE INTERNATIONAL
SAKHAROV HEARING

Published in 1977 by Smoloskyp Publishers,
a non-profit organization
P. O. Box 561
Ellicott City, Md. 21043, U.S.A.

Library of Congress Catalog Number: 77-020576

ISBN: 0-914834-11-8
       0-914834-12-6 (paperback)

Net royalties will be used in the interest of
political prisoners in the U.S.S.R.

Printed and bound in the United States of America

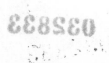

CONTENTS

ABBREVIATIONS

A.S.S.R.	Autonomous Soviet Socialist Republic
CC	Criminal Code
CC CPSU	Central Committee of the Communist Party of the Soviet Union
CC CPU	Central Committee of the Communist Party of the Ukrainian S.S.R.
CC Ukr.S.S.R.	Criminal Code of the Ukrainian S.S.R.
CPSU	Communist Party of the Soviet Union
CPU	Communist Party of the Ukrainian S.S.R.
KGB	Committee for State Security (*Komitet Gosudarstvennoy Bezopasnosti*)
Komsomol	Communist Youth League
R.S.F.S.R.	Russian Soviet Federative Socialist Republic
Ukr.S.S.R.	Ukrainian Soviet Socialist Republic

FOREWORD

The International Sakharov Hearing was held on October 17-19, 1975 in Copenhagen. The Hearing was sponsored by The Common Committee of East Exiles in Denmark and was financed by voluntary donations. The proceedings took place in Christiansborg, the Danish parliament building, and were chaired by Ib Thyregod, Barrister of the Danish Supreme Court.

The main objective of this Hearing was to examine recent violations of human rights in the U.S.S.R., especially those that occurred since Brezhnev's ascent to power. The witnesses, the Questioning Panel, and even the location were chosen so as to assure political impartiality. Denmark was selected because it is centrally located and is a politically neutral country. Denmark had already set a precedent for its neutrality when it served as the site of the debate over the role of the United States in the Vietnam war.

Coincidentally, the Hearing took place shortly after the sensational appearance of Solzhenitsyn's book, *Gulag Archipelago*, and during the very detailed press coverage of the Soviet government's hounding of Andrei Sakharov and his wife. These two events provided the momentum for the Hearing. Although the Final Act of the Helsinki Agreement had been signed only two months previously, it had not as yet generated the impact that it would during the first months of President Carter's administration.

Newspaper, radio and television coverage of the Hearing was extensive and headlines were made in Denmark as well as in other European countries. However, the Hearing was largely ignored in the United States, possibly because Secretary of State

Kissinger was still trying to expand his policy of detente. Probably the best criterion for assessing the significance of this Hearing was that the Soviet embassy in Copenhagen sponsored a counter-hearing to coincide with The International Sakharov Hearing and brought forth its usual witnesses.

The image of the Soviet Union, as described in the *Gulag Archipelago*, was confirmed and broadened by testimony during the Hearing. Even more important was the disclosure that violations of human rights are not just scattered instances occurring in isolated concentration camps that are relics of the Stalin era. The Hearing showed that abuse of human rights is widespread, systematic, sanctioned by the highest levels of authority, and that it is becoming increasingly sophisticated in methodology and in the official apparatus involved.

Most of all, as one reads testimony after testimony, one begins to sense that what is occurring in the U.S.S.R. is not just the growing pains of a peculiar political system that has as yet not adjusted to its social and economic environment. The Soviet Union appears to be another in a long list of totalitarian empires locked in the vicious circle of preserving itself at the cost of its multi-national citizenry.

— SMOLOSKYP PUBLISHERS

10

EDITOR'S NOTE

The testimonies in this book are translations from the original, unless the original was in English. Translations were prepared by the organizers of the Hearing and made available to the publishers. While most witnesses read from prepared texts, some spoke without text, which would explain the varying linguistic quality of individual testimonies.

Some of the testimonies are published here in slightly abridged form. Texts were edited only where it was necessary to achieve maximum clarity or to omit repetitious or extraneous testimony.

Although witnesses were queried at length on their testimony by a questioning panel, the questions and answers are not included in this book for reasons of space.

Biographical material, where available, has been added on dissidents mentioned in the testimonies, and on panelists and witnesses at the Sakharov Hearing.

ON THE EVE OF
THE INTERNATIONAL
SAKHAROV HEARING

The idea to hold an international tribunal dealing with violations of human rights in the Soviet Union was first suggested by a group of prominent Soviet dissidents, including Andrei Sakharov, on the day Alexander Solzhenitsyn was expelled from the U.S.S.R. in February 1974.

The idea, contained in an open appeal issued by the group of dissidents, was taken up and pursued by a group of East European exiles living in Denmark, the Common Committee of East Exiles.

The following are excerpts from a November 22, 1974 telephone conversation between the Committee and Andrei Sakharov:

A TELEPHONE CONVERSATION
WITH ANDREI SAKHAROV

Sakharov: "A hearing on human rights in the Soviet Union to take place in Copenhagen, near the center of Europe, is extremely important in order to obtain a true picture of the conditions in the Soviet Union. I welcome such a judicial hearing, and I am very grateful to the initiators of the hearing.

Today the sentence is pronounced in Ajkjenkan's case, and I appeal in this connection to the Danish political organizations for help in the defense of the accused Moroz, Plyushch, Dzhemilev, Abel, Hel, Lyubarsky, Makarenko, Ogurtsov—Soviet intellectuals, people who particularly need protection. They are in a very tragic situation.

I wish that the question of the right to free departure from and free return to the Soviet Union would be included in the discussion concerning these persecuted people. This is a right on which all other rights depend. Only by such a right to free departure and free return is it possible to remedy the violations of human rights that have happened.

Moreover, I ask that attention be drawn in particular to such a problem as the persecution of religious people in the Soviet Union. These persecutions have been heavily intensified, and a very great number of people have been arrested in the Baltic states. Many Baptists and Unitarians have been sentenced to prison."

Question: "What is in your opinion essential in connection with a hearing on human rights in the Soviet Union?"

15

Sakharov: "It is necessary to deal with the problem of free departure, and with the problems connected with the national minorities in the Baltic states, Ukraine, Armenia, Georgia, with the Crimean Tatars and Volga Germans. A third question is religious persecution, and it is important that the outside world be informed of the economic conditions of Soviet labor, where one man's pay never suffices for a family of four. Therefore the women always have to work, rendering the education of the children highly difficult, and creating enormous social problems. The number of working hours in order to earn one's living is several times greater in the Soviet Union than in any other European country. Also, things are not easy with regard to educational possibilities and medical treatment.

If it is possible during the hearing in Copenhagen to gather enough authoritative information on these problems, it will be of great importance, since in the outside world an enormous amount of false information is being circulated concerning the real economic conditions of the working people in our country, [or concerning] education, and housing problems. The worst housing problem in such cities as Moscow, Kiev, and other metropolitan areas has, of course, receded into the background, but in other places the problem is still very great when compared to the conditions [that exist] for the majority of workers in the West. I feel that such information will be very useful."

Question: "A personal question: Do you fear for your own personal security?"

Sakharov: "I only fear for my family. As for my own person, I am of the opinion that I no longer need to be afraid. I do not give any thought to these possibilities."

Question: "Will you have any possibility to take part in the human rights hearing in Copenhagen?"

Sakharov: "I do not think it will be possible. If an interest for my participation is expressed by the government or by various political organizations abroad, and if at the same time I am given reliable warrant for my return home after the hearing, I shall be delighted and flattered to participate. But I can do nothing for it myself."

ANDREI SAKHAROV:
MESSAGE TO THE SAKHAROV HEARING

A. Sakharov did not attend the Hearing because he feared Soviet authorities would deny him re-entry into the U.S.S.R. Instead, he transmitted a personal message which was read on the opening day of the Hearing.

I am grateful for the opportunity afforded me to address myself to this Hearing and for the fact that it has been named after me. I regard this as a recognition not only of my personal merits, but also as a recognition of all those in my country who strive for full publicity, for the realization of human rights, and especially of all those whose loss of freedom is the high price they pay for these endeavors. I am sure that the witnesses at this Hearing, on the basis of numerous documents and their personal experience, will be able to present a convincing picture of the way in which people are persecuted—both within and outside the process of law, as well as by imprisonment in psychiatric hospitals—for their convictions, national aspirations, and their wish to leave the country. I am sure that they will make known the harsh conditions in the places of imprisonment, which are impermissible in the world of today; and that they will tell about the continuing violation of the rights of the Crimean Tatars and of many other nationalities, and about the suppression of freedom of conscience and the persecution of people for their religious beliefs.

Among the documents which are important for this Hearing I should like to single out in particular the *Chronicle of Current Events,* a journal of information published in samizdat in the U.S.S.R. The problems I have mentioned are reflected in detail, and in my opinion objectively, in its pages. Of particular importance is a special issue of this journal which deals with the tragic and intolerable situation in the camps and prisons of our country. In this connection I draw the attention of the participants of the Hearing to the increase of repressive measures against political prisoners.

In the last few months alone, many political prisoners have been transferred to Vladimir Prison, among them Rode, Superfin, Antonyuk, Khnokh, and Torik. Gluzman is threatened with further juridical proceedings in the camp.

I believe that the main theme of the Hearing should be the demand for a general political amnesty in the U.S.S.R., as formulated in the recent statement of Larissa Bogoraz, Anatoli Marchenko, and others. A political amnesty would be a supremely important factor in changing the moral and political climate of our country and would provide decisive support for the relaxation of tensions, both internally and externally. I am convinced that for every person in the West, the demand for a general political amnesty, for guarantees of the rights of man and for freedom of expression in the U.S.S.R., is not only a matter of conscience, but is also the safeguard of his own and his children's future. Now, after the Helsinki Conference, such demands are particularly opportune.

I consider it important that the Hearing should speak up in defense of those prisoners of conscience in the U.S.S.R. known to it—such as Leonid Plyushch, whose mind is being destroyed in the Dnipropetrovsk special psychiatric hospital, and such as the heroic inmates of Vladimir prison and of the Perm and Mordovian camps.

One of them is Vasyl Romanyuk, a priest who has been again sentenced in a closed court to 10 years for religious activities and for a few words of sympathy for Valentyn Moroz. Romanyuk was first arrested in 1944, and his first 10-year sentence did not even have the flimsy pretext of the latest sentence. The first was meted out in connection with the death of his father from hunger and the murder of his young brother. In 1959 Romanyuk was rehabilitated, yet at the time of his second trial in 1972 he was declared to be an especially dangerous recidivist. Romanyuk has carried out a prolonged hunger strike in protest against the injustice meted out to him. His life is now in danger. I call on the participants of this Hearing to do everything in their power to save Romanyuk and to alleviate the lot of his destitute family. The fate of Father Romanyuk is a true reflection of the position of religious life in our country.

It is most important that the Hearing speak out in defense of Sergei Kovalev and Andrei Tverdokhlebov, [members] of the Soviet group of Amnesty International, who were arrested in 1974 and 1975 respectively and who are now awaiting trial. A case is being brought against them because of their long and open service to the cause of human rights and of publicizing the truth. One of the charges leveled against Sergei Kovalev is that he circulated Solzhenitsyn's *Gulag Archipelago*. This is apparently one of the major charges against him. Solzhenitsyn's great book is considered slanderous. Such an attitude is self-incriminating and I can only hope that one day there will be a change. Kovalev, a talented biologist and a man of great honesty and integrity, is threatened with 7 years' imprisonment and 5 years of exile. I call upon the participants of the Hearing to adopt special resolutions in support of Kovalev, of Tverdokhlebov, of Mustafa Dzhemilev, who is dying of malnutrition caused by his being many months on a hunger strike and who is under threat of a fourth sentence, and in support of Vladimir Osipov, who was recently tried for the second time and sentenced to 8 years' imprisonment.

Of special urgency are also the demands for immediate liberation of women imprisoned on political charges; the liberation of all those sentenced to 25-year terms prior to the new legislation; and the relaxation of the regime under which all prisoners serve their sentences, including the observation of labor safety regulations and the cessation of forced labor, improvement in nutrition and medical services, and the granting of permission for prisoners to receive parcels containing medicines and vitamins.

The political prisoners in Mordovia have authorized me to speak in their name at the Hearing. I cannot reveal the names of the prisoners in question, but consider it my duty to acquaint the world, to the best of my ability, with their wishes. I hope that this Hearing will be featured prominently in the Danish and the international press and will serve as a major milestone in stepping up the struggle for human rights in the U.S.S.R.

DECLARATION OF THE ORGANIZERS

OF THE

INTERNATIONAL SAKHAROV HEARING

We appeal to the Government of the U.S.S.R. to review the means hitherto used so mercilessly to choke any form of dissent from state policy.

No ideals and no ideology can justify the cost in life and the suffering that have been brought upon countless individuals in Soviet prisons and labor camps.

We are convinced that your aims can only be achieved if you permit free exchange of opinion and freedom to travel inside and outside your country, grant national minorities the right to foster their cultural traditions, and religious bodies the right to practice and propagate their faith.

We appeal to you to change course, to acknowledge the mistakes and crimes of the past, and to liberate and rehabilitate all prisoners of conscience in prisons, camps, and psychiatric institutions.

A refusal to do so will render impossible a genuine detente, based on the growth of mutual trust among states, and will perpetuate the hideous mockery of justice which the "adherence" of the Soviet government to the U.N. Declaration of Human Rights has hitherto signified.

LET OUR PEOPLE GO.

Make the world a better place for all mankind!

THE QUESTIONING PANEL

BJOL, ERLING—Denmark

Born on December 11, 1918. Since 1963 professor of Political Science at the University of Aarhus in Denmark. His publications include *Sult og Sol* (1961), on the Mezzogiorno problem in Italy; *La France Devant L'Europe* (1966), on the European policies of the French Fourth Republic; and *Verdenshistorien Siden 1945 I-III* (1972-73).

BOURDEAUX, MICHAEL—England

Born in 1934; brought up in Cornwall, England. Rev. Bourdeaux is Director of Keston College, which houses the Center for the Study of Religion and Communism. An authority on religion in communist countries, especially the U.S.S.R., his most noted publications include *Religious Ferment in Russia, Patriarch and Prophets,* and *Faith on Trial In Russia.*

GERSTENMAIER, CORNELIA—West Germany

Born in 1943. Editor from 1966 to 1969 of the journal *Ost Probleme.* One of the founding members of the Brussel's Committee for the Defense of Human Rights in the U.S.S.R.; chairperson of the Association for Human Rights. Her publications include: *Die Stimme der Stummen: Die demokratische Bewegung in der Sowjetunion* (1971) and *Vladimir Bukovsky—der unbequeme Zeuge* (1972).

IONESCO, EUGENE—France

French avant-garde dramatist, born in Romania in 1912. Author of numerous "comic dramas" and "tragic farces," most notably *Les Chaises* (1951), *Amedee, ou comment s'en debarrasser* (1953), *Tueur sans gages* (1957), and more recently *Macbett* (1972); also author of the novel *Le Solitaire* (1973) and several books for children. In 1971 Ionesco became a member of the Academie Francaise.

21

JANOUCH, FRANTISEK—Sweden

Czechoslovak physicist. Known for his activities in defense of human rights in Czechoslovakia and elsewhere. Emigrated from Czechoslovakia, resides in Stockholm, Sweden.

LIE, HAAKON—Norway

Born on September 22, 1905. Secretary general of the Workers' Education Association from 1932-1940. Secretary general of the Norwegian Labor Party from 1945-1969. Served as the secretary general of the European Movement in Norway in 1973.

SCHAKOVSKAYA, ZINAIDA—France

Born in Moscow in 1906. Emigrated from Russia in 1919. Writer and journalist; editor-in-chief of the Russian weekly *Russkaya Mysl*, published in Paris. Author of 18 books. Twice named Laureat of the French Academy for her works on Russian history.

SHTROMAS, A.—England

Born in 1931 in Lithuania. Emigrated from the U.S.S.R. in 1973. Senior Research Fellow in Peace Studies at the University of Bradford in England since 1974; expert on Soviet law; author of four books on comparative law and numerous articles on political history, criminal law, criminal procedure, forensic science and legal cybernetics.

SPARRE, VICTOR—Norway

Born in 1919. Norwegian artist; activist in the Norwegian Solidarity Committee for Intellectual Freedom. Author of the book *The Stones Will Shout*, a work about art and freedom.

STYPULKOWSKI, ZBIGNIEW—England

Born in 1904. Member of the Polish Parliament from 1930 to 1935; headed the Polish National Armed Forces during WWII. One of the leading officials of Free Poland in Exile. Author of the book *Invitation to Moscow*, an analysis of the techniques of brainwashing.

SWIANIEWICZ, S.—England

Born in 1899. Professor emeritus at St. Mary's University in Halifax, Canada. Former prisoner of war in the Soviet Union. Economist and one of the foremost Polish experts on the Soviet Union. His publications include: *Forced Labour and Economic Development: An Enquiry into the Experience of Soviet Industrialization.*

WIESENTHAL, SIMON—Austria

Born in 1908. Head of the Jewish Center of Documentation and chairman of the Association of Jews Persecuted by the Nazi Regime. Author of several books, including *KZ Matthausen* and*Head-Mufti Head Agent of the Axis*. His awards include the Diploma of Honor of the League of the United Nations.

23

Clockwise from upper left: Erling Bjol, Michael Bourdeaux, Cornelia Gerstenmaier, Haakon Lie, Zinaida Schakovskaya, A. Shtromas, Victor Sparre, Zbigniew Stypulkowski, S. Swianiewicz, Simon Wiesenthal.
In the center: Andrei Sakharov.

BRIEF COMMENT ON SOVIET LAW

According to the Soviet Constitution, any legislation comes into force only after being published in the official press. Apart from these laws, there exists an entire system of regulations not intended for publication. However, in the practical application of penal jurisdiction and in practically all spheres regulating Soviet society, these regulations, which because they are unpublished do not have legal force, enjoy priority over the official legislation.

Let's take the following example: According to the Soviet Constitution, the citizens have the right to freedom of conscience and religion. According to unpublished instructions, however, a number of religious denominations are prohibited. In the practice of penal law-proceedings, to belong to such a denomination constitutes one of the "actions" listed in Art. 142 of the Penal Code of the R.S.F.S.R. (and in the analogous articles of the penal codes of the other Union republics).

This means that these people are being arbitrarily accused of violating the law on the separation of church and state. The same article is applied also in other cases, *e.g.* in the case of A. Levitin-Krasnov in May 1971. In this latter case, the fact that the defendant had been writing articles was evaluated as an activity falling under Art. 142 of the Penal Code of the R.S.F.S.R.

This extended interpretation of the articles of the penal code is a rather widespread practice. It is obviously not by chance that *the Scientific-Practical Commentary to the Penal Code of*

25

the Ukrainian S.S.R., acknowledged as official commentary for lawyers, defines "anti-Soviet literature" as follows:

"In the sense of Art. 66 of the Penal Code of the Ukrainian S.S.R. [anti-Soviet agitation and propaganda; A. G.], by literature of anti-Soviet content is understood brochures, leaflets, periodicals, and likewise *paintings, graphic works and sculptures* . . . [emphasis added—A.G.]

On the request of the Hearing's witnesses:

ANDREI GRIGORENKO

CHAPTER I

*Political Oppression and
the Persecution of Dissidents*

ANATOLI LEVITIN-KRASNOV

"... The U.S.S.R. is a typical police state."

LEVITIN, Anatoli (pen name KRASNOV)

Born September 21, 1915 in Baku (the Caucasus) into the family of a justice of peace. Graduated from the A. I. Herzen Pedagogical Institute in Leningrad, and was later employed as a lecturer at the city's Theatrical Institute. Schoolteacher by profession.

Deeply religious from childhood, Levitin took an active part in church life. In 1943, after being evacuated to Simbirsk, he became a deacon and secretary of the revivalist movement in the Russian Orthodox Church. Arrested in June 1949 as an "anti-Soviet" clergyman and sentenced to 10 years' imprisonment. Following his release and rehabilitation in 1956, Levitin became a contributor to the "Journal of the Moscow Patriarchate." During the anti-religious campaign of 1958 Levitin, under the pen name "Krasnov," turned to "unofficial" writing, thus founding the religious samizdat.

In 1967 Levitin became an active participant in the Russian democratic movement, and in May 1969 he joined the Initiative Group in defense of human rights. These activities were temporarily interrupted when in September 1969 Levitin was again arrested and subsequently imprisoned for 11 months.

On May 8, 1971 Levitin was arrested for a third time and sentenced, according to Article 190—"for calumny of the Soviet socio-political system"—to 3 years imprisonment, with 11 months reduction because of his pre-trial detainment. Released after completion of sentence in June 1973. Threatened with new arrest, Levitin emigrated from the U.S.S.R. in September 1974.

Levitin-Krasnov is a prolific religious writer. He is the author of the three-volume "History of the Revival Movement in the Russian Orthodox Church" and of numerous articles on religious history and apologetics.

THE POLICE STATE

The following account represents the second part of Levitin-Krasnov's testimony. The first part, dealing with religious oppression, is given on page 143 to 150.

. . . The U.S.S.R. is a typical police state. Every person lives as if in an aquarium, under vigilant surveillance by the authorities. The focus of attention is centered on a category of people that has been designated as follows: "Being under KGB surveillance." All correspondence of such individuals is rigidly checked. All their telephone conversations are monitored. And when it comes to persons the KGB is especially interested in, there's a device which can record domestic conversations.

In 1952, Marshal Vorozheykin's wife found herself in a prison camp in Kargopol. At the time of her court investigation she had been charged on the basis of a conversation she had had with her husband while both were lying in bed together.

In 1960, Metropolitan Nikolai Yarushevich was confronted in the Council for Religious Affairs with a word-for-word playback of a private conversation he had had with one of his co-workers. When the bewildered Metropolitan asked how it was known what he had said, he was answered: "You're living in the 20th century."

Shortly before my departure, Major Shilkin, a KGB representative with whom I was having a discussion, quoted to me verbatim a sentence from a phone conversation I had had some days before.

31

A listening device was also placed in my apartment on 7 Zhukovsky St., Moscow. At one time the device malfunctioned and for one hour a din was heard throughout the flat.

The KGB, however, only deals with citizens who are politically unreliable. For all the others there's the militia which embraces the whole country like an octopus. The militia's staff has been increased considerably in recent times. Each militia department has a so-called "prophylactic division" whose job it is to keep a close eye on persons who have returned from prison. Each residential quarter has its own militia base whose function is to spy on people living in that quarter. The militia is everywhere except where it should be. You won't see a militiaman in dark back alleys that are controlled by hooligans and robbers, and you would appeal in vain to a militiaman for protection against a bandit. When there's a murder committed somewhere, the militia's investigation department hastens to declare it a suicide or an accident.

The so-called propiska[1] plays a special role in the life of a Soviet person.

Let's assume you live in Pushkino (15 km from Moscow) and you want to move to Moscow. This is as impossible as going to America: You have a propiska for the province, but not for Moscow. It's even more difficult to move to the regions of Moscow, Leningrad, Kiev or Odessa from other (adjacent) regions. All these regions are off-limits. It is incredibly difficult to move even from one town to another, for instance from Kuybishev to Saratov. An endless questioning begins: Why are you moving, for what reason, do you have relatives in that town, do you have a place to live, etc.? And if you don't give the necessary information, you don't get a propiska.

For a person who lives in the country, in a kolkhoz,[2] it's almost impossible to get a propiska. Even in the days of serfdom there were no such forms of binding a person to the soil.

True, these statutory provisions can nevertheless be circumvented (by fictitious marriages, by entering the militia or the fire brigade, and sometimes by lulling the vigilance of the custodians of order with the help of not quite legal means); however, to paraphrase Beaumarchais, one can say that in order to obtain a propiska, ordinary people have to spend as much effort, talent, and ingenuity as would be sufficient to govern five Spains.

32

Things are equally absurd where work is concerned. Pursuant to the Act relating to "idlers," passed in the time of Khrushchev and then somewhat modified, every citizen who in the course of a month does not work is subject to compulsory provision of employment. If he leaves this employment before one year is out, his case will automatically be submitted to the public prosecutor, and the "idler" will be sentenced to 2-3 years' imprisonment in a camp.

This system makes it largely possible to deal with people with noncomformist views. I myself have experienced this more than once. When in 1959 I was deprived of the opportunity to work in my special field as a teacher, I was unable to find work thereafter because, in order to find employment, one has to produce a work-book. My work-book, however, aroused general perplexity. Why does a highly qualified teacher suddenly look for work as a librarian, postman, or watchman? Potential employers did not hire me so as to avoid getting in trouble themselves. Meanwhile the militia bombarded me with demands that I settle my working status, giving me a grace period of 2-3 weeks. I found a way out of my predicament by making use of my connections in ecclesiastical circles. I tried to keep busy, sometimes working as a sexton, sometimes as stoker, and later I was forced to work as a floor-polisher at the Restaurant No. 2 in Moscow's Bauman district.

But not everybody had the same luck as I. Valentin Sergeyevich Prozorov, a history teacher from Astrakhan (Tatishchev St. 85), was dismissed from work in 1959—the same year I was fired—because of his religious convictions. Because Prozorov was not able to find work, he was deported to the Krasnoyarsk territory, where he was forced to do hard physical work. He exerted himself beyond his strength and suffered a paralytic stroke. He now lives with his sister, has lost his power of speech, and receives a humiliating "pension"—30 rubles a month. (The cheapest suit costs 60-70 rubles.)

As regards the common working people who have had no run-ins with the authorities, their lot is equally a hard one. The state's trade unions are just a fiction; nobody takes them seriously. An administration's mere wish to get rid of a worker is sufficient to have him dismissed on any pretext: the staff is being cut down, labor discipline was lax, etc. The trade unions almost always agree with the administration. But even if the trade unionists

33

were to take sides with the dismissed, the administration would not be too worried; an appeal could always be taken to court, and the court as a rule sides with the administration.

* * *

Enough has already been written on the situation of political prisoners. I can scarcely say anything new here. What I would like to do, however, is to describe the situation of those who were convicted pursuant to the so-called articles of "everyday life." In this connection I would like to point out that such "offenses" exist only in the U.S.S.R. and nowhere else in the world.

A female resident of the town of Armavir, visiting Rostov-on-Don, bought some children's bodices there because they were unavailable in Armavir. When she returned home, she sold the bodices to a neighboring woman at a price somewhat higher than that set by the state. Result: she was sentenced to 5 years' imprisonment for "speculation." Other examples:

You've exchanged apartments and taken a small additional payment because your flat was in a better district. Result: 5 or 10 years in prison for housing speculation.

You've quarreled with your wife. You've shouted at her. She, in a fit of anger, complained to the local police officer. Result: 5 years for "hooliganism," even though you and your wife were reconciled the very next day.

I know of a case where a mother, in order to scare her impudent fellow of a son who had sold her galoshes, denounced him to the court. The court sentenced the 15-year-old boy to 5 years' imprisonment. The mother fainted on the spot.

Of course there are also the downright criminal. But irrespective of the convicts' guilt, they are detained under conditions reminiscent of the darkest times of the Middle Ages.

* * *

Presently there are four prisons in Moscow: The Lefortovo Prison (for political prisoners); the Butirky Prison; a prison on Matrosskaya Tishina St. and the deportation prison, Krasnaya Presnya. Since in the last 6 years I found myself in all four prisons, I am in a position to give my opinion on what goes on in them.

The most tolerable prison, as far as living conditions are concerned, is the Lefortovo Prison, which is under KGB authority. Each cell there houses no more than two or three prisoners. Sani-

tary facilities are good, the food is more or less decent. The Butirky Prison is overcrowded: 70-80 prisoners to each cell. A new
arrival is often forced to sleep on the floor until a berth becomes
free. The dimensions of the building bring some reprieve, however. Erected during the reign of Catherine II, the building has
roomy, lofty cells, and so the air is not particularly stuffy. On the
other hand, the prison on Matrosskaya Tishina St. is regular hell.
Some 20-30 prisoners are packed into each of the tiny cells. At
times a prisoner has a mere 2 square meters to himself. The air is
incredibly stuffy. People are held under such conditions up to
5-6 months.

The cells swarm with vermin: fleas, bugs, sometimes also lice.
It's impossible to summon a doctor. He visits the cells only once
in the course of a 2-3 week period. Only those who are seriously
ill receive real medical help. Prison officials are incredibly rude;
time and again they repeat the same obscenities. For any trans-
gression of regulations, the guilty party is dragged out into the
hallway and mercilessly beaten. An atmosphere of terror perme-
ates the cells: Thieves with sadistic dispositions play the masters
and beat prisoners without mercy. The custom of the so-called
propiska deserves particular mention: Every newcomer (up to
age 40; older people are spared) gets "20 kotsov," that is, 20
kicks. The administration knows of all that is going on, but not
only does it not prevent it, it even encourages it. The prison
warden, Major Ivanov, distinguishes himself by his unusual rude-
ness.

In the Krasnaya Presnya prison, matters stand somewhat better;
Prison officials there are more cultured and do not permit themselves to be overly rude. Sanitary conditions, however, are not
in the least better. An infinite number of people are packed into
the tiny cells. The prison presents a more than usually dreadful
picture in the summer months. Half-naked people, steeped in
stinking perspiration, their eyes stupefied, find themselves in a
semiconscious state. The smoke of makhorka[3] poisons the atmosphere even more. It is literally a hell.

Much the same conditions exist in the prison at Rostov-on-Don
and in Armavir, where I spent 10 months in 1969-1970. In the
summer months people there lose consciousness regularly. They
are then dragged out into the corridors, splashed with cold water,
and crammed back into their cell.

The town of Sochi has no prison. Persons whose cases are being investigated are kept in the prison of Armavir; periodically, however, they are taken to Sochi for interrogation, where the militia keeps them in the Kamera Predvaritelnogo Zaklyucheniya (KPZ).[4] Here, in cells that measure 18-19 square meters, as many as 15 prisoners are often placed. It is impossible for them to stretch out their legs. They cannot get fresh air. A filthy toilet bucket stands in the corner. People spend 3-4 weeks under such conditions. The militiamen shamelessly rob the prisoners. When prisoners (those who have relatives in Sochi) receive parcels, the militiamen appropriate half. And all this takes place in a fashionable health resort, crowded with foreigners.

❋ ❋ ❋

In conclusion I would like to touch upon conditions in corrective labor camps and psychiatric hospitals for prisoners, such as I have had the opportunity to experience in recent times.

I was kept in a camp for criminals from 1971 to 1973. I was sentenced under Article 190.1—slander of the Soviet socio-political system . . . The camp was located in the town of Sychevka, Smolensk district, and I can talk in detail about this camp (I was released on June 8, 1973).

All prisoners work 8 hours, practically without any days off, since a day off is granted only once every 3-4 weeks. I was in a group whose job it was to assemble wooden boxes. At any time of the year (the climate is rigorous in the winter season—about 40 degrees below zero when the wind blows) the work is performed inside an unheated shed made of planks. Because of the fire hazard it is categorically forbidden to kindle a camp fire. It is also forbidden to visit a heated shop in order to warm oneself.

In the morning we ate porridge (5-6 spoons). For dinner, a soup of dried potatoes, sometimes cabbage soup. As a second course—again porridge or potatoes. In the evening, porridge (5-6 spoons). For healthy young fellows occupied with manual work in the open air this is absolutely a starvation diet.

Among the camp officers there are decent people who treat the prisoners with humanity (such as Major Petrov and 1st Lieutenant Ivan Ivanovich—a teacher by profession, whose surname I unfortunately do not remember). I am glad to speak well of them. They are, however, practically powerless. The tone is set by the head of the regime, Major Mikshakov, a sadist and a rude fellow. He personally beats the prisoners mercilessly when making his inspection rounds. What's more, he actually uses torture, making use of handcuffs as instruments of torture. The handcuffs are put on the hands and then tightened to such an extent that the prisoner feels an inconceivable pain. The prisoner is left like this for about an hour. Mikshakov used these measures particularly often in the summer of 1972 when a new stone fence around the camp was being built and there was a rush to get the job completed.

Mikshakov used this method as "encouragement." He reminded us of this treatment frequently, just when the prisoners were falling into formation. His usual phrase was: "I will put the handcuffs on you; and when I turn my back on you—then you will weep a little!"

The wardens endeavored to emulate their superior. But I must say that Mikshakov is still not the worst of the Gulag staff. He possesses one good quality: he is no coward and no formalist. He does not like people to have their lives spoiled, and he usually gives prisoners good testimonials when they leave the camp. Other prison officers (in order to play it safe) give people bad testimonials, with the result that when the prisoners leave camp they become subject to special surveillance by the militia.

There are no real medical services in the camp. There is an infirmary with a closet and two cots. The number of prisoners in the camp fluctuates between 700 and 1300. The head physician, Vasili Ivanovich Yermakov, is a rough, absolutely ignorant man —he cynically declares that he does not want to waste valuable medicines on offenders. He virtually does not give sick persons any help.

On August 28, 1972, I stepped on a rusty nail that was protruding from a log. The nail penetrated the hemp sole of my camp boot and pierced my foot deeply. I asked to be inoculated against tetanus. Yermakov refused to do so, saying this was the nurse's business. The nurse came only 2 days later and inoculated me, when the inoculation was practically already senseless. I must point out the custom of placing into the same cells criminals and persons who were convicted pursuant to Article 190.1 (political prisoners, most of them intellectuals). I myself did not at all suffer from this and cannot complain of having been treated badly by my fellow prisoners. On the contrary, they treated me with an affection I did not deserve.

But it is not always like that. For instance, a licentiate of mathematical sciences, Burmistrovich (a member of the democratic movement) was subjected during his confinement in camp to malicious humiliation and even beatings by criminals out of anti-Semitism. Similar things also happened on many other occasions.

Adjacent to the camp in Sychevka is a psychiatric hospital for prisoners. I have not been there myself, but the conditions in that hosiptal were well known to me because about 200 of our lads were working there as hospital attendants, and not only did they tell me in detail about the system there, but they also often brought me letters from patients-prisoners and delivered my letters to them.

The "hospital" is located on the premises of a former prison that was built during the reign of Catherine II. It's tale-telling that during the German occupation (1942-1944) the building was also used as a prison. The "hospital" has 14 wards, housing about 1500 patients who come here from various prisons and camps. The most dreadful wards are those for patients with indefinite terms, wards 7 and 14, which house mainly persons who were sent there because of their religious and political convictions. Yuri Byelov, a young writer, has been kept there for 3 years now. He was closely associated with democratic circles and his stories have been published in *Grani*.[5] He was transferred there in May 1972 from Vladimir Prison.

Some 12-15 patients are housed in each section of wards 7 and 14. There's only one pair of slippers at the disposal of all 15 patients. Patients are forced to stay in bed for days on end. They do not receive any reading material. No radios are provided. Going to the lavatory poses quite a problem because patients have to be accompanied by one of the attendants, and the attendants are too "occupied." For hours the patients beseech them to take them out and let them "put themselves in order," but for an answer they often get their faces slapped. Thrashing of patients is very common because criminals with sadistic dispositions are selected as attendants. Let me repeat for you the remarks of three attendants:

Said a fellow of 24 with expressionless eyes: "It's good to work in the hospital. There's always somebody to smash on the snout."

"Why so, smash?"

"Not for anything special, it's so boring. You're standing all day in the corridor. Then you see a fool (that is what the attendants usually call the patients) coming along—give him a box on the ear."

Another attendant, a healthy man of 30 with an athletic appearance: "My hands are hurting today. I thrashed a fool."

A 40-year-old attendant, Ivan Petrovich, who now lives in Moscow: "The physician came and said: 'The floor is dirty.' At once I gave the first fool who came along a box on the ear: 'Wash the floor'."

He also said: "The fools ask for a cigarette. You light it for them—then, to make things even, 20 flicks on the nose or 20 hot ones with the belt (belt-buckle)." I heard about this procedure from at least 10 persons.

All this is well known to the administration and the physicians, but they do absolutely nothing about it. On the contrary, they display even more cruelty themselves. For even the slightest disobedience, patients are tied to their cots for as long as 24 hours. This is called to "keep on leash." In order to repress them, patients are often injected with drugs which torment them for hours on end.

In November 1971, a mentally deranged person managed to escape from the hospital during the night. When he was recaptured and brought back to the hospital, he was mercilessly beaten by Lamich, the head physician, and some three dozen attendants. After this beating, the escapee was severely and permanently crippled.

It is an open secret that completely healthy people are being confined in this hospital. Even the representative of the operative department of the MVD, Leontovich, makes no secret of this. Said he to Yuri Byelov: "We do not treat you for a disease, but for convictions. And I am your physician. As long as you do not renounce your past you will not get out of here."

* * *

The picture would be incomplete if I did not also mention the transfer of prisoners. Transport from one camp to another is the greatest torment. Thirty to forty prisoners are crammed into each carriage compartment. People who are exhausted with thirst get nothing to drink. And when at last the guards have "pity" on them, they let five persons have water from one mug, without taking into consideration that among the offenders (criminals) there are many syphilitics. Upon arrival, the prisoners are jostled into a "voronok," an armored lorry in which the prisoners are squeezed together and are not able to move. In Sochi and Armavir, prisoners are subjected to a humiliating procedure: after leaving the carriage, while they are waiting for the "voronok," all prisoners are compelled to kneel or squat to prevent anyone from escaping.

These are facts which I witnessed in person. Not only have I avoided any exaggeration, but I have also left out many things because of lack of space and out of a sense of decency, not wishing to offend your feelings.

* * *

As to the material conditions of citizens in the U.S.S.R., some progress has been made lately. The housing situation has improved considerably, shops have more to offer and, at last, the lot of the collective farmers has improved markedly. Nevertheless, conditions are still very difficult for the average man.

There has not been a single price reduction since 1953. Prices remain at incredibly high levels, and not only are wages not being increased, but they are showing a tendency to decrease in value in relation to the higher productivity.

The average wage of a qualified worker amounts to 200 rubles. Let us take an ordinary working family: husband, wife, two children. One needs a minimum of seven rubles a day to feed such a family. This adds up to 210 rubles a month. Additional expenditures are needed for housing and municipal services (although in the U.S.S.R. they amount to considerably less than in Western Europe), which amount to 10 rubles: 5 rubles for housing, 3 for electricity, 2 for transportation. Clothes are expensive. Ten rubles a month are needed for children's clothes. Parents, even if they live very modestly, must spend an average of 20 rubles a month on themselves to look at least halfway respectable. To receive guests, entertain them, drinks—20 more rubles. All this time we are operating with minimum figures. Thus the subsistence level, given the most modest living standard, stands at 300 rubles. As a consequence the wife must also look for a job. Children are left alone, without supervision. What's more, that kind of a budget does not permit one to have more than two children. A normal sex life is therefore impossible. There's constant trouble with abortions, and nerves are strained for various reasons.

To be sure, there's money after all; nobody dies of hunger, but one has to work to the point of exhaustion.

Even worse is the lot of the working intelligentsia. Teachers and physicians are in the most precarious situation. A workman always has a way out of his predicament. He can improve his norms through uninterrupted input. He can earn money by working on the side; for example, he can repair someone's summerhouse or chop wood. Teachers and physicians, on the other hand, work at standard wages, and their work is so enervating and exhausting that they do not have energy left for anything else. The standard wage for secondary school teachers and for physicians (one feels ashamed to say it) comes to 100-120 rubles.

But there are people even worse off: Elementary school teachers (standard wage: 80-90 rubles), doctor's assistants, nurses, labworkers (60-70 rubles).

One is perfectly justified to call these people the intellectual proletariat and to admire their heroic deeds. They educate to the best of their abilities the ignorant, almost illiterate masses, and treat sick people perhaps no worse than well-paid foreign physicians do.

I have endeavored to be as objective as possible. I have not stated one single thing which I have doubted. I do not draw any conclusions and do not pronounce any judgment.

That is not the business of a witness. That is the business of the court. I hope that the court will pass a just and impartial sentence.

---

1) Propiska—a residence permit that must be obtained from the militia.
2) Kolkhoz—a collective farm.
3) Makhorka—a very low grade of tobacco.
4) KPZ—ward for pre-trial detention.
5) *Grani—A Journal of Literature, Art, Social Sciences and Social Political Thought* published by a Russian emigre group in Frankfurt, West Germany.

AVRAHAM SHIFRIN

" . . . almost every industry in the Soviet Union is founded on prison labor . . . "

SHIFRIN, *Avraham*

Born 1923 in Minsk, Byelorussian S.S.R. Spent childhood in Moscow.

In 1941, mobilized into the Soviet Army in which he served until 1945. Twice wounded on the front and decorated. After the war, finished the Moscow Juridical Institute and worked as senior legal counsel in the Soviet Ministry of Armaments.

Arrested in Moscow in June 1953 on charges of "Israeli-American espionage." Sentenced by the war tribunal of the Moscow garrison to death by firing squad. Sentence commuted to 25 years in labor camps, 5 years in exile and 5 years' deprivation of rights. Of the 25 years, Shifrin served 10 years and spent 4 years in exile.

Emigrated to Israel in 1970, where he remains active in the defense of political prisoners in the U.S.S.R. Heads an information center in Israel, which collects material on present conditions in Soviet labor camps for political prisoners. Author of the book *Fourth Dimension*, which depicts life in Soviet prison camps.

44

PRISON LABOR:
THE BACKBONE OF
SOVIET INDUSTRY

In order to clarify why I shall be speaking not only of my personal experiences but also of the experiences of my friends, I should like to commence by giving a brief outline of the sources for my testimony.

From 1945 to 1953, I held several posts within the framework of Soviet jurisprudence. My legal training enabled me to assess violations of both Soviet law and the Universal Declaration of Human Rights with the eye of a specialist, both in my own case and in the case of others.

In 1953, I was arrested by the KGB in Moscow, and subsequently sentenced to death. This sentence was later commuted to 25 years of special regime labor camps, 5 years of exile and 5 years of deprivation of rights. However, I was born under a lucky star (my being still alive and present here today is sufficient evidence of this!), and in fact served only 10 years of my sentence in camps and prisons, with 4 years in exile. This may not seem much by comparison with the 25-year sentences served out fully by some of my friends, but it was long enough for me to become thoroughly familiar with Soviet penal institutions.

From 1953 until 1957, I was held as a political prisoner (even though such a "status" does not exist officially in the U.S.S.R.) in 9 prisons, 18 camps for political prisoners (strict and special regimes), in 2 special type prisons, and also in many BURs (barracks with stricter regime) and ShIZOs (punitory solitary confinement cells). Apart from this, I was exiled to Kazakhstan.

After being released from camp, I made two lengthy trips—one to Siberia, and one through the Asiatic republics, the Caucasus and Ukraine. My aim was to locate prisons and camps I knew of only by hearsay, and also to re-establish contact with friends who had remained, after their release, in areas to which they had originally come as prisoners.

Although I have been in Israel since 1970, I still maintain contacts with friends from my labor camp days—friends who are still in the U.S.S.R., and even those who are to this day incarcerated in prisons and camps. . . .

In 1975, a group of former political prisoners from Soviet camps organized a small centre in Israel to collect information from new immigrants recently released from Soviet camps concerning conditions of confinement, questioning methods, and trial procedures in the Soviet Union today.

I should like to commence with my personal testimony. My first encounter with the relentless Soviet system of crushing the individual occurred when I was 14 years old. My father was arrested, and my mother, sister and I automatically became the family of one of the "enemies of the people." Twenty years later, my father was posthumously rehabilitated. He was an ordinary engineer, engaged in factory construction. He was still in camp at the time when I, as the son of an "enemy of the people," was sent to the war front in a penal battalion which consisted of the sons of political prisoners. We were obviously sent off to be exterminated. The 500 of us were issued 100 rifles and advised to "obtain further arms from the enemy." But I survived, and returned home at the end of the war.

I was arrested on June 6, 1953, after Stalin's death. At this time I was working as a senior legal counsel in the Ministry of Strategic Industries of the U.S.S.R., which in those days was more accurately known as the Ministry of Armaments.

I was detained on a Moscow street and taken in a KGB car to the central prison on Dzerzhinsky Square, better known to the world as Lubyanka Prison.

I was served with no arrest warrant, but brutally searched and thrown into a cell. For the next month I was subjected to interrogation, with still no evidence of an arrest warrant and without being informed of the charges against me. During this entire period I was not permitted to contact my family (as far as they knew, I had simply "disappeared"), nor was I allowed to call in a lawyer: Soviet jurisprudence does not call for the presence of a lawyer during interrogation; he can be present only at the actual trial. As a rule, interrogation sessions were conducted during the night, but during the day I was given no chance to sleep in my cell, for permission to sleep was used as inducement for me to "confess" that I was an Israeli-American spy. One piece of "indisputable" evidence produced by the interrogator was that upon joining the Ministry of Armaments, I had concealed the fact that my father—Isaac Shifrin—had been arrested on a political charge (anti-Soviet agitation) in accordance with Article 58.10 of the Criminal Code of the R.S.F.S.R. Furthermore, I had concealed this fact both in the army and upon receiving my documents after discharge from military service.

All this was construed as proof that I had obtained a position of trust in order to engage in "activities hostile to the Soviet state."

It should be noted that at this time Soviet jurisprudence was still adhering to the absurd principle, laid down by the Prosecutor General of the U.S.S.R. Vishinsky, that the accused could be tried and sentenced on circumstantial evidence in the absence of direct proof.

At no time during my preliminary questioning was I formally charged with stealing or passing specific Soviet military secrets, either verbally or in documentary form, to a foreign power. But my interrogators insisted that I "knew secrets" and "had met with foreigners." This led them to the conclusion that I was a spy, for with a biography like mine it would be impossible for me not to turn over any secrets I might know to the enemy. Characteristically, this arose from one of the basic principles of Soviet criminal investigation and trial—"socialist consciousness." Soviet courts are obliged to be guided in their deliberations by "Bolshevist institution" and by the above mentioned "socialist consciousness," that is, to try the accused according to his attitude toward the Soviet state.

I was held in detention and periodically interrogated from June to December 1953. During this time, as well as being given no opportunity to sleep for a whole month, I spent 28 days and nights in a "standing cell," which is a cell constructed to keep the prisoner on his feet. Ankle deep in malodorous, stagnant water, I was naturally unable to stand all the time. After a while I had spells of unconsciousness when I would slump down as far as I could in that cramped space. Sometimes, consciousness would return fleetingly, only to be swamped out by blackness again.

My life was virtually saved by the arrests of Beria, Kabulov, Merkulov, Vladzimirsky and other KGB "brass," some of whom had been among my interrogators. After their fall, the prison authorities had me removed from the "standing cell," as all my prosecutors were now prisoners themselves. However, although this saved my life, it did not bring about my release, for new interrogators appeared to replace the old.

Some 35 to 40 days after my arrest I was finally served with a warrant, which had been back-dated and carried the signature and seal of the special deputy to the prosecutor-general of the U.S.S.R. for special affairs, *i.e.*, the only person in the prosecutor's office who had access to KGB files.

It is necessary to stress that according to Soviet legislation, the KGB is an "investigative agency," and preliminary interrogation of a prisoner must be carried out under the instruction and supervision of the prosecutor's-general office. In actual fact, this function is performed by an agent appointed by the KGB, and this "special deputy" seizes arrest warrants and protocols upon completion of preliminary interrogation. In this way, outward appearances are maintained, and the KGB is not inconvenienced.

In December 1953, I was brought before the military tribunal of the MVD in Moscow and, at the end of a closed hearing, was sentenced to death by firing squad.

The trial itself was a mere formality. My judges were obviously not interested in the case, and turned a deaf ear to my protestations that someone being tried for spying should at least be apprised of what secrets he delivered, or attempted to deliver, to a foreign power. The three officers of the internal MVD forces remained unmoved and obviously bored, and then the chairman of the hearing read out my sentence.

I believe one can safely say that by this time the death penalty had also become a formality. Neither I, nor many people who had been similarly sentenced, lodged any appeals for clemency, yet were informed—days, weeks or months later—that our sentences had been reviewed and commuted to 25 years' confine-

48

ment to penal institutions with subsequent exile and deprivation of civil rights.

I should also add that the death sentence at this time carried a rider concerning confiscation of the defendant's property. Thus the death sentence was a source of profit to the state in its role as executioner.

Conditions of confinement undergo a change after the trial. The prisoner is transferred from his solitary cell to a communal one, holding some 50-70 people. This was my first encounter with other political prisoners since my arrest. I shall describe the prisoners typical for this period later.

A common feature of all Soviet prisons is hunger. The ordinary rations are inadequate, and hunger is used as a tool for further punishment. "Transgressors" are placed in cold punitory cells, on even lower rations than usual—300 grams of bread and 2 cups of water every 24 hours. This form of punishment is also resorted to in the labor camps, with the added aggravation of forcing the starving prisoner to work during the day and spend his nights in the punitory cell.

Transportation of prisoners from prison to camp is rife with not just violations of human rights, but even of the most basic rights of any living being. As many as 25-30 persons, with all their belongings, are packed into "Black Marias" (in Russian, colloquially known as "voronki") built to hold a maximum of 10-11 people. The last in line are literally wedged in by the convoy staff onto the heads of those already in the van. It is quite common for those in the van, packed in and in total darkness, to lose consciousness from lack of space and air.

When the van pulls up by the special railway carriage into which the prisoners are to be transferred, things become even worse; from 22 to 25 prisoners are herded into compartments consisting of eight seats and four sleeping berths. They are literally made to sit on top of one another.

The journey to the camp takes weeks, and during this time the prisoners receive nothing but dry or stale bread and herring. There is no water, and visits to the toilet are permitted only twice in 24 hours.

It is difficult to give an adequate description of purely physical suffering. During transportation people begin to lose all vestiges of human dignity, reduced to begging indifferent guards to allow them to use the toilet. This, I repeat, is not just a violation of human rights, it is a violation of the basic rights of any living being.

For purposes of comparison, I should like to recall paragraph 12 of the Rules for Treatment of Prisoners[1] which were adopted by the United Nations on August 30, 1955, which stipulates that sanitary installations should be adequate to allow *all* prisoners to relieve their physical needs in a *proper* manner *whenever they wish*. Every time I see these words, I am inevitably reminded of the common latrines for use by 50-60 people, inhabited by grotesque, fat rats . . . but that was in the camps.

Upon arrival in camp, the prisoner must don special garb. For instance, a political prisoner sentenced to special regime has his number on the front of his shirt. In my time, the number was also on the back, on the cap, and on the right trouser leg at thigh-level.

Escorted by armed guards and their dogs, the prisoners are daily driven out to work. The working day is 10 hours, but is lengthened by some further 3 hours because of searches before and after work, and the time required to get to the work-site from camp and back. Labor laws do not extend to political prisoners. As there is enough material on violation of labor laws in the Soviet Union for a separate lecture, I am handing over to this Hearing a special report I compiled on this subject at the request of the president of the AFL-CIO, Mr. George Meany.

It was not until I found myself in camp that I fully realized what an agony it is to be deprived of correspondence and the hope of being able to see one's family. The KGB, drawing on its many years of experience, has brought about such a situation that, although the prisoner has certain rights on paper, in actual fact he can never avail himself of these rights.

For example, a prisoner may write one, sometimes even two letters a month. However, as orders specify that such mail must be to "close relatives," the censor may refuse to pass the letter on the grounds that the addressee is not a "close" enough connection. Any letter can also be confiscated because of its allegedly "unsuitable" contents.

The same rules apply to letters coming into the camp—very few of them reach the addressee. I have in my possession a letter from prisoner A.A., in which he writes in 1975 that six of his letters were confiscated. I also have experienced this, and former political prisoners among recent arrivals in the West testify that conditions are lately becoming even more stringent. I am dwelling on this problem at some length because I know from personal experience what it means to a prisoner to be deprived of even this tenuous contact with his dear ones.

Deprivation of the right to correspond, moreover, is not inherent in the prisoner's sentence, and is not based on any existing law: it is an instruction issued by the KGB and the MVD.

Another privilege of which prisoners are systematically deprived is the right to receive parcels containing food or other essential articles. One food parcel not exceeding 5 kilograms is allowed per annum, and can be received only by prisoners who have served at least half their sentence. This, at least, is the official version. In practice, any guard can deny a prisoner the right to receive his annual parcel for "disruption" of camp discipline. "Disruption of camp discipline" can mean many things, among them—unfulfillment of work quotas (and they are virtually unfulfillable), non-attendance at political study sessions (imagine how prisoners feel being forced to listen about the happiness and light pervading the Soviet Union), not removing one's cap at the approach of any member of the camp administration —all these, to name a few, are considered to be breaches of camp discipline.

Jews, whose religious law forbids them to uncover their heads, are thus systematically deprived of all rights, to the accompaniment of jibes: "We're only teaching you manners!"

I should like to stress that Soviet law contains no provisions for the torture of prisoners by hunger and by deprivation of parcels—these are the illegal maneuvers of the KGB and the MVD.

Much has been written about food in the camps, and other speakers will be discussing this subject in detail at this Hearing. Therefore I shall touch upon only one aspect of the problem— how it affects believers who, by their religious laws, cannot eat pork, are vegetarians, or (as in the case of Jews) are forbidden non-kosher foods.

Prisoners such as these were usually arrested for their religious beliefs in the first place, and therefore felt obliged to adhere to the rules their religion dictated about their food intake. The majority of them were indifferent to external conditions, and among them could be found Jews, Muslims, Buddhists, Hindus, Seventh Day Adventists and members of other Christian sects. Later I shall discuss the problem faced by Jews in this situation.

Another matter of paramount importance to the prisoner is the right to meet his relatives or close ones. This privilege is granted only if the prisoner has no recorded breaches of camp discipline. As a rule, the meeting lasts only a few hours, and is carried out in the presence of a guard. A meeting in a separate room without a guard is granted only as a special privilege or reward. After I had spent 8 years in labor camps, my mother was permitted to come and see me for 2 hours. Before she was permitted to see me, she, a free citizen, was subjected to a humiliating search accompanied by insulting references to her criminal son. I have just mentioned that a meeting could be granted as a "reward"; this is used by the administration as an inducement for prisoners to cooperate with the KGB. It is an astounding but irrefutable fact that there is a sort of internal police force composed of prisoners in the camps, known as "brigades of internal order." They are made up of prisoners whose spirit has broken due to systematic deprivation of food, correspondence, parcels and meetings with relatives.

As one of the telling examples of demagoguery and the humiliation of prisoners, I am handing the Hearing an internal camp newspaper. This paper is published by the KGB, but the articles it contains are written by political prisoners who have "come to see the error of their ways." An analysis of the contents shows that the authors of these articles are the weak, and often former collaborators with the Nazis.

For those who refuse to bend or break, however, there are plenty of forms of punishment set out in secret instructions, yet not to be found in the official legislation of the land of "victorious socialism." These methods are well known to the prisoners through personal experience. To name just several, there is the punitory solitary cell (ShIZO), the barrack with particularly strict regime (BUR), and the prison regime (closed prison). Do not be misled by the name of the latter into thinking that there are any other kinds of prisons in the U.S.S.R., such as the "open" kind one finds, for example, in Sweden. Soviet terminology can be deceptive and meaningless.

52

The ShIZO and BUR, as one prisoner accurately put it, are "prisons within a prison." They consist of a special penal barrack in a fenced-off section of the camp zone. Intransigent prisoners are consigned to the cells of such barracks for 10, 15, 20, and even 30 days as punishment. During this period, moreover, they still have to work as usual. They are also deprived of the right to move around the camp zone, and although this may not sound too bad, for a prisoner this is a great deprivation. Their food ration is lowered drastically, and after some 10-15 days they emerge "thin, sharp and transparent" (as camp parlance puts it), swaying as they walk. . . .

But all this is a mere bagatelle by comparison to the closed prison to which one is dispatched for a "malicious" breach of camp regulations. Most political prisoners are sent to the jail in Vladimir, but this is by no means the only place catering to such "offenders." I was sent to the prisons in Semipalatinsk, Ust-Kamenogorsk and to the one at Vikhorevka in the Irkutsk region. These prisons vary from old to new. The horrors of old prison buildings in Siberia are adequately described in literature. They are characterized by stench, dirt and darkness. Nowadays, however, they have been "improved": Windows have been bricked up to half their original size, and the remaining space covered with opaque shields. The new prisons have their special features, too. They are built out of reinforced concrete, to which large amounts of salt have been added to accelerate setting. As a result, in summer they are invariably damp, and in winter walls freeze right through, covering the interior of the cells with ice. The prison at Vikhorevka was a typical example, and it is still operational to this day. I have evidence of this in a letter received this year from a former prisoner, who is still living in that area.

How can one reconcile the addition of salt to concrete as mentioned above with any accepted human rights norms? The Soviet Union is indeed "a land of unlimited possibilities" as we were wont to say—and still do.

It would be a highly educational experience for prisoners from the West to be taken on an excursion through such Soviet prisons —a word of advice in the ear of Western prison authorities, plagued by prisoners revolting for being served chicken instead

53

of steak! It would also be a very instructive experience for the Communist assassin we read of in the papers recently, who protested violently against the inhumanity of his incarceration on the grounds that his color television set was broken. If one were to recount this to someone confined in a Soviet prison, he would have no hope of being taken seriously.

The administration of Soviet camps and prisons is, nevertheless, afraid of the prisoners, for there have been many instances when, driven beyond the bounds of all endurance, unarmed men have thrown themselves upon their armed oppressors—and won!

A wave of uprising and strikes swept through Norilsk, Vorkuta, Kingir and other areas with large concentrations of prisoners in 1953 and 1954. I hope this tribunal will hear the testimony of witnesses of these events and of the mass executions which followed them. I have only heard about them from people who were there at the time, and am touching upon the matter with the aim of showing how the KGB, in an attempt to weaken and exterminate its enemies—the prisoners—tries to turn them against each other.

It might be timely to stress at this point the difference between guarding prisoners in the West and in the U.S.S.R. In the Soviet Union, the KGB deliberately cultivates and encourages cruelty, sadism and inhumanity by guards towards prisoners. For example, when going off duty, the outgoing guard declares: "Handing over duty of guarding enemies of the people!" to which the new guard replies: "Taking over duty of guarding enemies of the people!"

And what of the execution of prisoners supposedly making an escape attempt? For shooting down such a prisoner, the guard is granted two weeks leave with the right to visit his family! And what of setting dogs on a prisoner who lags behind the column? And of searches, necessitating the removal of all clothing in temperatures of 30-40 degrees below zero? Or showing a starving prisoner the food parcel sent by his family and then telling him that it has been confiscated? I have seen countless instances of such sadism and brutality.

I should like to recount several instances of prisoner turning against prisoner at the instigation of the camp authorities. In the Kamyshlag group of camps, in camp No. 3 to be precise, in the winter of 1954, I watched KGB envoys spread rumors about an armed attack that the Russian prisoners were supposedly planning against the Ukrainian prisoners. Naturally, the Russian prisoners were also "warned." The method employed was amazingly simple: a KGB agent, a Ukrainian national, would "accidentally" let slip to a Ukrainian prisoner that he knew that "the Russians are out to get you all soon." In the meantime, a Russian KGB agent would be "accidentally" telling a Russian prisoner that "It burns me up to see those Ukrainians getting ready to slit your throats."

The atmosphere in the camp became tense. On the surface, nobody believed the "well-wishers," but the careful ones began sharpening their knives just in case—after all, one has to defend oneself should the need arise!

The hostility of Ukrainians, the Baltic nations, the Georgians and others towards the Russians (whom they see as invaders) has always been deliberately fanned by the authorities, even outside the prisons and camps, in accordance with the principle of "divide and rule."

Thus the remarks of the KGB men fell upon fertile soil, with the result that one morning at 6 o'clock, while it was still dark and the prisoners were assembling for the trek to work, a massacre broke out. It would seem that many had already "marked their man," and attacked in silence. Only the moans of the wounded indicated what was going on. I was knocked off my feet in the melee and was lying prostrate with several bodies on top of me when the administration, deciding that the time was right, flooded the entire area with spotlights, and the guards opened up machinegun fire on the prisoners. More than two hundred men died for nothing that morning and about six others (the first to fall into the hands of the guards when the shooting stopped) were sentenced to death as "ringleaders."

I witnessed a second instance of mass-killing between prisoners at Ozerlag in the Irkutsk region. Prisoners from dozens of camps were brought together to one work site near Angarsk, where a huge synthetic fuel combine was being constructed. Many of the prisoners were from the Caucasus region—Chechens, Ingushes, Kabardinians.

To this day, I do not know how the KGB managed to provoke the slaughter of these "blacks" by the combined "whites," but I think it was probably triggered off by the KGB appointing these prisoners from the Caucasus to jobs connected with the distribution of food and clothing, thereby making them hated by the others.

But no matter how it was done, the fact remains that one lot of dying men was turned against another, and three to four thousand innocent people perished in broad daylight in the resultant slaughter. I cannot vouch for the exact number of dead, but those prisoners who were tried later as "ringleaders" reported that these were figures mentioned by the prosecutor at the trial.

In this way, by deliberately aggravating national differences, the Soviet authorities get their enemies to destroy each other.

In the case of the Jews, the Soviet authorities leave no stone unturned, no opportunity unexploited.

In the first place, Jews are intentionally put in cells with prisoners who were sentenced in the 1945-1950 period for collaborating with the Nazis. These people are devoured by hatred, and their intellectual and moral level has sunk to a semi-human level. They are the erstwhile "Polizei" and those who served in special execution squads for Jews.

I shall digress briefly here to remind that Article 9, paragraph 2 of the Rules for the Treatment of Prisoners referred to earlier states that prisoners sharing communal sleeping quarters should be *carefully selected* to ensure their compatibility under such circumstances. How naive this sounds when one recalls Soviet camps—almost like a cruel joke.

I once heard a calm discussion between two such prisoners that went like this:

"What did they put you in for?"

"For nothing."

"Go on! What does it say in your sentence?"

"They wrote down that I killed people during the war."

"And didn't you?"

"O course I didn't. I killed Yids, not people."

I could recount many examples of the moral degradation of these people, people who could, while aiming a stone at a bird to bring it down for fun, exclaim excitedly: "I'll get you, you Yid bastard!"

This is what the Jew who is sent to a Soviet camp must contend with. I am not speaking here of the many fine, noble people of all nationalities whom I met in camps, and whose friendship I treasure to this day. To speak of them would not be germane to the issues being examined at this forum. We are testifying to the crimes of the Soviet regime against the very concept of humanity, and I am consequently concentrating upon the darkest aspects of the horrifying existence which is still the lot of many of my friends.

Another measure hostile to Jews and widely employed by the KGB is to send them to camps containing inmates sentenced for membership in neo-Nazi and fascist youth organizations. Groups of such prisoners began to arrive in camps from 1957 onwards. I remember one such group of students from Leningrad. Their anti-Semitism was ideological in character. They believed what they had read in the "Protocols of the Elders of Zion," and that Jews were the mainstay of the Soviet regime. In 1961 they tried to organize a pogrom in camp No. 7. They went around the barracks lobbying for support, addressing themselves mainly to those prisoners who had been in cahoots with German Nazi assassins. It was only because of the stiff opposition we Jews put up with the support of our friends that we escaped becoming victims.

The camp authorities and the KGB, who could not have been ignorant of what was going on, preferred to turn a blind eye instead of punishing the initiators. But if a fight had broken out, all the participants would have been brought to trial, irrespective of who was the aggressor, and who the victim. The authorities always try to extract as much profit as they can for themselves out of these situations, and have no scruples about the means employed.

I know many instances of KGB "stool-pigeons" spreading damaging rumors about the more "active" prisoners. Frequently the prospective victims were my friends, Jews. Once I, too, became the target of such an operation. It should be stressed that this was in 1955, and at that time, the rumor that one was an informer was the equivalent of a death-warrant—the prisoners themselves would slit the suspect's throat that very night.

Therefore, on the day my friends and I learned that such a rumor was circulating about me, we began an immediate search for the source. After going from prisoner to prisoner, we finally tracked down the culprit. My friends forced him into a secluded corner, and by putting a knife to his throat learned that he had been given an assignment by one of the KGB men to put this rumor into circulation.

My friends then marched him forcibly through all the barracks, and made him repeat what he had told them before hundreds of prisoners. After this they released him, and he fled back to his masters for fear of reprisals. My life was saved—but how many innocent people have lost their lives through these tactics?

Jewish prisoners in camps are subject to special surveillance by the KGB. Should two or three Jews gather together, they are immediately forced to disperse by guards shouting, "Come on, break up your Zionist clutch!"

Should several Jews participate in a hunger strike, or should there be a preponderance of them in a labor-gang that has not fulfilled its quota or turned out for work, the authorities try to formulate criminal charges against a "Zionist group."

Furthermore, Jews are categorically forbidden to celebrate religious holidays; they are not allowed to gather for Passover or for the New Year, nor are they permitted to bake or receive unleavened bread.

Once again, I should like to stress that in the Rules for the Treatment of Prisoners adopted by both the U.S.S.R. and the U.N., Articles 41 and 42 state that ministers of religion representing the faiths adhered to by the inmates must be admitted to camps in order to perform religious services, and that each prisoner has the inviolable right to satisfy his spiritual requirements and to have religious literature concerning his own faith in his possession. I have a vivid recollection of the bonfires the camp guards made with Bibles confiscated from the faithful. It would seem that they were unaware of the U.N. Rules. . . .

On two occasions I participated in secret sessions of baking unleavened bread, symbolic scraps of which were later distributed among the Jewish prisoners. I well remember how careful we all were not to give the KGB the slightest chance to begin proceedings against us as "Zionist conspirators."

Jews who have been sent to camps for their religious beliefs, or Orthodox Jews who attempt to carry out rituals prescribed by their faith, find themselves in an unbearable situation. They cannot eat in the communal dining area, as the food served there is not kosher. Their requests to be issued dry rations are met with jeering refusals.

58

The administration obviously acts in accordance with secret instructions from higher up, and it is only rarely that some head of the supply section will allow these literally starving believers to draw dry rations for a month or two. Otherwise, they eat nothing but dry bread and water—for years, at that! I have personally witnessed this in the cases of prisoners N. Kaganov, L. Rablovich, L. Teplinsky and many others.

Jewish believers are subjected to special persecution for the observance of religious rituals such as prayer, obligatory washing and the wearing of a headdress. They are forbidden to pray in seclusion, and especially to carry out the Law of Moses—forming a group of ten Jews to pray. On Fridays they are forbidden to visit the bathhouse in order to perform their ablutions before the Sabbath. Overseers tear off Jews' headdresses in the dining hall and in the barracks, and go out of their way to taunt and humiliate those Jews who attempt to grow beards and sidecurls. In Ozerlag, Kamyshlag and Dubrovlag I saw many times how guards would handcuff and drag Jews to the guardhouse, where they were forcibly shaved clean. Incidentally, there is nothing in Soviet law to forbid the wearing of beards and sidecurls, but this does not prevent Jews or Christian priests from being forcibly shaven. I hope that the persecutions they suffer shall be dealt with separately at this Hearing, and will not enlarge upon the theme myself.

Suffice it to say that the indignities described above are perpetrated in order to destroy the victim's human dignity and to violate the basic human right to spiritual freedom.

During transportation, the camp authorities and the convoy guards do their best to set prisoners sentenced on criminal charges on to the Jews, although I cannot say whether this is done in accordance with instructions or through personal sadistic inclinations.

During transportation from the hospital at the Vikhorevka camp in 1959 (this is not far from the famous Bratsk, which was built by prisoners) to Penal Camp No. 307, I was unable to walk on my badly swollen legs. Some convoy guards dragged me along the ground from the camp to the railway, swearing and jeering. Having reached the siding, they flung me down beside a group of criminal prisoners, and the head guard told them to "Belt the guts out of that Yid so that he'll stop malingering!"

Gladdened by this signal to "have a bit of fun," and probably not stopping to consider what they were doing, they flung themselves at me with a will. My life was saved by the arrival of the train and the order to commence boarding. I lost consciousness, and do not know what happened after that.

I can personally testify to the deliberate humiliation and persecution of Jews, and from reports made by Jews released from camps in 1973-1975, and now living in the West, I can say that they persist to this day. I am offering the testimonies of these former prisoners to the participants of the Hearing for perusal.

Another matter I should like to speak of is the burial of prisoners in accordance with certain instructions devised by the authorities.

Several times it fell to my lot to be in the funeral-detail at Ozerlag. It was generally considered that those who died in summer were "lucky." In summer, the corpses are thrown into a pit, with a wooden slat tied to an ankle of each body. This slat does not bear the prisoner's name, but the prison file number of the deceased. A marker with the numbers of those interred is placed over each pit when it is filled in.

But before the cart bearing the bodies of the dead is allowed to leave the precincts of the camp, there is a grisly ritual to be performed. According to some unknown (to us), but patently existing directive, the guards must assure themselves that no live prisoner has managed to hide among the corpses in the cart.

Checking procedures vary from camp to camp. In some, the cranium of each corpse is broken with a hammer-blow, in others a red-hot steel rod is driven through each body before the dead prisoners are granted their final "release." . . .

In winter, the corpses were simply removed some distance from the camp and piled up in a heap in the snow. It is impossible to dig any kind of grave in the frozen earth when temperatures fall 40-50 degrees below zero. Returning to the same spot several days later we would find no trace of the bodies we had left, for by then they would have been completely devoured by the wild animals of the taiga. We all knew—for the guards made no secret of it—that traps were set and hunting expeditions were organized around the "cemetery." The pelts of captured foxes, sables and other scavengers would later find their way to the state-owned fur industry. I have mentioned this frequently since my arrival in the free world, but wherever I go in Paris, London, New York or any other large city, I see crowds of carefree women in shops selling "Russian furs." These shops do a soaring trade. . .

However, let us now turn to more pleasant subjects. For instance, how one is released from camp.

Release from a camp or prison in the U.S.S.R. is merely the signal for further violations of one's human rights. Up until 1955, the "liberated" prisoner was sent under guard along a prescribed route, through prisons and checkpoints, to his appointed place of exile. Sometimes it could take him months to travel a distance of two to three thousand kilometers. Before 1955, no one was ever allowed to return home upon completion of the sentence.

From 1955-1956 onwards, released prisoners travel to their place of exile alone. They are issued train tickets and told the route they must follow. Should the newly-released prisoner chance to be delayed en route, he is faced with the threat of imprisonment and a new trial on charges of violating passport laws. I know of many cases when just this did happen. For example, Vladimir Rishal was sentenced to a further year in prison for detouring to Moscow to see his wife and children, from whom he had been separated for 14 years.

Upon release, the prisoner is issued with a document, which is exchanged for a passport when he reaches his destination. However, in some cases the authorities may issue him a passport immediately upon release. It should be noted that every passport issued to a former prisoner contains an entry specifying the bearer's travel limitations. Even if the prisoner was not sentenced to exile, his passport upon release will still be endorsed with an article number from the passport law, which will prevent him from registering for residence in certain towns and cities. There is an article, colloquially known as "Minus 16," which means that the bearer of the passport is forbidden to reside in republic capitals. There are others, too, such as "Minus 30" and "Minus 40," which indicate that the bearer may not live in 30 or 40 specified towns.

In actual practice, persons who have completed their period of exile, or have had the period shortened, can register for residence only in provincial areas. Should they venture into larger centers, the police will order them to leave immediately. A second offense can mean a trial on charges of violating passport laws, with a sentence of one to two years in prison or exile. This happened to Anatoli Marchenko.

Apart from exiles, there are persons sentenced to live for a specified time away from large population centers. We know that lately both methods are being practiced by the Soviet authorities. In recent months this was the fate of Jewish activists B. Tsitlenok and M. Nashpits.

These are names we know. But how many others are there who are still unknown to us?

For instance, according to reliable sources, there are 7 large prisons and 32 labor camps in the Krasnodar region in the south of the U.S.S.R. This is no Siberia, it is an area of gardens and holiday resorts. These prisons and camps hold some 30,000 prisoners, who work on tree-felling and the construction of towns and canals. I am supplying evidence of this from ex-prisoner D. B. for perusal by the participants of this Hearing.

What, then, must be the true picture in areas like Irkutsk, Krasnoyar, Vorkuta, Kazakhstan and Kolyma? At present, there is a huge project under way in the U.S.S.R.—the construction of the Baikal-Amur Railroad, the BAM. I should think there is not a single person in the Soviet Union who has not heard of the Bamlag group of camps. For many years this construction was carried out by prisoners—it was so in my time, in 1956-1963. At present, free labor has been brought in to carry on the work commenced by the prisoners, therefore the project is being widely publicized. But before this, hundreds of thousands of prisoners slaved along the five to six thousand kilometer tract, drowning in swamps and freezing to death in winter on mountain passes.

It is impossible to make a full estimate of the number of prisoners incarcerated in Soviet prisons and camps. One can only make educated guesses until the truth becomes known at some future Nuremberg trial, which will have access to the files of the KGB.

However, let us return to the incidence of violation of even basic Soviet laws at the time of release from camp or prison.

It is fairly widely known that it was common practice in the U.S.S.R. to send people to prison according to the decision of the OSO—the Troika[2]—without trial, without the observance of any formalities, and without the summoning and interrogation of the accused. But is it equally well-known that in 1956 Khrushchev

Commissions released prisoners from camps along the same arbitrary principles?

I was a witness of this procedure, which, due to my legal training, was of special interest to me.

In March 1956, an official announcement was made in the Ozerlag group of camps that a Special Commission of the Supreme Soviet of the U.S.S.R. was expected from Moscow. This commission was authorized to review the "cases" of the prisoners, to decide the authenticity of the charges against them, and to either repeal or confirm their sentences.

At this time, most of the inmates of the camps were serving 25-year sentences in labor reform colonies or special regime camps. Those whose sentences were for 15 or 10 years were considered "short-termers," and at times were even allowed to break convoy for work outside the camp zone. Sentences handed down to patently innocent people bristled with monstrous charges of terrorism, espionage and sabotage. To substantiate my statements, I shall give a number of examples. A certain prisoner, Gorman by name, was sentenced to 25 years on charges of espionage. He told me about the beatings he had been subjected to during questioning, while his interrogators demanded that he admit to being a spy. When he finally "admitted" this, they demanded that he name the country for which he had spied. Gorman told them they could put down any country they liked, but his interrogators sadistically insisted that he must name it himself. Gorman knew that to name a large and powerful country, such as the U.S., would mean instant execution by firing squad. He thought quickly, and named—Guatemala. And this was entered into the protocol—"spied for Guatemala." So Guatemala can stand advised that it had in the Soviet Union a volunteer spy of which it knew nothing. . . .

Another case was even more grotesque. Three tribesmen of the wild Chukchi tribe, which had never seen electricity, or air planes, were sentenced to 25 years of special regime camps for mounting "an armed attack against the Soviet military fleet." Sounds imposing, doesn't it? Yet what actually happened was this: While out in a boat, these tribesmen saw what they thought was a whale, and began to throw harpoons at it. One of them opened fire with a hunting rifle. To kill a whale would keep the whole tribe supplied with food for about a year! But suddenly the "whale" began to shoot back, smashed their small boat, and (to use their own words) "swallowed" them. Inside the "whale" they found lots of people, who took them somewhere where they were tried and sentenced. The "whale," as you will have guessed by now, was a Soviet submarine. Every word of this story is true—I would say that anyone who was a prisoner at Ozerlag at that time knew about these three tribesmen.

I have cited the above examples in order to show what an impossible task faced the Special Commission. The prison files contained only the sentence, which listed bare "facts"—spy, saboteur, terrorist, anti-Soviet propagandist, and other no less "serious" charges. Copies of the proceedings in each case were not and could not be made available to the commission: they would have had to be sorted according to camps and delivered by the trainload, for at that time there were millions of political prisoners.

Nevertheless, the Soviet legal apparatus found an easy way out of the dilemma. Upon arrival in our camp, the commission would interview some 60 prisoners daily, questioning each one for 2 to 3 minutes. After verifying the prisoner's name, surname and date of birth, the commission would ask the prisoner whether he admitted to being guilty. Then the members would "confer" for a few minutes and announce: "You are to be released and rehabilitated!"

There were no supplementary documents, interrogation, or protocols—a veritable triumph over bureaucracy. But even this proved insufficient, for the number of prisoners was astronomical, and it would have taken the commission years to complete its work. . . .

Therefore, some 12-15 days after the commission began its work, an announcement (undoubtedly sanctioned by Moscow) was made over the camp loudspeakers: "All prisoners sentenced by the OSO are declared rehabilitated, and are to assemble by the guard-room with their belongings for issue of documents testifying to their release . . ."

In this way, about 30 per cent of the prisoners were freed immediately, and the commission set to work on sorting out the remainder. Thus, the same OSO which was responsible for sending people to camps in the first place eventually became the token for their release. The cases of these patently innocent prisoners needed no reviewing.

It is typical for the Soviet Union that two or three weeks later the commission packed up and left, although the cases of 25-30 per cent of the prisoners had not been reviewed.

It is quite likely that Khrushchev decided that he had done enough window-dressing for the rest of the world. Millions of prisoners had returned to their homes, and this was given broad coverage by Western media. The ones who were still in camps could therefore stay put and go on working.

My surname, commencing as it does with the Russian letter "Sh," comes towards the end of the alphabet, and the commission had not gotten that far at the time of the mass releases. When I finally did come up before the commission, it was in the last days, and releases had stopped. All I had was the cold comfort of supposing that perhaps I would be among the last to be summoned before a firing squad should executions also be performed in alphabetical order . . .

And now, a few words about the types of people making up the population of the camps up to 1963.

Going by my personal observations after my arrest in 1953, I would break down into the following general categories the political prisoners in the many camps, prisons and other detention centers I passed through. (I repeat that I cannot claim statistical accuracy, but am merely stating my personal conclusions.)

1. The greater part of the prisoners were soldiers and officers from Vlasov's army, and nationalists. Of the latter, the most plentiful were the Ukrainians, although there was a fair number of Lithuanians, Latvians, Chechens, Ingushes, Tatars and other national minorities. All those listed above seemed to comprise some 60-70 per cent of camp and prison inmates from 1953-1955.

2. Koreans and Chinese formed a considerable part of the sum total—my estimate is 7-8 per cent.

3. Jews did not stand out noticeably: I would say that in camps with a population of 2,000 I would encounter some 100 Jews. However, if one takes into account that Jews comprise only 1-2 per cent of the population of the U.S.S.R., the "per capita" intake of Jews into camps was very high. In relation to the overall figure of prisoners, I would estimate that 5 per cent were Jews.

4. Foreigners were very conspicuous in the camps. Especially numerous were Germans, Rumanians, Spaniards and Japanese

prisoners-of-war. I was told that I was seeing the tail-end: it was said that some 100,00 prisoners-of-war relegated to camps had perished on the Taishet "Death Trail." I saw about 7,000-8,000 of them. I remember this figure because they were repatriated in 1955, and a fairly accurate estimate could be made of their numbers judging by the number of railway carriages brought up to transport them.

5. There were also foreigners who had been kidnapped abroad and spirited into the U.S.S.R. The majority of them had been kidnapped in Austria in the Soviet Occupied Zone. Among them I particularly recall Americans such as General Dubik, Frenchmen such as Vincent de Santerre, and Swiss such as Henri Gewurz. Furthermore, there were many foreign Communists who had come to the U.S.S.R. in good faith to assist in the construction of communism. There were also Spaniards, who had been brought to the Soviet Union as children in 1937 and had expressed the desire to return to their homeland. For this desire they were promptly sent to prison.

To this day, there are nationals of most countries among the inmates of Soviet labor camps. I am turning over to the Hearing the testimony of former prisoner I. K., who arrived in the West in 1974. This testimony contains a list of names which prove that there are still Japanese, Americans, and even citizens of "friendly" Arab countries in Soviet camps. The authorities practice no racial discrimination when it comes to imprisonment . . .

I should also wish to point out that according to the testimony of former prisoner I. M., there are still many foreigners in the camp on Wrangel Island. The authorities keep their names a closely guarded secret.

6. The remainder of the prisoners were an endless miscellany: there were students and schoolchildren, sentenced for adolescent discussions about government policies; their professors and teachers, who had allowed the education of their charges to diverge from the general party line; orthodox Communists who had come forward with proposals for bolstering the Soviet system (among these I recall the secretary of the party organization in Leningrad); Soviet officials from all levels who had lost out in the settling of scores. I also remember seeing the former Secretary of the Communist Party in Armenia, Grigori Tsaturian. He would recount vividly how at Stalin's direction he, Beria and

Mikoyan would compile lists of persons to be summarily executed in the Caucasus area.

There were many young people who had been apprehended while attempting to escape across the border, or who had planned such escapes. You all know that it is virtually impossible to leave the Soviet Union without the knowledge and sanction of the KGB. It is only in recent years that Jews have made a small breach in this truly Iron Curtain. But in those days, a request to leave the country would never have been granted. Therefore, many tried to escape—and got caught—and found themselves in prison. Although the maximum penalty for an attempt to cross the border illegally was 3 years, these people were nevertheless sentenced to 25 year terms on charges of "high treason!"

Among the prisoners I also encountered those who had voluntarily returned to the Soviet Union from the West. I think that few of these victims of nostalgia managed to miss out on a "cure" in Soviet camps. Between them, they knew the names of all the voluntary repatriates, and would go over them. I am afraid that a similar fate awaits those who, at present, wish to return to the Soviet Union because they have been unable to adjust to a democratic way of life.

Now I should like to touch upon the composition of contemporary camps.

To begin with, I shall describe one of the crudest violations of Soviet law I have ever witnessed in the U.S.S.R.

Some time ago—I believe it was in 1958—the Supreme Soviet of the U.S.S.R. ruled that the maximum period of penal confinement be reduced from 25 to 15 years. In theory, this was to apply automatically to all prisoners who had earlier been sentenced to 25 years. In practice we were informed that our cases were "being reviewed" in the light of the new legislation. All of us who were serving 25-year sentences were individually informed one, two or three years later of our "amended" terms. In 1961, when I had long given up waiting, I was advised that my sentence had been commuted to 10 years.

Even though I had had to wait a long time to hear this, I was one of the fortunate. Many prisoners never did get their sentences commuted, although legally they were eligible for automatic reduction of their terms. I can name among my friends those who completed serving 25-year sentences as recently as

1974 and 1975, although officially there is no longer such a term in the U.S.S.R. This happened, for example, to Solomon Berkovich, one of the activists of the Jewish Bund; and to Ukrainian nationalist Volodymyr Horbovy. Mykhaylo Soroka did not live to be released—he died having served 25 years of his sentence, but his wife, Kateryna Zarytska, survived and completed her 25 year sentence in 1974. But Rabbi Yankel Meyerovich died in camp before release (I remember that a sadistic KGB interrogator tore out half of his beard during questioning) . . .

Such is the attitude of the Soviet authorities towards the observance of their own laws . . .

I once heard a prisoner ask the head of the camp administration in Ozerlag why the authorities do not enforce implementation of their own legislation. The reply was that "It's more peaceful for us to have you all behind bars." This is the true position of the authorities, and as for laws—they are a blind for public opinion, for foreigners, just like the Bolshoi Ballet and the performances of the Beryozka Ensemble.

Getting back to today's political prisoners, I want to stress yet again that they number among them people who have been in confinement for 20 or more years. But there is also what one might call a "new generation" of prisoners. From 1960 to 1963, I encountered students who had been arrested for protesting against the crushing of the Hungarian uprising. Western leftist demonstrators would do well to ponder a little about this: in the U.S.S.R. they would not last an hour before finding themselves behind bars. And the "demonstration" of the Soviet students was not even a demonstration by Western standards—they had merely met for a discussion about events in Hungary. Yet although there was no demonstration, there were mass arrests. It is an ancient truth that youth is rarely intimidated by threats of repression. You are all familiar with the fact that these years saw the birth of the so-called democratic movement in the U.S.S.R. It was "crimes" such as these that brought a new wave of prisoners to the camps in 1960-1963.

Among these groups there was again, alas, a preponderance of Jews. I use the word "alas" deliberately, because in my personal opinion Jews should concentrate on being good Zionists, and not get mixed up in other people's revolutions. But this restless, fermenting element, which has played a part in all revolutions and counter-revolutions, remained true to form yet again. Although lately there have been declarations in the West that the Jews in the U.S.S.R. are only out for themselves, such statements are contradicted by facts.

One only needs to recall the names of the more prominent Jewish democrats to see this. Among the first are Edward Kuznetsov and Ilya Bokshtein, participants of the poetry-reading on Mayakovsky Square in 1961. Also among the first (and, regrettably, last)—Pyotr Yakir. Then there are such well-known figures as Julias Telesin, Litvinov, Ginzburg, Rigerman, Yakobson, Fainberg, Gorbach, Superfin, Gershovich, Tumerman, Shakhovich, Vishnevskaya, Zilberberg, and many others, not forgetting Galich, whose role it would be hard to overestimate.

It is not necessary to waste time explaining that the only "crime" these people ever committed against the Soviet state was that they had the temerity to think in a way not prescribed by Soviet authorities, and at times expressed these thoughts either verbally or on paper. If they did demonstrate, these were silent manifestations unaccompanied by slogans, such as the annual demonstration on Pushkin Square on Human Rights Day, when people simply stood in silence, with bared heads.

Among the new wave arriving in the camps appeared those who wanted to leave illegally for Israel—one such was A. Gluzman, an officer of the Soviet armed forces. There were also those who had tried to create an awareness in the West of the persecution of Jews in the U.S.S.R. and had circulated unsigned articles about state-sponsored anti-Semitism. In this connection I particularly recall the Podolsky family—Dora and Simon and their son Boris. Tina Brodetskaya was one of this group, too. The camps absorbed B. Kochubiyevsky, who had declared at a factory meeting that Israel was not an aggressor. Another group of Jews dispatched to the camps consisted of neo-Zionists such as Khavkin, Schneider and others. They were further supplemented by Orthodox Jews who had protested against the enforced closing of synagogues. It would be impossible to list the hundreds of names I know, and I have mentioned only a few of them to show that people who would have been considered innocent of any crime in the free world were arrested and sentenced to penal servitude in the Soviet Union in 1960-1963.

The striving of Jews to gain freedom and observance of human rights in many cases found its outlet in neo-Zionism, a purely nationalistic movement aimed at emigration to Israel. I believe that the Soviet authorities feared this movement would serve as a precedent for the creation of others.[3] It is true that many national groups in the U.S.S.R. have learned a lesson from the Jewish movement, and are demanding the right to emigrate as well as observance of their human rights.

The wariness of the Soviet authorities towards the neo-Zionists did not manifest itself in an instant wave of arrests. On the contrary, Brezhnev, who in 1964-1970 was still fairly new in his post and was marshalling his forces, even allowed some of the more active Jews to emigrate to Israel. But after 1970 we see a mushrooming of KGB operations against Jews, and many arrests. Among the better-known examples is the "Leningrad trial" of 12 Jews, charged with planning to hijack a plane (all were sentenced to maximum terms and even the death sentence was handed down). We know of scores of arrests and trials in Riga, Kishinev and again in Leningrad; those of Galperin, Voloshin and Boguslavsky are just several of them. There was also a trial of Reiza Palatnik, who was charged in Odessa for typing and distributing samizdat; and of Grisha Berman and those who followed him in refusing to serve in the Soviet army which is being geared to attack Israel. In Kiev, proceedings were instituted against A. Feldman on trumped-up charges of "hooliganism" in 1973.

It should be noted that the Soviet authorities have of late frequently resorted to bringing criminal charges against Zionists and democrats, not even hesitating to employ false witnesses. This method ensures dual profit: the Western world cannot intercede on behalf of criminals, and the defendants can be sent to camps for criminals, and not for political prisoners. Once the prisoner is in the camp, the authorities set the criminal element against him. At the same time, the movement the prisoner belonged to would appear somewhat discredited in the eyes of the West. Prominent victims of these new tactics have been Kukuy in Sverdlovsk, and Zabelishensky, who was crippled in the camp. Typical also is the trial of Ya. Khantsis, who was tried for his desire to emigrate to Israel, but was officially charged with hooliganism; as a result of beatings received in camp, he became a complete cripple. I am handing over to the Hearing materials containing comprehensive coverage of these trials, and the verdicts brought in. These materials contain evidence of violation of Soviet law as well as of general, human laws. Not without reason has a bitter saying appeared in the Russian language since the Soviets came to power: "Find us a man, and we'll find a charge to pin on him." As well as materials mentioned earlier, I am turning over to the Hearing, for wide dissemination, letters from Jewish political prisoners, and the testimonies of those who have been lucky enough to emerge alive from this hell on earth.

As there is no possibility of presenting all the materials fully, I shall merely give a brief summary of their contents. They all show that conditions in the camps today serve to facilitate the physical destruction of the prisoners. For example, in camp No. 7 of the Perm group, there is a glass factory, in which the prisoners cut and polish glass for 10 hours a day. The building is not ventilated, so all that time they are breathing in glass dust, which indisputably leads to silicosis and other lung ailments. Furthermore, the factory and the prisoners' living quarters are under the same roof, so even during their sleeping hours the prisoners are inhaling glass dust which filters through from the factory area.

Arrests of Jews wishing to emigrate to Israel continue. The arrest of Roitburd in July of this year is a case in point.

The list of arrested grows daily, and there are many about whom we do not get to hear, as news of closed trials in provincial areas rarely reaches the West. It was only recently that we learned, quite by chance, about the trial of two Jews in Odessa—Khenkin and Rubinstein—although the KGB had them sent to camps early in 1975.

A similar case is that of two brothers, Arkady and Leonid Weiman from Kharkiv. These two 23-year-old cellists applied to the appropriate Soviet authorities for exit visas to Israel in 1972, but we knew nothing about them as they had no affidavit from Israel. Criminal proceedings were instituted against them immediately, and due to the testimony of witnesses who did not hesitate to commit perjury, they were sentenced to 4 years of strict regime camps on charges of hooliganism.

I also feel that I should mention the case of a Sverlovsk engineer, V. Markman, who was very energetic in his efforts to obtain an exit visa to Israel. The KGB cast around for some reason to arrest him, but Markman was being exceedingly cautious. Eventually, unable to find another excuse, the KGB arrested him for making a telephone call to Israel. Yes, in 1972 the U.S.S.R. had its own "Watergate scandal": the KGB admittedly tapped Markman's telephone, and a telephonist from the local telephone exchange appeared as one of the witnesses for the prosecution. She testified that Markman used obscene language during a telephone conversation. The court ruled that Markman was guilty of hooliganism, and sentenced him to 3 years in prison.

There is another case deserving attention out of the rich collection available. An Israeli citizen, *not* a citizen of the U.S.-S.R., I. Kogan, went to the Soviet Union in 1963 to visit his brother, whom he had not seen since 1941. They had been separated by the war, and the brother had been thrown into a German camp. Upon arrival in the U.S.S.R., I. Kogan was arrested and sentenced to 10 years of camps—for desertion from the Soviet army. The KGB "explained" that as in 1945 Kogan was fighting with a partisan group in Poland (which since the war is considered to be Soviet territory), and as the group was under Soviet command, Kogan's failure to return to the U.S.S.R. and subsequent settlement in Israel [then Palestine—Ed.] in 1945, without permission from the Soviet authorities, made him a deserter as he had not been demobilized. The absurdity of these "legal" arguments is plain for all to see. Apart from this, it ought to be noted that in 1945, the Supreme Soviet of the U.S.S.R. issued a directive concerning amnesty of deserters from the Soviet army, and Kogan, even if he had been a deserter, would have been covered by that amnesty. But no. Nothing was taken into account in sentencing Kogan against all reason and existing Soviet legislation. He subsequently spent 10 years in Soviet prisons, to be released in 1973. At present, thank God, he is back in Israel.

I should like to request that all the documentation concerning the above mentioned trials be incorporated in the final documentation of this trial of the U.S.S.R. as proof of malicious, deliberate violation of both human rights and Soviet law in the U.S.S.R.

Another matter I should like to mention is that apart from the camps we know of in the Soviet Union, there are also camps whose existence is cloaked in secrecy: nobody knows any details about the inhabitants of camps on Novaya Zemlya and on Wrangel and Schmidt Islands. About camps in the Far North near Solikhard we know nothing save the fact that they exist—no information is available concerning their inmates.

72

Unspeakable deeds are perpetrated there, beyond the Arctic Circle—they are being perpetrated today! By the time we learn all there is to know about them, they will have passed into the realm of history, and nobody shall be unduly disturbed by these past horrors. But I adjure you to remember—there are extermination camps in the Soviet Union this very day. A witness to these events, Kh. Moshinsky, has testified that on Wrangel Island, Soviet "scientists" carry out experiments on prisoners. These experiments, in the interest of "science," are concerned with such things, for instance, as the cosmos: they determine endurance thresholds of the human organism, how it responds to an insufficient supply of oxygen, to motion, to weightlessness. . . . But the prophets of detente—at any price!—do not wish to know of such matters. It is to be hoped that American astronauts who link up with their Soviet colleagues in space get to hear about these monstrous experiments. The world encourages the blackmailers and bandits holding power in the U.S.S.R. No normal society would condemn a man for defending his home against a group of bandits, even though he may have to resort to use of arms: nobody would be likely to accuse the householder of unjustifiable interference into the "internal affairs" of the bandits. And yet bandits who have in the course of their reign of terror exterminated more than 60 million people are thriving and prospering, and attending diplomatic banquets organized in their honor. Nations trade with them willingly and fall over each other to grant them loans and increase their strength.

Does the (as yet) free world realize that almost every industry in the Soviet Union is founded on prison labor? We are presently engaged in a study of this matter, and here are some of our preliminary findings.

The timber and oil industries, as well as the mining of gold and other precious metals, are largely dependent on labor drawn from the camps. Even black caviar, so popular in the West, passes through the hands of prisoners in the area around Gurev. Prison labor is also employed in the manufacture of gold and silver jewelry, in the carving of ornaments from bone and horn, in the production of souvenirs such as the well-known "Matreshki" dolls, wooden spoons, and painted boxes. But the West blithely goes on buying all these articles, lining the pockets of the slave-owners. It is no secret that the U.S. and Europe built up Soviet

73

industry in the 1920-1930 period, and later rescued the Soviet Union with its economic aid in the war years 1941-1945. They have thrice averted widespread hunger in the U.S.S.R. in postwar years, and today are assisting in the construction of huge factories which are primarily of strategic value. It is a well-established fact that an automobile plant can change over to production of tanks in a matter of a few days. The development of trade with the U.S.S.R. is nothing less than suicide for the democratic world.

Lenin once remarked that it woud be the capitalist countries "who shall sell us the rope on which we will hang them" . . .

We, who have managed to break out of this dark world which is preparing to slay you and your children, find it especially frightening to see the world's encouragement of this realm of murderers.

I shall consider myself rightly rewarded if my testimony and the bitter experiences of political prisoners shall provide food for thought for those who are in a position to impede the Soviet butchers and liquidate the terrible threat from the East.

---

1) Shifrin is referring to the *Standard Minimum Rules for the Treatment of Prisoners* which were adopted by the first U.N. Congress on the Prevention of Crime and the Treatment of Offenders held in 1955. They were later submitted to the eleventh session of the Social Commission in May 1957, which recommended their adoption. The Economic and Social Council approved these rules in 1957.
2) OSO (Osobovye Sovyeshchaniye)—In April 1918, the Cheka (secret police) set up its own three-man courts, the Troikas, to formalize its actions, including executions.
3) Strong nationalist sentiments continue to exist in Ukraine, the Baltic republics, Armenia and among other non-Russian nations.

LEV KWATSCHEVSKY

"... one's trial is clearly a farce ..."

KWATSCHEVSKY, Lev

Born in 1939. Biochemical engineer. Arrested in Leningrad in August 1968 for attempting to write a letter—with a group of other Leningraders—to the citizens of Czechoslovakia. Tried Dec. 17-26, 1968 and sentenced to 4 years in strict-regime camps for "anti-Soviet agitation and propaganda."

Spent part of his imprisonment in a Mordovian concentration camp. Incarcerated in Vladimir Prison near Moscow from May 1970 until his release.

ON THE SYSTEM OF JUSTICE

There are at least 3.5 million people engaged in forced labor in the Soviet Union. Directly or indirectly, they participate in the production of industrial technology and consumer goods: for example, in the timber and mining industries as well as in the metallurgical, chemical, and automobile industries. The above-mentioned number does not coincide with the overall number [of prisoners] in camps, although theoretically the 3,000 camps, each capable of holding 800-1,200 persons (the new-type camps of 1965-1968), and the existing prisons, could easily accommodate these 3.5 million.

A new method was introduced in Khrushchev's time and is still being successfully applied under Brezhnev. It entails the early release of prisoners, who had been tried on criminal charges, on the condition that they go to work on large construction projects. This method was obviously aimed at obtaining increased productivity from people permitted a certain amount of freedom of movement within a specified area, and who nominally are paid a full wage.

But whatever the motivation, it can be confidently asserted that there is not a single large construction project on which there are no "chemical workers" (as they were nicknamed in Khrushchev's time) employed. This nickname has stuck, although nowadays few of these "chemical workers" have anything to do with chemistry. They are employed on the construction of the Kama Automobile Works (KAMAZ), the Baikal-Amur Railroad (BAM), and the Ust-Ilima and Krasnoyarsk aluminum works.

I have personally witnessed the inauguration of three large plants in Leningrad Region which were constructed over the past 4-5 years: the Kirishi oil refinery and biochemical complex, the Fosforit works at Kingissepp, and the Belkozin in the Luzhsk area.

The role played by political prisoners in this picture is a comparatively minor one, if only because of their numbers. I think it would be a reasonable estimate to say that there are some eight to twelve thousand political prisoners, if one includes in this number all believers and all those tried under Articles 190, 79, and 206.

In any case, one can say that certain parts of all automated transport modes in the U.S.S.R.—be it buses, cars, tractors or bulldozers—were most likely manufactured by political prisoners in camp ZhKh/385/1-3. From 1969 to 1972, all steeringwheels were manufactured by political prisoners. Many owners of television sets manufactured by the Aleksandrovsk factory in Vladimir region have sets which were partially assembled by political prisoners. It must be noted that the working "conditions" here were later found to be "unsuitable" for political prisoners, and they were taken off this work. The furniture manufactured in Perm camps and in the factory of camp ZhKh 385/19 is also widely distributed.

However, as the overall contribution made by political prisoners to the development of the "national economy" is fairly small, it is clear that the arrests made by the KGB cannot be likened to the earlier arrests sanctioned by the Troikas, the aim of which was to labor for Communist construction projects. But the actual number of political prisoners so employed is not known.

It is a little-known fact that for every one person arrested in the Soviet Union, there are 10-12 being subjected to so-called "prophylactic measures." As this is a very interesting manifestation, I propose to go into it in some detail. I maintain that the KGB goes to work as follows:

The KGB representatives and operatives in factories, offices, institutions of higher education, armed forces, and so on, implement "prophylactic measures" against persons suspected of disloyalty towards the regime. In this they receive the full support of personnel officers (the majority of whom are former KGB men) and of the management.

They then proceed to compile dossiers and circulate false information about those found "wanting" in the screening process. They tap telephones, "bug" living quarters, infiltrate and co-opt informers. "Prophylactic measures" generally yield a certain amount of information, for the object of this kind of "attention" must do certain things to prove that he has "reformed" or that he is loyal to the regime:

—He must write a confession addressed to the KGB administration, setting out all he knows about the circulation of samizdat and the expressed opinions of certain persons. He must also "voluntarily" surrender any samizdat materials he may have in his possession.

—The "best" among these objects of "prophylactic measures" agree to become informers.

The worst, along with those marked for arrest and therefore not undergoing "prophylaxis," become subjects of secret dossiers, and eventually find themselves facing preliminary investigation.

I claim that the KGB could have prevented the Ronkin and Khakhayev case, the VSKhSON (Ogurtsov) and "Hijackers'" cases, had it wished to do so, without resorting to arrests.

Despite the much-vaunted "drop in the crime rate" annually boasted of by the MVD, these twin organs (especially the KGB) are not interested in the liquidation of crime. The Soviet system encourages the MVD and the KGB to promote the occurrence of "important cases," and they have a vested interest in the upsurge of crime (even if it is "manufactured") because this is the only way to assure the establishment of new departments, promotions, and good pensions.

Thus, on the one hand the KGB implements preventive measures, and on the other hand it "stimulates" the very activities it is supposed to combat (e.g. in Bukovsky's case, where the KGB sent along its stool pigeon to suggest the setting-up of an underground press).

In the face of such active work by the interior sections of the KGB, what is left for the preliminary investigation to determine?

I maintain that the investigator is not required to determine the guilt or the innocence of the accused. Arrest by the KGB serves as sufficient evidence of guilt.

I maintain that the final ruling of the court is determined by the preliminary investigation, and that the actual trial serves a purely cosmetic function. (One of my fellow-accused knew his sentence—3 years—long before his trial, and conveyed this information to his wife 2 months before he faced the court.)

At times, the court ruling changes the predetermined sentence within the range of 1-2 years, but the guilt of the accused remains unchallenged. Changes in terms usually occur if the prisoner has not been "broken" by the preliminary investigation, and the authorities hope to get some more out of him at the trial.

The investigator is also obliged to "correct" any faults not eliminated by "prophylactic measures" employed earlier. In strict isolation, at times lengthy solitary confinement (for example, Zelikson of the "Kolokol case"[1] spent 7 months in solitary confinement), the prisoner must be made to feel his utter helplessness, and his total inability to prove anything at all. He must be convinced of the startling fact that the investigator can interpret the Criminal Code in any way he pleases, and can cause irreparable harm to the prisoner's family.

I believe the KGB does not resort these days to physical violence to obtain its objectives, although it can always employ indirect means, such as planting one of its agents in a prisoner's cell. The agent can then beat up the prisoner on the pretext of a private quarrel.

I further maintain that during preliminary investigation, the KGB does not resort to direct administration of drugs (injections, etc.), although it is possible that certain narcotics are added to the prisoner's food in order to lower thresholds of resistance. I myself experienced periods of acute and inexplicable desire to talk to anyone at all while I was under preliminary investigation.

I therefore believe that many of the "confessions" made by persons under investigation are motivated by fear (even if it is purely subconscious) of the KGB apparatus, fear for one's future. At times, "confessions" are made by agreement with the investigators, who are not interested in whether the prisoner has changed his convictions, but only in obtaining a public declaration that he has done so. In cases like this, everything is decided and legalized out of court, and the trial is nothing but a revolting farce in which the executioners and the victims alike know the outcome beforehand (e.g., the Yakir and Krasin trial).

The situation is quite different if the accused refuses to cooperate, for it brings to light the inadequacy of the investigative organs, their total inability to do anything apart from sending agents after their quarry, their incapability of presenting any convincing arguments because of ignorance and a lack of stable personal convictions—a quality not needed by investigators.

The KGB works subtly and efficiently when it comes to violating its own official rules in accordance with secret instructions (cross-examination of witnesses, blackmail, planting its informers in prison cells).

I maintain that not one political trial during the past 10 years was carried out without the participation of informers planted in the cells of prisoners who were under preliminary investigation. During the period of my own preliminary investigation (August-December 1968), I came across the following KGB informers: Kustov, a black-marketeer; P. Kogan, an engineer who was caught dealing in illegal currency and platinum operations; A. Chernenko, a small-time black-marketeer; Khachaturyan, who was dealing in illegal currency operations; Sugrobov, who seemed to be a former employee of the Internal Affairs Administration. All such scum are fitting examples of the high ideals on which the Soviet penal system is based.

In all the 8 years of my "involvement" with this system, I did not meet a single "reformed character." However, I did meet many average people who had become criminals under the influence of the penal system. In a broad sense, therefore, one could say that it was the Soviet system that had made them what they were.

I maintain that the KGB deliberately leaves some loose ends in most cases, referring them to operatives to be used as a basis for the fabrication of new arrests. Part of the available information is filed away "for a rainy day." In view of all that I said earlier, this is hardly surprising.

I should like to list the names of some of the employees of the Leningrad KGB administration, which, in my experience, is the most competent (and therefore most negative) department of its kind. In my time, the "star" of this division was one Colonel Syshchikov (presently he is "boss" of Orel region). There was also Captain Kislykh, a nonenity who "struck gold" with the first issues of the *Chronicle of Current Events,* and is now a Major working in Moscow (the Krasin case), and likely to rise to even dizzier heights. Then there was Lieutenant-Colonel Elesin; Majors Menshikov, Stepanov, Shchadny and Ryabchuk; Captains Groshev, Vishnyak and Kartashov, and many others.

All the above-mentioned gentry, despite being hardened cynics, suffer from inferiority complexes and insecurity. And therein lies the explanation of the extraordinary lengths they are prepared to go to in their efforts to break the morale of their victims —for they feel that they have managed to bring the prisoner closer to their own moral level.

Although one's trial is clearly a farce, it is nonetheless a torturing experience. Each new court case inevitably raises certain hopes, for, who knows?—maybe this time more truth will be allowed to surface and a miracle will occur: instead of being dispatched to camp, perhaps the accused will be given a suspended sentence?

But to get off in. this way, one must stoop to unbelievable depths of degradation—and even then nothing can be taken for granted. Occasionally, hopes are pinned on being completely candid. However, with the exception of the Heifetz trial in Leningrad, it has been impossible to gain admission to such trials.

I had enough disappointments in connection with trials (even before my own) in 1967. The KGB guards surrounding the court building are not to be caught napping. The court hearing is an educational experience, and proceedings are consequently attended by budding KGB lawyers and selected "workers" anxious to demonstrate their faith in the legal system and the party (not to mention the beloved "organs").

So far I have been speaking only of my own observations and experiences, but this does not mean to say that I have forgotten many others—spiritually I am still with them. Therefore I should like to grant them the one small service in my power—to publicize their names to the world.

It must not be forgotten that G. Rode is serving a third term in Vladimir Prison, where he almost died of peritonitis in 1972. It would be unforgivable to forget the ailing Father Boris Zalivako, who, because of the purity of his soul, wept when a member of the prison administration, one Obrubov, cynically suggested that Father Boris should turn informer.

One should also remember Zinoviy Krasivsky—intelligent and

82

cheerful despite an acute stomach ailment; lame I. Yu. Federov, who was declared insane and forcibly placed in a psychiatric hospital, yet never lost his willingness to participate in hunger strikes in the cause of truth; and reed-thin Gabriel Superfin, who "knows of everything in the world."

Neither should we forget Moroz and Ogurtsov, irrespective of whether we share their views or not.

I should like to remind you, once again, of the names of the "Vladimirovites" Lyubarsky, Bukovsky, Butman, Vudka, Davydov, Pavlenkov, Bondar, Lukyanenko, Makarenko, Budulak, Zdorovy, Safronov, Shakirov; and of some of the inmates of the Perm and Potma camps—Kuznetsov, Chornovil, Svitlychny, Antonyuk, Kalynets, Khnokh, Mendelevich, Ayrikyan, Navasardyan, Shakhverdyan, Penson, Fedorov, Murzhenko; the names of the suffering Belov, Terelya, Chinnov; the names of Lupynis, Plakhotnyuk, Plyushch.

It is impossible to maintain indifference when remembering the weary, yet determined, face of Sergei Kovalev as I saw it 4 days before his arrest.

A thorough study of the fate of all these people, these hostages, inevitably leads to the only possible conclusion about the true worth of all the declarations we constantly hear in Soviet broadcasts about freedom, democracy and socialism.

---

1) "Kolokol case"—*Kolokol* was a publication of the Union of Communards, a neo-Bolshevik youth group based in Leningrad. Four issues appeared before the KGB broke up the group in 1965.

VICTOR BALASHOV

*". . . release from prison . . . can be more easily obtained
if the names of the political victims are publicized . . ."*

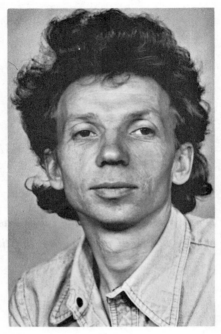

BALASHOV, Victor

Born February 10, 1942 into the family of an officer. In 1953 Balashov entered the Suvorov Officer School in Kiev, but decided against a military career after the Hungarian uprising and left the Officer School in 1960. That same year he entered Moscow University, where he studied in the Department of Theoretical and Applied Linguistics. In 1961 Balashov founded the Union for Intellectual Freedom which drew up a manifest calling for the "liberation of philosophy, creative ideology and culture from control by Party dogma and ideological dictatorship." He was arrested in 1962 with other Union members, tried on charges of anti-Sovietism, and sentenced to 10 years imprisonment, which he spent in Vladimir Prison, psychiatric institutions, and labor camps. After release he spent two years (1972-1973) in exile in Yerevan, Armenia.

Balashov left the Soviet Union in December 1973 and came to the U.S. in April 1974. He was briefly employed as translator at the Harvard Law School. In 1975, he was employed as an instructor of Russian Literature and Language at Bennington College in Vermont, then took a position at the Slavic Institute of the State University of New York in Albany.

86

THE PRISONS

Having witnessed for over 10 years violations of human rights, liberty, and dignity in the Soviet Union, I undertake to tell nothing but the truth about the people I encountered and my experiences during that time.

I should like to begin with a few words about myself, and then pass on to my experience in prison, where I was sent for my intellectual and spiritual opposition to the ideological dictatorship of the party and political regime in the U.S.S.R.

I was born in Moscow on February 10, 1942. My father, a tank-construction engineer and officer in the armed forces, was killed in the battle of Vienna in 1945. In 1953, I entered the Suvorov Officer School in Kiev. The son of an officer, I wished to serve my country as my father had done before me.

However, when I saw the crushing of the Hungarian uprising —with the active participation of Soviet officers—I changed my mind about a professional career in the army and left the officer school in 1960, without having taken the oath of allegiance.

When I returned to Moscow, I obtained work as a technical photographer and translator in the Bureau of Foreign Military Literature of the Defense Ministry and General Armed Forces Headquarters. At the same time I enrolled as a part-time student at Moscow University.

In 1961, I founded the Union for Intellectual Freedom, which was composed of former students of the Officer School. Some of them had graduated, others had transferred to colleges, universities, and various military academies. We drew up and circulated a manifesto of intellectual liberties, directed mainly at the intelligentsia, the officer class, and the student body. This manifesto called for the liberation of philosophy, creative ideology, and culture from control by party dogma and ideological dictatorship.

In 1962, we were all arrested and tried on charges of anti-Sovietism. Not one of us pleaded guilty, as we had not aimed at an overthrow or change of the regime. Our aim was the intellectual and spiritual liberation of the entire nation from the tyranny of ideological monopoloy of the CPSU.

I spent 10 years as a political prisoner in the KGB prisons of Moscow and Vladimir, in the Serbsky Psychiatric Institute, and in camps of strict regime in Potma and Mordovia.

Throughout all those years my friends and I remained loyal to our ideals of intellectual and spiritual freedom and freedom of conscience. We demanded the right to continue intellectual activity in prison. We all demanded that we be acknowledged as political prisoners, and not be labeled traitors and particularly dangerous recidivists.

After release, all former political prisoners become permanent exiles, deprived of all the civil rights enjoyed by free citizens, and live under constant administrative and secret police surveillance. I spent 2 years of "freedom," from 1972 to 1973, under such surveillance in the Trans-Caucasus area. All this time I was under the threat of psychological and political blackmail by the KGB, and under the threat of new arrest, because I had not discarded my former ideas nor the principles of intellectual and spiritual freedom.

I managed to obtain the right to emigrate only by maintaining an unwavering stability of principle in my applications and in my meetings with government officials in Yerevan.

Those of my former associates from the Union for Intellectual Freedom and my friends from prison days who unsuccessfully attempted to leave the Soviet Union—Edward Kuznetsov, Yuri Federov, Oleksiy Murzhenko—were all arrested again and sentenced to 15-year terms, deprived of their rights, and doomed to deprivation of human dignity in the political camps of the KGB in which I had spent 10 years, and in which they had all served previous 5- to 7-year sentences after their first arrest and conviction for being "political deviationists."

I shall name some of those whom I personally encountered in special regime prisons, and of whose spiritual purity and intellectual conscience I have no doubts. They were confined solely for their political, nationalist, and religious beliefs, yet are apparently doomed to life imprisonment without even the dignity of being acknowledged as political prisoners. Instead, the authorities brand them traitors and particularly dangerous recidivists. To their number belong two deeply religious and "truly Orthodox" monks: Mikhail Yershov and Vasili Kalinin. Father Mikhail had spent 30 years in prison. He was twice sentenced to 25-year terms (his second sentence was handed down in Kazan in 1958). Father Vasili had also been imprisoned for 30 years, having been sentenced to two 25-year terms. Then there were the Russian nationalists—religious philosophers and believers:

Igor Ogurtsov—sentenced to 15 years in 1967.

Vladimir Osipov—sentenced to 7 years (1962-1969), soon to face yet another trial.

Sergei Solovyov—who has completed 20 years of a 25-year sentence for serving as an officer in the Vlasov Army. He was sentenced to a further 10 years for anti-Soviet activities.

Victor Tartynsky—who has been imprisoned for 21 years. Originally sentenced to 25 years on criminal charges, he received an additional sentence of 10 years for "anti-Sovietism" when he became converted to the Russian Orthodox faith.

There were also Lithuanian Catholic nationalists:

Pyatras Paulaitis—has served 20 years. Originally sentenced to 25 years for anti-Soviet activities, but was released before the end of his term. Later he was tried again on the same charges and sentenced to 10 years.

Lyudvikas Simutis—has served 20 years of a 25-year sentence for participating in a nationalist liberation movement in Lithuania.

I also encountered the following Ukrainian nationalists:

Oleksandr Vodenyuk—who was twice sentenced to 10-year terms on charges of anti-Soviet activities.

Dmytro Synyak—has been imprisoned for 17 years. Originally sentenced to 15 years, he received an additional 15-year sentence in 1967.

Konstantyn Didenko—sentenced in 1970 for attempting to emigrate from the U.S.S.R. during the 1967 Middle East War.

When I was in the Serbsky Psychiatric Institute in 1962 I met several people who were later dispatched to the psychiatric prison in Kazan for solitary confinement. They were:

Writer Pyotr Stebelev, a construction engineer and a former colonel whom I had known before my arrest when he worked in the Publications Department of the Ministry of Defense. He was arrested on orders from the prosecutor-general of the U.S.S.R. for a book he had written, *Battle of Nations*. The Ministry of Defense, to which he had submitted his manuscript for publication, decided that it was "ideologically incorrect."

Poet Valentin Bezymenny, who was charged with anti-Sovietism for writing epigrams about the Politburo.

Father Mikhail Yershov (one of the monks I have mentioned earlier), who spent many years in the psychiatric prison in Kazan, as well as terms in ordinary prisons.

I should like to say something of the conditions in Vladimir Prison where I was confined from 1963 until 1966, and of the Potma Special regime camp No. 10, where I was from 1966 until 1972.

The regime for political prisoners remains unchanged to this day. It is based on physical deprivation and psychological terror practiced by the prison authorities.

The prisoner is allowed 500 grams of bread daily. In fact, this is all the nourishment he gets, because the "swill" served with the bread is unfit for human consumption. The bread itself is of such poor quality that prisoners have declared hunger strikes in protest.

The forced labor one performs in prison can be equated with slave labor, for it pays the prisoner 2.5 rubles a month. This meager sum is all he has with which to buy additional food from the prison store.

Prisoners in special regime camps receive a monthly wage of 5-10 rubles, out of which they may spend a maximum of 3-4 rubles in the camp store. The work the prisoners carry out, for example machine building, is very profitable for the government, therefore the authorities have no scruples to employ the slave labor of political prisoners.

The conditions under which political prisoners are forced to exist provoke continual hunger strikes as signs of protest. Among the "criminal element" these protests usually find expression in self-inflicted tattoos, such as "Slave of the CPSU," or profane slogans concerning the Soviet regime, general secretaries of the CPSU, and Lenin. Such protests are usually quelled by trials (15-year sentences or solitary confinement in psychiatric institutions), or death by execution. Such are the punitive measures the authorities resort to against those who dare raise their voice in protest.

In 1963 I made a purely symbolic escape attempt as a sign of my refusal to acknowledge myself guilty of the charges leveled against me. For this I was sentenced to serve my term in special regime prisons (Vladimir Prison and Potma Special Prison No. 10) until the end of my sentence in January 1972.

In 1963, there were 470 political prisoners on special regime in Vladimir Prison and Potma Special Prison No. 10; by 1972, this number had shrunk to 180. Not more than 100 of them survived to be released, as I was, upon expiration of their sentences. Some 90 to 95 of them were executed because they participated in protests and escape attempts; others died due to illness. But these latter deaths cannot be regarded as natural ones, for political prisoners do not receive any medical attention without the special sanction of the KGB. The remaining 100 or so were scattered throughout camps in Siberia and Potma, holding mostly criminals, and were forced to recant and condemn their own "criminal past." In this way they achieved not liberation, but reclassification as criminals.

Of the 180 political prisoners on special regime in January 1972, more than 100 could be considered "life termers." They had served 15 years of their sentences and were faced with a further 10 to 15 years. The psycho-administrative terror practiced by prison bosses and the political blackmail by KGB agents provoke protests among political prisoners, which result in corresponding punitive measures by the authorities.

Release from prison upon completion of a sentence on special regime is something approaching a miracle, and an outcome few even dare to hope for. Every day on special regime can easily be one's last, or can bring an additional sentence. But the miracle of release can be more easily obtained if the names of the political victims of the Soviet regime are publicized and not forgotten by free citizens both in Russia [U.S.S.R.] and in the West. This is the hope that kept us alive.

The work done by Sakharov, and others like him who struggle selflessly in the name of freedom, human rights and observance of human dignity, is the highest ideal of those who believe in the individual's right to political freedom.

Thank you for your attention. I hope that our testimonies, the sincere testimonies of former political prisoners, about the greatest foe of human rights and liberty—the Soviet regime—will be heard by all those who wish to know the truth about our life in the U.S.S.R.

BORIS SHRAGIN

*" . . . the fear of being unemployed accounts for the sub-
missiveness of public opinion in the country . . ."*

SHRAGIN, Boris

Born in 1926 in Smolensk Region, R.S.F.S.R., into the family of an army physician. In 1949, Shragin graduated from the Department of Philosophy at Moscow University. In 1966 he received a Candidate of Science degree—roughly equivalent to a Ph.D.—in philosophy. From 1958 to 1968 Shragin worked at the Moscow Institute of Art History, the last years as its director. Shragin has published in the Soviet press some forty works dealing with art history, aesthetics and literary criticism.

In 1968 Shragin co-signed the *Open Letter of Twelve to World Communist Leaders* regarding the violation of human rights in the Soviet Union. That same year, he signed with other Moscow scholars and professionals a protest against the "violation of legality" in the trial of Ginzburg, Galanskov, and others.

In 1968 Shragin was dismissed from the Institute of Art History on grounds of "ideological incompatibility." That same year he was expelled from the Communist Party and was subsequently unable to get his works published in the Soviet press, although he did publish them in the samizdat.

Not able to find employment in the Soviet Union, Shragin emigrated to the U.S.A. in March 1974.

94

ON THE RIGHT TO WORK

In his essay *My Country and the World,* Andrei Sakharov writes about the persecution of dissidents in the Soviet Union: "In addition to judicial persecution of dissidents, there are such extralegal acts as discharge from work, obstruction of free access to education and employment, etc. It seems to me," adds Professor Sakharov, "that the West does not realize the seriousness of it all in our totalitarian state."

My testimony concerns the loss of employment. Of course there are many other ruthless methods in the Soviet Union, like blackmail, terror and suppression of freedom of speech and opinion. However, discharge from work has proved to be a convenient and effective weapon in the hands of the government. It needs no legal procedure, does not attract attention, and is discreet. At the same time, it offers an inexhaustible range of possibilities for arbitrariness and harassment. The fear of being unemployed accounts for the submissiveness of public opinion in the country. Professor Sakharov rightly states that losing work on ideological grounds in a country in which all sources of income are held by the state is in no way comparable to being out of a job in the West. The situation eloquently reflects the dangers involved in a so-called "socialism," a socialism that leads to the concentration of all power in irresponsible hands.

Little attention has been paid so far to this subject. I shall attempt to shed light on that hidden corner of the Soviet system by virtue of the right of every person to work according to one's training and abilities.

I consider myself qualified to discuss this matter because I had been denied the right to work on ideological grounds, and also because many of my friends are subject to this illegal practice. I speak from firsthand experience.

On April 17, 1968, I was relieved of my duties at the Institute of the History of Art on the ground of "incompatibility with the requirements for scientific workers of an ideological character." This rather illiterate statement implied that I was politically unreliable and thus would be deprived of the opportunity and the right to exercise my profession in the field of the philosophy of art. The language of the discharge order shows that literacy is not a requirement for a "scientific worker of an ideological character" and not even for the post of director of the Institute of Art History. I have been unable to get work for 6 years and I left my country in March 1974. Had I not left the country I would have stayed unemployed for the rest of my life.

The only other job I held, for a mere 6 months, was at the Institute of Industrial Art, where I had taught post-graduate courses since 1957. I was dismissed without any explanation, and subsequently it became quite obvious that I would be under continuous surveillance to make sure that I would not get a job and live normally.

What had I done? Together with 11 Soviet citizens I addressed a letter to the Communist Party Conference in Budapest, describing the violation of human rights in the Soviet Union. The illegal discharge from work was also mentioned. Furthermore, I joined my signature to that of 67 Moscow scientists who described the "hooliganism" of the authorities at the trial of Galanskov, Ginzburg and others. The letter was addressed to the state prosecutor and to the Supreme Court of the U.S.S.R. I was shown a photocopy of our letter with the seal of the Supreme Court of the U.S.S.R., which took no action on it but forwarded the letter to the employers whose job it was to stifle the dissident authors. Yu. A. Dmitriyevich, secretary of the local party chapter at the Institute of Art History, tried to talk me into disavowing all responsibility for the letter. All I had to do was to declare that I had been misled by bourgeois propaganda and that no violations had ever occurred in the Soviet Union. Dismissal was the alternative offered. That is sheer blackmail. No attempt was made to disprove the contents of the letter, whereas immediate dismissal was threatened. When I pointed out that such intimidation was dishonest, I was discharged. I also lost my post at the Seminar for Stage Direction where I lectured on aesthetics. My articles which used to appear regularly in leading journals were no longer published.

The preceding victim was Yu. Ya. Glazov, Candidate of Philological Sciences; he also signed the letter and consequently was discharged from his post at the Institute of the Peoples of Asia of the U.S.S.R. Academy of Sciences. To get rid of him, the courses in Tamil at Moscow University were suddenly suspended, Glazov being the only one to teach that rare language. Glazov, a father of three, fell seriously ill. Yet, he was summoned to the police, questioned, and told to get work immediately or he would be declared a parasite, which would mean that he would no longer be allowed to live in Moscow. Needless to say, nobody was interested in the reasons for his unemployment.

The problem of work and occupation invites special attention. In the Soviet Union anyone deprived of the right to exercise a profession is continuously exposed to the danger of relentless and ruthless persecution for being unemployed. Since dismissal from work for ideological reasons is illegal, the state authorities refuse to acknowledge the very fact of such dismissal.

Yu. Ya. Glazov was not successful in getting work and had to leave the Soviet Union. At present, he is a department head at Dalhouse University in Canada.

L. Z. Kopelev, Candidate of Philological Sciences and one of the most eminent specialists in German literature, was relieved of his duties at the Institute of the History of Art soon after my dismissal. He had written an article for the Austrian communist press in which he stated that a return to Stalinism was no longer possible. Today, Kopelev has no steady income and his work remains unpublished. He once spent 10 years in a Stalinist concentration camp.

Two young editors of the journal *Iskusstvo* [Art], Alexander Morozov and Dimitri Muravyov, lost their jobs at about the same time. Their only crime consisted in the signing of a protest against the verdict of the Galanskov trial. However, officially they were told that their work was unsatisfactory. Although the employers were unable to produce proof for the alleged inefficiency, the court upheld the decision. Both young men have not found employment since. Their lives are ruined. Dimitri Muravyov is sick and suffers from epileptic fits.

If needed, I can cite many more such cases.

I should like to know why we were subjected to harassment and prosecution. Why were we branded as politically unreliable? Certainly not for disagreeing with the proclaimed official ideology of the Soviet state, but for bringing to light the hidden crimes of the regime. In the Soviet Union, one has to remain silent in the face of blatant injustice committed by the state in order to qualify as politically reliable and enjoy the right to work.

Only few voices were raised in defense of Andrei Sakharov when a campaign of defamation was unleashed against him. Among the few were Pavel Litvinov and I—but neither of us had anything to lose. We were both without occupation. Valentin Turchin, Doctor of Physical and Mathematical Sciences, came forth with a restrained and moderate statement in support of Sakharov. The regional Party Committee immediately reacted by pressing for his discharge, but his superiors did not give in. He was demoted and stripped of all privileges—a compromise reached between the administration and the Party Committee. Yet he did lose his job later, and he is still out of work. He was refused an exit visa despite an invitation by Columbia University in New York. The situation is without hope in the Soviet Union for all those who wish to be at peace with their conscience.

Take the case of Yuri Fedorovich Orlov, an outstanding physicist and a corresponding member of the Armenian Academy of Sciences. After the launching of the press campaign against Academician Sakharov he wrote an open letter to Brezhnev, but in lieu of a reply he was relieved of his duties. We all know what work means to a scientist—not only a means to earn a living but life itself.

It is therefore no surprise that most of the intellectuals in our country keep silent, although they know and see what we know and see. They are threatened with the prospect of losing their job. That is the price of their silence and their submissiveness. That is the reason for the uniform views, for the failure to criticize the government. Those whose voices are occasionally raised pay for it by sacrificing their work and the daily bread of their children.

But silence alone does not suffice. If you want to keep your post you must say what you are told. Recently one of the editors of *Mysl*, a publication of social and economic literature, expressed his wish to emigrate to Israel. The administration suggested to the staff members to condemn his act as a betrayal of the homeland. The six staff members refused to obey and were subsequently "sacked," while the department was closed down.

The same fate, the same endless unemployment awaits those who return from labor camps and exile. Constantin Babitsky, a Candidate of Philological Sciences who formerly taught at the Institute of the Russian Language of the Academy of Sciences, was exiled for having participated in a protest demonstration when Soviet tanks rolled into Czechoslovakia. He is still without occupation.

The Constitution of the Soviet Union asserts that the principle of socialism, "of each according to his ability and to each according to his work," has been implemented. This is untrue. Are not all that I have mentioned, and the many others alike, able and willing to work?

In the Soviet Union abilities do not count, unless its the ability to be dishonest and willing to participate in the government's crimes against its citizens.

What other conclusion can we draw?

Last but not least, the Soviet government ratified Convention No. 111, "Concerning Discrimination in Respect of Employment and Occupation," of the International Labor Organization.

In Article 2 of the Convention we read: "Each Member for which this Convention is in force undertakes to declare and pursue a national policy designed to promote . . . and practice equality of opportunity and treatment in respect of employment and occupation with a view to eliminating any discrimination in respect thereof."

Through the representatives of the press at this Hearing I should like to ask a question of a venerable organization like the International Labor Organization: How do you reconcile the commitment of the Soviet Union to eradicate discrimination in respect to employment with a national policy which elevates this very discrimination to a principle?

Why is it that you do not object to serving as a smoke screen for acts of discrimination? Are you afraid of losing your job, too?

DIMITRI PANIN

" ... the (Soviet) illegalities and crimes have reached massive proportions ... "

PANIN, Dimitri

Born 1911 into the family of a lawyer. Graduated from the Institute of Technology as a mechanical engineer.

Arrested in 1940 for speaking out against the regime among a close circle of friends (One of Panin's friends turned out to be a KGB informer). Sentenced without trial to 5 years in labor camps. In 1943, while in a labor camp, his sentence was extended for another 10 years on the charge that he allegedly organized an armed uprising. In 1953, Panin, was deported to Siberia for lifelong exile. After the death of Stalin in 1956, he was partially rehabilitated, and came to live and work in Moscow as an engineer-contractor.

In 1972, Panin left the U.S.S.R. for the West to, as he says, be able to publish his works. Has published works in Russian, French, German, and English. Panin currently resides in Switzerland.

ILLEGALITY AND ARBITRARY RULE IN THE U.S.S.R.

The illegalities and crimes which the Soviet authorities have committed and continue to commit have reached massive proportions. The astronomical magnitude of the numbers involved can be checked with the help of statistical data. The great number of facts available makes it possible to reach accurate conclusions and to disperse certain myths which exist in the free world.

1) The myth of the great and virtuous Lenin. This myth makes it necessary for me to recall the true state of affairs:

Lenin's seizure of power in October 1917; the machine of terror in December of that same year that was set into motion with the creation of VCLN—the All-Russian Special Commission, the "Cheka" or secret police; the forcible dissolution of the Constituent Assembly in January 1918: All these events plunged the country into a state of lawlessness and rule by force. . . .

Lenin gave his approval to executions without trial, to torture, to the shooting of hostages, to excesses committed by local officials, to the shooting down of workers' demonstrations, to the armed pillage of the countryside in a period when the economy was disintegrating, when starvation and disease were rife due to the civil war. In the years 1917 to 1923, some 20 million people perished, and by 1953 another 60 million had died, not counting war losses. These are the figures. They speak for themselves.

I have drawn up a table showing these deaths in my book *Notes of Sologdin*, which was published in France in 1975.

Lenin imposed a regime of continuous terror on his country;

he created and approved the notorious Article 58 as part of the Criminal Code. Its many paragraphs made it easy to find an excuse to arrest anybody.

2) The myth of the evil Stalin, who perverted the good Lenin's teaching, should also be destroyed. Stalin was, of course, a monster, but he himself invented nothing. He was Lenin's diligent pupil who consistently carried out the precepts of his teacher.

I myself have had experience with Stalin's prisons, camps, penal colonies and exile regions during the years 1940 to 1956, and I have described the first part of my imprisonment in Volume One of *Notes of Sologdin*.

3) The myth of the liberal Khrushchev. This myth was created by the Communists for propaganda purposes.

Khrushchev was forced to release prisoners because a series of uprisings in the camps had made the further imprisonment of 15 million people behind barbed wire impossible. The first such uprising took place in 1952, while Stalin was still at the height of his power, at the penal colony of Ekibastus, and I describe it in *Notes of Sologdin*. After Stalin's death other uprisings followed in Vorkuta, Kingir, Dzheskasgan and other labor camps. Had Khrushchev not released a great number of prisoners he would have had to keep a division of soldiers near every labor camp.

The release of these prisoners made it necessary to decide the question of their pensions, and to begin housing developments.

Denunciation of Stalin and partial rehabilitation of political prisoners were necessary to Khrushchev in his struggle for power.

At the same time, Khrushchev's novel methods in agriculture and other spheres brought great hardships to the population. This is why the people hate Khrushchev at least as much as Stalin.

The following incident was one example of Khrushchev's "liberalism" in 1963-1964. After atomic bomb tests were carried out above the Arctic Circle, the Eskimos and other northern nationalities were subjected to radiation and the effects of radioactive deposits. A rapid decrease in the numbers of reindeer also began at this time. Not understanding what was happening, these people decided to go to Yakutsk to ask for help, medicines, and food. A few kilometers outside the town, the crowd was met by a punitive detachment of secret police who ordered them all to go home—to certain death. The people tried to explain the desperate position they were in, but the inhuman orders were merely repeated to them and they were given 30 minutes to think it over. When time ran out, the secret police opened fire with machineguns and automatic rifles on the unarmed, peaceful crowd of people, ill and worn out by their journey. Only a few survived, ran into the taiga and later entered the town, avoiding the main roads which were guarded.

I only heard about this mass murder of northern ethnic minorities in 1970, from a geologist who had just returned from an expedition to Yakutia. He had been told about it by his relatives, Tatars who had been resettled in Yakutia. A stranger would never have gotten to know about these events. Thousands of similar incidents take place under the rule of Brezhnev, but remain unknown to the Soviet population as a whole and to the rest of mankind.

4) The myth of Brezhnev's smile. This myth is strongly supported by those who uphold detente. In fact, illegality has merely taken other forms; it has even increased to some extent.

The number of political prisoners currently is not less than 1,700,000 and the overall number of those imprisoned is 3,500,-000. The system now includes the detention of dissidents in psychiatric institutions. As a result they are overcrowded. I shall give two typical examples of the lack of human rights in the era of Brezhnev.

a) In the 1960's Brezhnev's regime crushed in blood a number of strikes and mass demonstrations by the discontented populace. The whole world knows this. One such rebellion took place in the town of Karaganda, at the metallurgical factory construction site. As usual, the cause was the chronic insufficiency of food supplies, even of bread in this case. Milk products and vegetables rarely appeared in the shops, and when they did, they were sold out in a few hours. In the shops only vodka was in plentiful supply, and even it was of low quality. The angry workers took over the factory and then the town itself. Discussions achieved nothing. The rebelling workers fought against special punitive detachments. The rebellion was finally crushed with the help of tanks, artillery, and helicopters. Work at the factory was resumed only when workers from other factories were forcibly mobilized. Because of the terror they were subjected to, the families of those who suffered during these staggering events are afraid to speak out about them. I met one of the engineers from this metallurgical factory, a witness of these events, in Paris in 1974. Unfortunately, I cannot give his name because he has relatives still living in the U.S.S.R.

It should be noted that the custom of considering certain people as hostages is typical in the context of terror and illegality. This custom was started by Lenin and continues through today. In recent years, many of those forced to live abroad have limited their statements about living conditions under the Soviet regime. In the overwhelming majority of cases it's because they fear for their relatives in the U.S.S.R. I am convinced that the same fear for their relatives is characteristic of the so-called second emigration, those who failed to return to the U.S.S.R. after the 1941-1945 war.

b) After I reached the West, an eyewitness told me of certain events which took place in Siberia near the Chinese border. The local inhabitants were employed in the timber industry and in a sawmill. In 1969 and 1970 the food-supply situation worsened catastrophically (it had been bad enough up to then), but all appeals were in vain. Faced with imminent starvation, the whole adult population, accompanied by children and old people, began to move to the nearest town. The border guards decided that the crowd must be trying to get to China. Without thinking it over for long, they opened fire and shot nearly all of them.

Thousands of similar episodes are hushed up and pass unnoticed even by the Soviet population. There are rumors, insignificant details. Only the larger rebellions surface, such as those in Temirtau, Novocherkassk and Dniprodzerzhinsk, which the regime cannot hide because they took place not far from major cities and because the working class paid more attention to them. But in all more distant places, in regions thousands of miles away, the "Law of the Taiga" reigns supreme. It permits any illegality or tyranny on the part of the local authorities. People there laugh at the Soviet constitution and have never heard of the Declaration of Human Rights.

The U.S.S.R. is a realm of exploitation. In my book *The Oscillating World,* published in French in 1974, I described six forms of murderous, total exploitation in the U.S.S.R. . . .

Our people have developed quite effective means of indirect economic struggle and opposition. Although the workers have been deprived of the right to strike—and participation in strikes is regarded as a grave political crime—it is no longer so rare for strikes to occur, even in large industrial centers. In 1970, Brezhnev's administration introduced new measures in its battle against strike movements. Armed brigades of guards were organized at the larger factories. They terrorized the workers with searches in hallways of the factories, openly walked about the workshops during work, spread rumors, and so on. Thus it was that disorganization and fear were rife during the first, most dangerous, period of strike action, when the strikers meet and talk with each other. The ringleaders would be identified and isolated until the strike was over. The guards were recruited largely from the secret police, who retire at the age of 40 to 45, since service in the KGB brings with it all kinds of privileges and advantages. Secret policemen who retire on a pension in the prime of life are allowed to take jobs as guards, and their wages are added to their pensions.

Under Brezhnev, wide use was made of the "druzhinniki,"[1] an organization founded by Khrushchev. They were originally not a bad idea since the country was suffering from a huge wave of crime, hooliganism, and drunkenness. In their spare time, druzhinniki, usually members of the party or Komsomol, were supposed to keep order in public places. But now they are mainly employed in the struggle against dissidents and religion. Brezhnev's storm-troopers are no different from Hitler's storm-troopers. They often provoke an incident on the streets in order to detain some dissident. They search him, check the contents of his wallet, confiscate his books, beat him up, and threaten him with the worst kind of violence. There have been well-known instances where druzhinniki were used to close down monasteries, or to disrupt religious assemblies and religious services. It happens particularly in the provinces that such a detachment breaks into the house of any citizen on the pretext of searching for forbidden underground literature.

It is in this way that the mass outrages, begun under Lenin, underwent change during Stalin's purges (in those years they were centralized in the hands of the NKVD, the former KGB), and later were perfected under Brezhnev. Nowadays the KGB carries out its work with the help of druzhinniki and psychiatric staff.

5) One of the regime's worst crimes is the way in which it indoctrinates people ideologically from childhood on. At the same time as family ties are being weakened in every possible way, Marxism and godlessness are forcibly inculcated. The main aim is to break down the inner man, to make him obedient to any orders, to reduce his ideals to those of a robot, blindly approving all decisions made by the party and government. The education one receives is designed to deprive people of the pangs of conscience, of painful self-recrimination; it aids them in accepting the crimes of the regime and participating in those crimes.

When the regime had been raging for only 20 years, people had not yet lost their sense of decency. Comparable happenings were looked at in 1937 in a different way than nowadays. I remember a meeting that took place during the Stalinist purges at the Moscow Institute of Chemical Engineering, where I was a graduate student. Like other workers, we had to vote for the resolution condemning Tukhachevsky and other military leaders to death, as they had been declared enemies of the people and denounced in the worst kind of language. I was amazed to see people rushing out of the assembly hall as if they had been scalded; the faces of many lecturers and workers were twisted with emotion. The risk of behaving like this was great, because in those years people were often arrested for not looking enthusiastic at such meetings.

In 1938, as I was waiting for a friend who worked at the People's Commissariat of Machine Engineering, I saw a middle-aged man reading a newspaper account of the trial of Bukharin and the right-wing deviationists. The middle-aged man had obviously given up pretending: his lips and hands were trembling, he was muttering half-aloud denunciations of the executioners who had forced the accused to make monstrous self-accusations.

Thirty years later, in the same circles, the picture was completely different. In 1968, some young engineers at the Moscow Institute of Construction and Road-Transport Machines, where I was working at the time, talked quite freely about the Soviet invasion of Czechoslovakia and allowed themselves to use words like "revolution," "constitution," "socialism with a human face."

A Brezhnev court sentenced the chief speaker to 3 years' imprisonment, which in itself proved he had not belonged to any organization and had no particular aims. After the trial a general assembly was organized at the institute, which amazed me by its baseness. For reasons of cowardice and amorality, and in the interests of careerism, people of various ages who had nothing to fear vied with each other in pretending to be shocked, in making denunciatory or sham-patriotic speeches. The regime has had great success in perverting people, in inculcating in them a lack of resistance to injustice, in trampling underfoot the idea of personal dignity.

In the same institute, toward the end of the 1960's, a beautiful typist suddenly disappeared. Some time later one of the engineers told me that she was a fervent Christian and together with her brother and father had been committed to a psychiatric hospital because of her belief. I had not involved myself in open political activity after my imprisonment, as I was devoting all my free time to developing a different kind of world-order. But in this case I proposed that the engineer and I should protest publicly, if we could get some others, at least two former soldiers, to join our protest. The engineer's reaction to my proposal was to sharply reject it. This same man had told me earlier that he had ordered his son to remove a cross he had been wearing because of the influence of his grandmother. This engineer's behavior is typical, he has disarmed himself, he is afraid to even think of opposing open oppression.

The inculcation of an inner slave-mentality should be considered the regime's worst crime against the people. We are however far more often troubled by outer manifestations of oppression, illegality and erosion of human rights, and we do not always notice this terrible work of destruction.

The regime's nature gives no grounds to hope that democratization and liberalization will come about. But the peoples of our country still have sufficient strength and inner independence to create a steppingstone for their liberation. The inner "slave-mentality" can be combated with the help of the "spiritual revolution." This is one of the more peaceful methods of achieving an essential respect for human rights in our country. . . .

---

1) Druzhinniki—Volunteer militia youth groups organized to assist local police in dealing with criminal and delinquent offenders.

LEONID ZABELISHENSKY

" . . . The Soviet Union . . . is in fact nothing more than an enormous concentration camp . . . "

ZABELISHENSKY, Leonid

Born January 1, 1941 in Sverdlovsk in the Urals. Graduated from the Technical College in Sverdlovsk in 1959. In 1964, Zabelishensky received a Master of Science degree in electronics from the Ural Polytechnic Institute.

Was employed as a senior engineer at the Ural Polytechnic Institute, and in 1965 became an Assistant at that Institute's Department of Computer Technology.

In 1971, after having applied for an emigration visa to Israel, Zabelishensky was dismissed from work at the Polytechnic Institute. From then on all subsequent efforts to find a job were unsuccessful.

In October 1973 Zabelishensky was arrested and charged under Article 209 of the R.S.F.S.R. Criminal Code with "malicious refusal to act on an order to take a job and cease leading a parasitic existence." He was sentenced to 6 months' hard labor.

He was released in April of 1974, and in August of that year emigrated with his family to Israel.

ON THE RIGHT TO EMIGRATE

My testimony shall be devoted to one of the most blatant abuses of human rights in the Soviet Union today—the denial of right to emigrate. My testimony is based on my own experience, and on the experiences of others who have made statements which I am submitting for incorporation into evidence gathered at this Hearing.

In mid-September 1971 I lodged an application to emigrate to Israel. Thereafter I witnessed numerous violations of human rights and Soviet law by the authorities. At that time I was living in Sverdlovsk, a city closed to foreigners, which has a population of one million, of which some 14,000 were Jews.

A Soviet citizen wishing to emigrate is obliged to produce an affidavit from relatives residing in the country to which he wishes to emigrate. I was informed that without such an affidavit my application would not even be considered. I would like to stress that the necessity to produce this affidavit is a violation of Article 13, paragraph 2 of the Universal Declaration of Human Rights, and of the International Covenant on Civil and Political Rights, for it limits the right of emigration to those who have relatives living abroad.

Realizing the futility of expecting the Soviet authorities to observe human rights, I resigned myself to waiting for the affidavit from relatives in Israel. Weeks passed, however, and the affidavit sent to me from Israel was not delivered. It transpired that the KGB had ordered the authorities to withhold my affidavit, thereby violating international postal rules, Articles 12 of the Universal Declaration of Human Rights (inviolability of private correspondence), and Soviet law, which forbids the withholding of private mail without the sanction of the prosecutor-general. As a result, I could not lodge an application to emigrate. At the same time, I was advised that I would have to supply a personal reference from my place of employment.

Such a demand is illegal. Also illegal is the demand to obtain written consent to emigrate from one's nearest relatives (parents, children, divorced spouses) in the U.S.S.R. All these illegal methods are being used to impede emigration and provide a pretext for launching repressions against potential emigrants.

While I was still vainly waiting for my affidavit from Israel, the campaign against me got under way with my dismissal from the Ural Polytechnic, where I had been employed as an assistant in the School of Computer Technology. All my attempts to find a new job in my professional field (radio engineering) were unsuccessful as the KGB had issued instructions precluding my employment anywhere. My wife was forced to resign from her job, for she had been given to understand that she would be dismissed, with consequences similar to mine, if she did not hand in a voluntary resignation. Thus we both became unemployed in a country where there is no unemployment compensation. We had to make ends meet by taking odd jobs—for instance, I occasionally managed to get casual work as a loader, until the authorities would discover what I was doing and arrange for my dismissal.

Finally, my numerous protests against the withholding of my affidavit by the KGB yielded results, and some 2½ months later the affidavit was delivered. And so I was able to submit the necessary documents for permission to emigrate. I thought that all I had to do now was to wait for the permission to come through in the near future (according to a resolution of the Presidium of the Supreme Soviet—no more than one month), and that there could be no further obstacles to prevent my family from emigrating. It turned out, however, that the harassments I had been subjected to after lodging my original application were only the first of a long chain which was to follow.

Before going into this in detail, I should like to remind this Hearing that many emigration applicants in the U.S.S.R. wait for their affidavits for months, and even years. During that time they are subjected to dismissal from work, public denunciation at meetings, and are denied the chance to find other employment. It would be impossible to list the names of the hundreds of people in this predicament, so I shall remind you of just a few: A. Feldman from Kiev and the Weiman twins from Kharkiv (all three have been convicted and are serving sentences), and also Khavkin, A. Rubin, I. Schneider, and A. Shifrin who is here today.

Occasionally no affidavits at all reach the addressees in certain cities. This was the case in Kiev at the beginning of 1971, and is currently so in Leningrad. The KGB pressures relatives of would-be emigrants to withhold consent for their kinsmen to emigrate. Recent and widely publicized examples of this were the refusal of ballerina Galina Panov's mother to allow her daughter to emigrate, and the case of the Tiomkin family, when Tiomkin's wife refused to allow her daughter to emigrate with the father. One also recalls the Goldfarb family from Kiev: For a long time Mrs. Goldfarb could not obtain her parents' permission to leave. One also recalls the Weiman twins, who never did manage to get their parents' consent to emigrate, but ended up in court.

Sometimes it takes the would-be emigrant years to obtain a character reference from his last place of employment, even though he may have been dismissed from there a considerable time ago on orders from the KGB. This was so in the cases of V. Poltinnikova from Novosibirsk, A. Feldman from Kiev, A. Reichman from Odessa, and many others.

I should like to request inclusion of certain testimonies into the findings of this Hearing. They are testimonies of former Soviet citizens now residing in Israel, and testimonies of persons who have relatives still in the Soviet Union. They outline the repressive measures employed by the authorities against would-be emigrants.

Before proceeding to a description of the repressions I was subjected to, I should like to give a brief outline of the situation in Sverdlovsk from December 1970 on. At that time, 10 Jews had signed a protest against the sentences handed down in the so-called Hijackers' Trial in Leningrad.

This protest resulted in house searches, public denunciation at work, dismissals, and, finally, the arrest of Valeri Kukuy. Soon afterwards, Sverdlovsk newspapers began to publish articles denouncing Kukuy and others who, while they had not yet been arrested, had already been refused exit visas. In June 1971, Kukuy was "tried" and sentenced to 3 years' imprisonment, although all the witnesses stated in court that they had given false evidence under pressure from the KGB.

At the time when I had lodged my first application to emigrate, there was already a number of Jews in Sverdlovsk who had been denied exit visas, and who were being persecuted for their desire to leave the U.S.S.R. My dismissal from work made me one of this number. We were all kept under illegal surveillance, every letter addressed to us from abroad was scrutinized and copied by the KGB before it was delivered, our telephone conversations with relatives and friends abroad were taped. The KGB painstakingly compiled dossiers on all our open protests and appeals in which we described our desperate situation and the repressive measures of the Sverdlovsk authorities, who tried to infiltrate informers into our midst.

The official reply to my application to emigrate came in April 1972, i.e., 3½ months after it was lodged, and consisted of a refusal to grant my family exit visas. I was informed that the grounds for this refusal were, first, that I had had a security clearance to see secret information at the Ural Polytechnic; second, my father's objection to my proposed emigration; third, an absence of relatives in Israel (quoting my father, who supposedly declared that the affidavit I had received contained false information). My objections that I had never handled any secret documents (despite formal clearance to do so) were simply ignored, even after the administration of the Polytechnic confirmed this. My protests concerning the fact that my father's statement had been obtained under duress were also ignored. I found myself deprived of the opportunity to emigrate, and with no way of earning a living.

Not long afterwards, a new denunciatory article directed at us appeared in the *Vechernii Sverdlovsk,* and we guessed that a new arrest was imminent. Sure enough, a meeting was called at Vladimir Markman's place of employment. Markman had been vainly trying to obtain an exit visa to Israel for more than a year. At this meeting he was told that if he agreed to cease such "activities" forthwith, he would be promoted and given a new flat. Otherwise, he would be sent to prison.

Markman's reaction was to resign from his job. He was arrested several days later. He was accused of "slandering the Soviet Union," of "hooliganism" and of "spreading national hatred."

In May 1972, while Markman was awaiting his fate in Sverdlovsk prison, I was arrested and interrogated. The KGB tried to pressure me into giving them the evidence they wanted against Markman. My failure to do so was the signal for a new series of repressions against me.

In August 1972, Markman was "tried" and sentenced to 3 years of strict-regime camps. The authorities did not scruple to produce tapes of Markman's telephone conversations with Israel, which were made to indict him. One of the witnesses for the prosecution was a telephonist who unblushingly admitted to having listened in on Markman's calls on orders from the KGB. Neither were the "judges" disturbed by the fact that telephone-tapping is illegal under Soviet law. After all, they were not trying the KGB, they were "trying" Markman who wanted to emigrate to Israel. Therefore, all means were justified, even illegal ones, for his "guilt" had been predetermined. In violation of the Soviet criminal procedure code, the "court" ruled that criminal proceedings be instituted against me. Markman was sentenced.

The authorities continued to thwart all my attempts to obtain work. At the same time they repeatedly refused to grant me an exit visa. They also increased pressure on other Jews who wanted to emigrate. For example, just before Markman's "trial," his wife was dismissed from her job, which left her without any means of support.

In October 1972, I was summoned to the local militia division where I was threatened with criminal proceedings for "parasitism." These threats were repeated in November, although I was unemployed through no fault of my own.

When with great difficulty I managed to obtain a position in my own specialty in December, the authorities began a campaign against Markman's wife, accusing her of "parasitism" and "black-marketeering."

From December 1972 on, my application to emigrate to Israel was repeatedly turned down. All my mail from abroad (and that which I sent abroad) was intercepted, and I could neither make nor receive long-distance telephone calls. Surveillance continued.

In May 1973, I was again dismissed from work for participating with Moscow Jews in a sit-in demonstration in the foyer of the

117

Central Committee of the CPSU building. The demonstrators were demanding the release of all Jews imprisoned for wishing to emigrate to Israel. I was unable to find a new job, and my request to the Ministry of Internal Affairs for a review of my application to emigrate led to a new refusal.

The authorities made it impossible for me to secure work in Sverdlovsk. My mail was intercepted as before, and I remained under surveillance. Markman's wife lodged a complaint with the Ministry of Internal Affairs about the actions of the Sverdlovsk authorities. At the same time she was threatened with incarceration in the Sverdlovsk prison. Another Sverdlovsk Jew—Vladimir Zlotver—was refused permission to emigrate on the grounds that he had just completed military service in the Soviet army.

In August 1973, Markman's wife was unexpectedly granted an exit visa, and left for Israel. On the eve of her departure I was again summoned by the militia and threatened with imprisonment for "parasitism." When in September the authorities failed to secure a conviction of Vladimir Zlotver on charges of participating in a robbery, he was issued an exit visa in October 1973, and left for Israel. I was arrested and charged with "parasitism" just before his departure.

At this time the authorities in many Soviet cities had decided to prefer purely criminal charges against Jews wishing to emigrate from the U.S.S.R. In this way, for instance, proceedings were instituted against A. Feldman in Kiev on trumped-up charges of "hooliganism." Similar cases were being fabricated in Vynnytsya and Bendery. Right up to the present moment, with very few exceptions, Jews are brought to court as "hooligans" and "parasites" in most areas.

At the time of my arrest, however, this new technique had not been fully implemented, and the Sverdlovsk authorities intended to charge me with slandering the Soviet Union. From the day of my arrest until the end of November, I remained in prison without being questioned or having any other formal charges brought against me. During that time I was twice transferred to cells for political prisoners, which seemed to indicate that new, more serious charges were being formulated against me.

At my first interrogation session at the end of November, I realized that my "case" was ready, for the file on me was thick and questioning was obviously a mere formality. During the third interrogation session I learned that my home had been searched on the day following my arrest; this was an illegal act, because I was not present during the search. But the search had yielded no evidence that could justify charging me with more serious "crimes." Furthermore (as I learned later), my arrest had caused protests among Jews abroad. This must have prompted the authorities to stick to the original charge of "parasitism," even though it would only carry a maximum term of 1 year in prison.

At the end of December I was brought to "trial," in the course of which my judges received numerous telegrams of protest from abroad. The court hearing lasted 4 days. The authorities refused to allow a lawyer from Moscow to appear as my defense counsel, and also vetoed the calling of witnesses whose testimonies may have altered the outcome of the trial. Although the charges aginst me clearly lacked substance, I was sentenced to 6 months in labor camps.

Before the trial, and until my sentence was confirmed by the Sverdlovsk regional court toward the end of January, my wife was frequently threatened with imprisonment because news of the "trial" had reached the West.

In early February 1974, I was transferred from Sverdlovsk prison to general regime camp UShCh 349/43 in the Sverdlovsk region. On March 20, I and a group of prisoners were put to work on the construction of industrial liquid waste filters. I had to cart cement for shoring reinforced concrete foundation pits. To do so I had to carry my load on an unfenced concrete wall that divided the pit. Even the most elementary safety measures were absent.

I had lost a great deal of strength due to malnutrition and the foul air in prison, and was in no condition to perform such arduous tasks. After about 20 minutes on the job I was overcome by faintness, dropped my load, and, losing my balance, fell into the 6 meter deep pit. I managed to clamber out with great difficulty and demanded to be returned to camp, for I had excruciating pains in my back and head. Four hours later I was brought back to camp and placed in the sick-bay. Six days later I was discharged as "healthy and fit for work," although I continued to have severe pains in my back. My request to be X-rayed was refused. For several days after this I continued to demand further medical examination, but was denied medical assistance of

119

any kind. The head of the camp administration then decided to punish me for evading work and not fulfilling the required labor norm (I was to dig a deep pit in the frozen earth). My punishment was 10 days confinement in the punitive solitary cell. In all camps of this type this means incarceration in an unheated cell—with outside temperatures below the freezing point—of the "cement bag" type (1x2x3 meters). There is no bedding, no warm clothes. Hot food is issued once every 48 hours (water and stale bread the rest of the time), and no exercise in fresh air is permitted. The last 10 days and nights of my imprisonment thus proved to be the hardest. I began a hunger strike as a sign of protest. On the fourth day the duty prosecutor came to see me. He promised to review the legality of my punishment. I therefore called off my hunger strike, but his promise remained unfulfilled.

Three days before my release I was visited by an official from the Sverdlovsk KGB, one Major Abramov, who demanded that I stay away from Moscow for one month, warning me that if I did not obey I would be arrested again. On April 23, 1974, I was released from camp, and made my way home with great difficulty.

On the following day I sought medical help, and an X-ray showed extensive damage to the fifth vertebra of my spinal column. I was advised to enter the hospital for immediate treatment. I spent the next 3 weeks in a hospital, and upon discharge was advised to wear an orthopedic corset for 3 months. I was forbidden to sit or to travel on any kind of transport.

After my discharge from the hospital in July 1974, I was visited by a KGB official who informed me that I would shortly receive an exit visa, but that I was to stay out of Moscow during the Nixon visit. Two days after Nixon left Moscow I was advised that we had been granted exit visas valid until July 25, 1974. The authorities demanded that we depart almost immediately, knowing full well that I was in no state to travel. I was informed that doctors at the hospital where I had been treated had pronounced me fit and able to travel, although I had had no follow-up treatment.

We arrived in Israel on August 12, and I spent another month receiving medical treatment before I recovered completely.

In conclusion, I should like to draw the attention of the participants in this Hearing to the fact that repressions are continuing against persons wishing to emigrate from the Soviet Union. Many young people have been expelled from tertiary educational institutions only to be called up for military service. Thus, the young men cannot leave the country while they are on active duty. Afterwards they cannot emigrate because now they know Soviet military technology. Those who refuse to perform military service are arrested and sentenced to lengthy terms of imprisonment. A recent arrival in Israel, G. Berman, served a 3-year sentence for such a "crime." Some, such as L. Spivak and B. Mindel from Novosibirsk and I. Kolchinsky from Kharkiv, were drafted after they had applied for exit visas to Israel.

Yu. Tartakovsky was persecuted for a long time because he refused to ackowledge his draft as being legal, since he had passed the maximum call-up age and had earlier been excused from military service for reasons of health.

Authorities frequently use past military service as a pretext to deny applicants exit visas. For example, 5 years ago A. Feldman from Kiev worked as a construction worker for the army (doing digging and nothing else), yet he was denied an exit visa because of the "military secrets" he supposedly knew.

Many families have been striving vainly for years to get exit visas, e.g., the Slepak family in Moscow for 5 years, K. Friedman in Kiev—4 years, the Poltinnikov and Roitman families in Novosibirsk—4 years, the Soifer and Fainberg families, also from Novosibirsk—over 2 years, the Zlotvers in Sverdlovsk—over a year, M. Mager in Vynnytsya—more than 4 years. In all the above mentioned cases, half of the family is already in Israel.

These people have been living for years under constant surveillance. They must cope with imprisonment, confiscation of private correspondence, disconnection of private telephones, unemployment, and the loss of steady means of support.

At times the authorities refuse to grant exit visas for the sole reason that one member of the family may already be in the West without their sanction. For example, the family of the well-known cellist Victor Yuran has been receiving refusals since 1969.

There have been occasions when persons who wanted to emigrate were forcibly incarcerated in psychiatric institutions. There they are subjected to illegal experiments which lead to personality disorders. Chaim Gilel from Vilnius is an example. There have also been instances where parents were deprived of their parental rights—to make sure that the minors remained in the U.S.S.R. Example: Alexander Tiomkin and his daughter.

I am appending several documents concerning the authorities' refusal for years on end to allow families to emigrate. It is impossible to describe or even list all the cases, for according to official Israeli statistics, more than 150,000 families are awaiting permission to leave the U.S.S.R. This estimate was made by judging the number of as yet unrealized affidavits sent to the Soviet Union.

Even Soviet Foreign Minister Gromyko recently admitted during a press conference that some 1,700 persons have been denied permission to emigrate for reasons of "state security." The nature of this "security" can be assessed from the documents I have supplied about the case of Dr. Poltinnikov of Novosibirsk. He is an ophthalmologist, a pensioner since 1971. Nevertheless, the authorities refuse to allow him and his wife and daughter to emigrate, even though the head of the central visa office (OVIR), General Verein, admitted in 1973 that nobody in the family was in possession of any secrets prejudicial to the interests of state security.

Lately there have been more arrests of Jews who have not given up trying to obtain permission to emigrate despite repeated refusals over the course of years. They are all being sentenced to varying terms of imprisonment. This happened recently to Roitburd in Odessa, Malkin in Moscow, and Silnitzky in Krasnodar.

Everything I have recounted bears witness to the readiness of the Soviet authorities to employ all manner of repressions in order to intimidate Jews and make them decide against applying for exit visas. With this in mind, the KGB takes "preventive" measures in places where there are potential emigrants. Several families are being openly persecuted with threats, assassination attempts, beatings by "hooligans," illegal entry into their homes, intimidation at local KGB headquarters where they are warned that they could become victims of "hooligans," and so forth. At the same time, several families are allowed to emigrate as a sop to public opion abroad.

The Jews have become the primary target of the main drive

122

by the authorities against ethnic groups wishing to leave the U.S.S.R. This is probably due to the fact that they were the first to start fighting for their rights by legal means. This is why the Soviet authorities are ready to employ any means to halt the Jewish exodus, thereby cautioning all others who may be similarly inclined.

I hope that my testimony shall in some measure help people in the free world to understand at least a fraction of the horror of life in the Soviet Union, which, while priding itself upon being the epitome of democracy, is in fact nothing more than one enormous concentration camp.

MARIA SINYAVSKAYA

" . . . one should not forget that imprisoned dissidents have families, wives, and children . . ."

THE LOT OF FAMILIES
OF POLITICAL PRISONERS

. . . Following those terrible words which have just been said, my own experience, and what I am prepared to state here before you, would appear to be very modest, very insignificant, and of a very particular nature. I shall speak of how I was led to encounter the KGB, and will describe to you my encounter with the concentration camps—not as a prisoner, from within the camps, but from the other side of the barbed wire.

From the moment a person is imprisoned, especially in the case of a dissident, the whole family enters the prison—the wife, parents, brothers and sisters, and his children.

My experience started 10 years ago, in September 1965, when several extremely sophisticated, polite young men came to me with a search warrant. I am emphasizing here that these people were indeed very polite, very courteous, and throughout the 6 months of detention, the interrogator allowed himself to shout at me only once. Nevertheless, they did exert strong pressure on me and on my husband. They were professionals, and as such, they knew what kind of questions to ask.

When my husband was imprisoned, my son was 8 months old. Among the people who came to search our flat was a woman. She came to help me with my baby, so some unique "humanitarianism" was indeed demonstrated. But, from the very first interrogation, a slow, steady pressure was exerted on me. I was requested to answer very few, seemingly innocuous questions: What did I know about my husband's business? Did I help him send his works abroad? Did I recognize the evil my husband had done, and did I feel any remorse? Could I help them obtain certain works of Sinyavsky? They were not satisfied with my husband's answers, though he was ready to admit that he was indeed an author who had been published abroad.

He was required to repent, to admit that he had had certain malicious thoughts. But Sinyavsky did not want to repudiate his own work. He was then told in very polite terms that if he did not want to do that, his wife would be imprisoned. If she did not give the statements they wanted, then the child would be sent to a children's home.

I was told similar things at each interrogation. Many interrogations were carried out and the interrogator never said directly, "You are going to be arrested," but he made me understand that this issue in essence had already been settled, and that if it were not taken up today, it would surely be taken up in the course of the next interrogation. When I walked the streets I felt I was being followed. But it should be stated that our Chekists are very good at following people. They do it in a very, very concealed way, so this overt following was obviously a psychological weapon. After a few days I thought I was a victim of a persecution-mania. I was placed in a very difficult situation and this made me desperate. In desperation I wrote the following: "In the case of my death or arrest, or in the case of a lengthy absence, I request my friends to take care of my son and my books." I had no other property. One lawyer whom I went to see said that it was impossible to sign such a document. The next day when I returned to the interrogation—an average of 6 to 8 hours of questioning—I felt very desperate. I told the interrogator that I had written such a will. I told him that now he could keep me in prison. The interrogator then said: "Maria Vasilievna, dear Maria Vasilievna, do you think so badly of us? Do you indeed believe for one moment that we want to arrest you?" and then he began asking the same questions he had asked only 15 minutes ago. This was pure blackmail. It was a real threat, but I repeat that during the course of the 6 months of interrogation, all these threats were said in very calm tones and all the conversations between the interrogators and my husband and the interrogators and myself were carried out in a very amicable manner. This small detail I wanted to stress.

But in the case of Sinyavsky's friends, other methods were applied. Of course, it always depended on the psychology of the interrogator. Tania Makarova, for example, was not allowed to go to the toilet. This is a very small detail. The interrogator stated very simply: "Well, you will tell us what we want to know and then you can go to the toilet. At the moment though I can not allow you to go there."

Can I therefore accuse the authorities of having violated certain laws? I must say that all that was done was legal, but it still had an inhuman character to it.

Apart from this pressure which is exerted on relatives—particularly on women—there is also pressure exerted on the part of one's place of employment. Thus I lost my job in the very first month following Sinyavsky's arrest. I formerly taught art history at Moscow's Library Institute. I taught under contract. When my contract expired it was not renewed. Once again, from a legal point of view I had no grounds for complaint—no laws had been violated. However, I remained without any means of livelihood. At about the same time the publishing house "Iskusstvo" reneged on a contract I had signed for a book. The book had nothing to do with politics; it dealt with a Ukrainian artist. I had worked on it for a long time. Now it simply was excluded from the work plan of the publishing house. Again, I repeat, everything was done within the law, and the news that my contract had been cancelled was brought to me very politely.

News of the arrest of Sinyavsky and Daniel was spread abroad. The Western press started publicizing it. Apparently because of this my situation changed . . . Though Daniel's wife and I were living outside of what could be described as normal conditions—in fact we were living in a sort of state of siege, with certain privileges—our situation nevertheless could not be compared to that in which women found themselves in the 1930's and 1940's. Many of our friends refused to desert us. On the contrary, many of them supported us without fear. Our world appeared to have been divided: While the authorities were cruel, the intelligentsia showed its good will toward us. Many people whom I did not even know came to visit me, for example Alexander Volpin and Nadezhda Yakovleva Mandelshtam. People of different generations came to see me. Some of them had survived Stalin's camps and now they helped me live through my experience. But on the other hand, there were also people in the neighborhood who said: "If you want to live in a communal dwelling—and there are many such communal dwellings in the country—and since you're married to an enemy of the people, well then you can't use the communal kitchen to cook porridge for a son whose father is a criminal."

But the situation during the time of the interrogations is still not the worst for the wife of a prisoner, because despite what logic might dictate, one nevertheless hopes that in one way or the other, the case will come to an end. One should also not forget that interrogations are a sort of war game between the interrogators and the interrogated, and this of course distracts one's mind. But when the husband suddenly lands in prison because of the charges that were brought against him, then the entire day-to-day life changes totally. One starts to worry: How can I find out about him, where can I see him, how can I travel to the camp?

Visits take place in so-called "meeting houses." According to regulations at that time, a prisoner's wife was allowed two types of visits: On one hand the prisoner was entitled to a yearly personal visit lasting from one to three days, depending on how the prison authorities decided. In fact, there were many variables involved: A prisoner was permitted to see his wife if he was allowed "to get time off from his work." This means actually the following: When the wife during the course of the year comes to visit her husband-prisoner, it's completely up to the prison authorities or the KGB whether she can see him for one day or three. The authorities weigh this decision on the basis of a prisoner's behavior, that is to say, whether he was repentant or not

There is also the other type of visit, a general visit that was permitted three times a year, though that number has now been reduced. One was allowed to see the prisoner anywhere from one up to four hours, again depending on how the authorities decided. Again there were variables: Authorities could decide whether a table would be placed between the visitor and prisoner, whether one could bring the prisoner food or cigarettes, or whether someone from the prison staff would be present during the meeting.

A prisoner's wife must see the prison warden before the visit

130

takes place. During this meeting the head of the prison tries to "educate" the wife. He would tell me for example: "Well, why don't you ask your husband to repent, to recognize his fault? If you can do it, then you can see him for so many hours more." And so forth. And so one has to face a whole chain of attempts at blackmail.

On occasions the authorities assume they can obtain some information if a guard is not present during the visit. Of course they then switch on microphones and register every single word to use it against the prisoner at a later time.

Among the criteria [used to establish the conditions under which the visits take place] is the following: Is the prisoner on the path to "improving" himself? What does this mean? This means: Is he ready to cooperate with the KGB?

Still another method to violate the dignity of a prisoner's wife is the way she is searched. Now when you finally come for the three-day visit, it's obvious that you will bring with you as much food as possible. You'll try to give the prisoner all the necessary calories. You try to bring the best food possible. Some of your friends would accompany you to the camp because you'd be loaded down with huge parcels. Mr. Shragin, who is present here, can testify to this . . .

When I arrived at the camp and before I entered the "meeting house" I would be searched. It's interesting that during the course of these searches one can identify different types of guards. A guard is not always a sadist, although there were sadists among them. Many of them were pleasant and friendly people, I must say, and I had good relations with some of them, and could talk about my problems.

What is interesting is that when one is searched one is more frightened of a woman guard. Perhaps woman is a more cruel creature than man. There was a legendary woman guard, Sergeant Anya, in camp No. 11 in Potma. She would fully unclothe a prisoner's wife and search every stitch of the clothing before and after the visit. At any time during the preliminary search, the visit could be refused by the guard conducting the search, and so one was willing to submit to anything. But once, when Sergeant Anya wanted to search me after my visit with my husband was over, I asked her very calmly for a personal search warrant. You see, it was only after the visit that I spoke my mind, and in any case I had to wait 24 hours for the train . . .

The camp in which Ginzburg was being held was located some 90 kilometers from the Yavas railroad station. His mother who was coming to visit him asked the driver of a local school bus, which went by the camp, whether he could take her and her daughter-in-law to the camp. The women's request was refused. Why? They were told they might be a bad influence on the poor little children. The women finally found a truck that took them to the camp over the long and difficult terrain.

Let me repeat again that even here no laws are being violated by the authorities, but of course all this is typical of the inhumanity that reigns in our country.

A prisoner's wife has the added burden of explaining to her children their father's fate. I was very lucky in this respect because when my husband was arrested, our son was 8 months old. I had a few years to think about what I was going to tell him about his father. When the time came, I told my son that his father was living in a little house very far away and was doing very important work. As you see, it is difficult to speak with a child about the father's whereabouts. The homes of many families of prisoners are bugged with microphones, so one has to be very careful with words. When I once visited a camp near Moscow, a guard asked me: "Why do you tell your child all this nonsense about his father holding a responsible job? You know very well that he's carrying loads in this camp." What could I say? I looked the guard in the eyes and said: "Of course, but you also know that he is participating in a little bit of Russian history. And so I feel that he's doing important work" . . .

One should not forget that imprisoned dissidents have families, wives, and children. We should always remember them . . .

CHAPTER II

*The Fight Against Religion and
the Sufferings of the Faithful*

GERHARDT HAMM

" . . . our brothers and sisters are being persecuted for their faith in the Gospel . . . "

HAMM, Gerhardt

German. Born September 7, 1923 in Surova in the Urals. One of 20 children; received a religious upbringing.

In 1931, Hamm moved with his mother, brothers and sisters to Siberia, where his father was living in exile. In 1942 Hamm—like many other Germans during World War II—was interned and exiled to Vorkuta, a city in the northern Urals built by prisoners. He spent the next 5 years behind barbed wire and 10 more years under constant police surveillance.

From 1967 to 1974, Hamm, his wife, and their five children resided in Latvia.

In his own words, "Christian life in the Soviet Union is not an easy one," and because of his beliefs, Hamm was often exposed to harassment and persecutions.

On April 23, 1974 Hamm emigrated to West Germany, "a latecomer to the homeland," as he says, for which he is "very grateful."

136

ON THE LIFE OF THE RELIGIOUS IN THE U.S.S.R.

The Prophet Jeremiah said of old: "And seek the peace of the city whither I have caused you to be carried away captives, and pray unto the Lord for it; for in the peace thereof shall ye have peace." (Jer. 29:7)

Every Christian knows that he should pray for the place where he lives and for his country. I say with conviction that many people pray for Russia, in Russia itself and beyond its borders. Why is this so? The answer is simple. Russia is a multinational and greatly suffering land. In czarist Russia, Christians also suffered, and many gave up their lives for the Truth. We can read about this in books and hear about it from those who lived at that time. Believers who have emigrated from the U.S.S.R. not only pray for their motherland, they love her. They love their country because this is where they were born and where they left behind their father's house, their mother's love, and the concerns of their ancestors. I, too, love my motherland; I left there my dearest friends, my relatives, my best memories—both of joys and sorrows. Whoever does not love his country is not worthy of it. I do not intend to throw stones at it, to slander it; no, indeed not. I shall speak only of what is backed up by documentary evidence. Every state has its laws; so has the Soviet Union. From its many laws I shall quote only those that refer to religion.

Let me present a short rundown of laws that pertain to religion in the U.S.S.R.:

The Decree of the Soviet People's Commissars of January 23, 1918.

Paragraph 1:   The church is separate from the state.

Paragraph 2:   It is prohibited to enact on the territory of the republic local laws or regulations which would put any restraint upon or limit freedom of conscience, or establish any advantages or privileges on the grounds of the religion of citizens.

Paragraph 3:   Every citizen may confess any religion or no religion at all. Loss of any rights as the result of the confession of a religion or the absence of a religion shall be revoked.

Note: The mention in official papers of the religion of a citizen is not allowed.

Paragraph 9:   The school shall be separate from the church. Citizens may give and receive religious instruction privately.

The constitution, the fundamental law of our land, was published on the basis of the "Decree."

Paragraph 124:   The church in the U.S.S.R. shall be separate from the state, and the school from the church, to ensure freedom of conscience for all citizens. Freedom of religious worship and of anti-religious propaganda shall be recognized for all citizens, and the following freedoms are also guaranteed:

Freedom of Conscience;
Freedom of Speech;
Freedom of the Press;
Freedom of Assembly;
Freedom of Demonstration.

The constitution is merely a slogan for the benefit of other countries. In fact, faithful Christians in the U.S.S.R. are tried on the basis of the illegal Law on Religious Associations of 1929.

Paragraph 13:   Religious associations at their general assemblies elect by open ballot an executive body from among their members, consisting of: three members per religious society, and one representative per group of believers.

Paragraph 14:   The registering agencies are entitled to remove individual members from the executive body.

Paragraph 17:   Religious associations may not:
(a) set up funds for mutual aid
(b) grant material aid to their members
(c) organize religious or other meetings for children, young people and women, biblical or literary meetings, circles, groups, or handicraft circles, work circles, religion classes, etc., excursions, children's play-grounds, libraries, reading rooms, sanatoria, or medical care.

138

Paragraph 64: Surveillance over the activities of religious associations, as well as over the maintenance of prayer buildings and property leased to religious associations, shall be exercised by registering agencies, and in rural areas by village soviets.

The Law on Religious Associations is still in force, as the trials of Christians continuously demonstrate. Whoever does not accept this law meets difficulties, *i.e.*, comes into conflict with the authorities. A true believer cannot accept or carry out the Law on Religious Associations because this law directly contravenes the Bible, the constitution, and his own conscience. So the believer is either guilty before God and himself, or before the State. This is the situation Russian Christians find themselves in. This is the main source of all the sufferings of God's people.

I shall quote a few documented facts from the lives of Evangelical Christians and Baptists over the last 14 years:
1. Every local congregation must be on the authorized list, *i.e.*, it must be registered. This is legal and acceptable. Believers do not oppose registration on the basis of the constitution. This is attested to by thousands of petitions from local congregations addressed to the registering authorities. But, unfortunately, their requests are almost never granted. Why? The answer is that in Form No. 1, point 4, the following phrase occurs: "I am familiar with the Law on Religious Associations and I promise to act in accordance with it." This is the wording of the document. Believers cannot sign it, because the Law contravenes conscience, the Bible, and the constitution. As a result they refuse to register. This means that unregistered congregations are declared illegal and can be prosecuted. They have no support from the authorities, nor from the World Council of Evangelical Christians and Baptists, as the latter includes only registered congregations.

In 1968 the March Decree came into force: "For organizing an unlawful religious service, there is to be a monetary fine of up to 50 rubles and deprivation of liberty for up to 5 years." The fines have reached an inhuman level.

For example, in the town of Perm, G. P. Okunyer, a 79-year-old man, was fined a total of 1,225 rubles from 1969 to 1974.

In "Bulletin" No. 16, 1974, A. Gazov, a pensioner and total invalid, was reported to have had 150 rubles confiscated from his pension. S. P. Pirozhkov was fined 450 rubles. P. G. Sanychev was fined 250 rubles.

In January 1974, a small group of eight people was fined 320 rubles in one month. In Magnitogorsk, 34 people (21 of them pensioners) were fined 2,355 rubles; in the village of Mirolyubov-ka in Omsk region, where I grew up, a presbyter was fined 100 rubles on one occasion—he had 11 children in his family.

There are thousands of such cases. The total sum involved is over a million rubles, for which people have received receipts; even more money has been confiscated for which there is no documentary evidence, as it was merely taken off wages without any further proceedings.

2. There is no time to enumerate all the countless occasions on which religious services have been forcibly dispersed. Officials of the KGB, militiamen, druzhinniki laid their hands on people, dragging women out into the street by their hair, turned fire hoses on them, transported them in open lorries to a place 30 kilometers outside the town limits and dumped them there—to get home as best as they could. There are no words to describe this kind of lawless behavior which continues to this day.

3. As hundreds of prayerhouses and churches have been demolished, and permission to build new ones is rare, believers are forced to meet in private houses. In Omsk Oblast, for instance, there are 2 registered prayerhouses, and over 60 unregistered ones. This means that believers meet in private homes. Many such houses have been confiscated, or have been demolished by bulldozers, as happened in the towns of Barnaul, Novosibirsk, Alma-Ata, Frunze, Kishinev, Tula, and many other towns and villages.

4. As for the number of trials of believers over the last 14 years —there have been about 800, and of those tried, many were churchmen who were serving their fourth term in prisons and labor camps (both ordinary and strict regime). Alexander Solzhenitsyn describes the existence of prisoners in labor camps very clearly and truthfully in his book *Gulag Archipelago*. All the sufferings of Christians in the Soviet Union are almost unbearable.

Georgi Petrovich Vins, a pastor elected at a meeting in 1965 and re-elected in 1969, was sentenced for 10 years, 5 years in prison and 5 years in exile. At the moment he is in Yakutia. He was sentenced to a second term for not observing the Law on Religious Associations. We have already examined this illegal document; and until the Law on Religious Associations is abolished, there can be no guarantee of religious freedom in Russia. All accepted human rights are contravened in this illegal document. The constitution of the U.S.S.R. is not compatible with the Law on Religious Associations.

5. A very difficult problem is that of children. On July 6, 1973, a new Article (No. 52) of the Criminal Code was brought into force: "On marriage and the family." In accordance with Article 52 of the Criminal Code on the family and marriage in the R.S.-F.S.R., parents must bring up their children "in the spirit and moral code of the builders of communism." . . .

On the basis of this law, believers are being deprived of their parental rights, and the courts take their children away from them. Such episodes took place in the town of Perm. Romanovich and Zdorov were deprived of their parental rights. Such actions show the inhumanity of the authorities, but God will hear all the cries and [see all the] tears of widows and orphans, and the time will come when those responsible will have to answer for everything.

6. There have been a series of incidents where atheists, led by KGB officials, have tortured believers to death.

Nikolai Khmara, from Kulunda, was tortured on January 9, 1964, and his tongue was torn out.

Ivan Moiseyev was also tortured, then drowned in the sea near the town of Kerch on July 16, 1972.

Ivan Ostapenko, from the village of Shevchenko, was hanged in February 1974 for remaining true to his calling.

Dear listeners, it is very hard for me to speak of this, but I recall the story of Joseph. When he was in prison he said to Pharaoh's cup-bearer who was being released: "Think of me, when it shall be well with thee and show kindness, I pray thee, unto me, and make mention of me unto Pharaoh, and bring me out of this house." (Gen. 40:14)

There in Russia, our brothers and sisters are being persecuted for their faith in the Gospel, and our duty is to remember them, which we are doing today.

In the name of that great number of Christians, we ask the government of the U.S.S.R. to abolish the Law on Religious Associations, as it does not correspond to the law, that is, it is an unlawful law. We also ask that believers be allowed to live freely, in accordance with the Soviet constitution and the Declaration of Human Rights.

ANATOLI LEVITIN-KRASNOV

*" ... I have never been an enemy of the Soviet power,
and have always noted with joy the positive occurrences
that have taken place ... "*

THE STATE OF RELIGION
IN THE U.S.S.R.

. . . The Soviet system is the only state structure where a peaceful person, a school teacher, could be in prison for 10 years, held in 16 different jails and 12 different camps, forced to live for years in half-starvation, and in old age find himself in exile—only because of his religious-philosophical convictions and his adherence to democracy and Christian socialism. This alone is enough to characterize the system that exists in the Soviet Union.

And yet I have never been an enemy of the Soviet power, and have always noted with joy the positive occurrences that have taken place.

In the present case, however, I will tell you about the negative occurrences, since for the description of the positive occurrences the Soviets have a sufficient number of well paid, specially educated, though mostly not very clever, propagandists.

In doing so I will tell the truth, the whole truth, and nothing but the truth, so help me God! . . .

As is generally known, when the Communist Party of the Soviet Union came to power it officially proclaimed as its objective the annihilation of religion in the U.S.S.R.

In 1921, the authorities proceeded to organize a general physical extermination of the clergy. During the so-called "collectivization" period in 1929 and 1930, almost all churches were closed down and a wave of mass arrests of rural clergy swept through the country districts. The clergy, like the "kulaks,"[1] was declared to be a remnant from a hostile class structure. All rural clergymen were deported to camps . . .

145

The process of liquidation of the church in the U.S.S.R. was somewhat detained by the intervention of Pope Pius XI and his campaign in defense of religion.

But in 1932, a mass destruction of city churches began. The first blow was struck against the monastic clergy. On the 17th of February 1932, monks and nuns who previously had been driven out of the monasteries and now were serving in churches, were arrested. Some 20,000 were arrested in just one day. At the same time, the Orthodox and Catholic churches that were still open in the cities began to be closed in massive numbers.

Each of the following years saw mass arrests of clergy. The arrests were usually accompanied by large-scale closings of churches.

This kind of campaign was particularly evident in the autumn of 1935 and the spring of 1936, when prior to May 1, 1936 the following slogan was officially proclaimed: "Clergymen and sectarians want to poison our children with the venom of religion. Let us repulse the hostility of the churchmen and the sectarians."

At that time the religious became the target of a hysterical press campaign. All these events preceded the year 1937. Afterwards, only a small handful—some 200 to 250 persons—was all that was left of the Russian Orthodox clergy, which had numbered 100,000; and throughout the U.S.S.R., only a few dozen churches remained.

As is generally known, Stalin suddenly changed his attitude towards the church, partly under influence from abroad—Roosevelt played an important role here—and partly under the influence of the people's religious sentiment that showed itself clearly during the war.

But not one of the arrested bishops—and there were several hundred—and not one of the arrested clergymen or monks and nuns—of whom there were 100,000—were sent back, and all were physically annihilated in the camps.

At the same time, the authorities permitted churches everywhere to be reopened and some monasteries and seminaries to be restored.

As is generally known, Khrushchev, upon his ascension to power, set into motion the inhuman anti-religious campaign with the objective of exterminating religion in the U.S.S.R. within a short time span.

146

During the time that Khrushchev was in power (from 1959 to 1964), 12,800 of the 20,000 Orthodox churches were destroyed. To this may be added that the churches were closed down with brute force. Believers (elderly people) were hosed down, brutally jostled out of the churches, almost getting their arms broken. At the same time, dozens of monasteries and four seminaries were closed down . . .

All this is a thing of the past now. What is the present state of religion in the U.S.S.R.?

Further closing of the churches has been suspended for some time. But the remaining 7,200 churches are not enough to satisfy the needs of believers among the populace. There are entire districts where not a single church can be found, as for instance in the district of Kaliningrad (in Eastern Prussia) and also in nearly the whole of the Far East, where there's only one church for every stretch of 800 to 1000 kilometers.

All attempts by the faithful to have the churches reopened have been met with sharp rebuffs. When one considers that all prayer-meetings in private homes are strictly proscribed if one does not have the necessary registration, then it becomes clear that many millions of people are deprived of the possibility of satisfying their spiritual needs.

Things are no better in other districts. In the district of Leningrad, for instance, only a few churches remain open. In ancient Novgorod—a city of 200,000—only a little chapel, consecrated to the Holy Apostle Philip, is open. The chapel has only room enough for one-tenth of the faithful. Somewhat similar conditions also exist in Yaroslavl, in the cities of Gorky, Novosibirsk, and others.

At the same time, the church is under strict control and its activities are limited to the performance of religious rites alone. There's no separation of church and state despite the constitution.

Compulsory registration of persons christening their children or marrying in church was introduced in 1961. Parents who christen their children in church, or couples who get married in church, must produce their passports. All persons who get registered in this way are in for trouble because their names are passed on to the Rayispolkom,[2] and from there their names are transmitted to their place of work.

All clergymen (from the patriarch on down to the parish

clerk) must be registered with the mandatary of the Council for Religious Matters. This council has an unrestricted veto right. The mandataries have an equally unlimited veto power, both with respect to admissions to seminaries and clerical academies, as well as to activities of teachers there. This enables the KGB to flood seminaries and academies with agents of their own, and to blackmail seminary and academy students by threatening them that they will not be admitted to those institutions unles they become secret KGB collaborators.

Unusually many applications were handed in during August 1974 for entrance examinations to the Moscow Seminary: seven applications for each available seat. Twenty applications came from Moscow. But the Council for Religious Matters vetoed the most qualified applicants. The KGB in Moscow had established a very rigid standard: Only two persons were allowed to be admitted. All young people who had applied for admission were subjected to a series of repressions: They were fired from their place of work, after which the uniformed police declared them to be "idlers."

A religious person likewise has a very difficult position in Soviet life. Not only does he not enjoy "freedom of conscience," but on the contrary, he lives under conditions that involve continuous violence against his religious conscience.

Already in kindergarten children of religious parents are forbidden to wear small crosses. They are told that their parents are ignorant, illiterate people. In that way children, still under school age, are traumatized. The collision becomes even more traumatic in school where children of religious parents are forced to become pioneers [member of the Communist children's organization]; a pioneer, however, is obliged to be anti-religious.

When young people reach the age of 15, they are confronted with the question of whether to join the Komsomol, which is an anti-religious organization. But a young person who is not a member of the Komsomol has practically very little chance of getting into an institute of higher learning. All teachers have a duty to make anti-religious propaganda. While it is true that most teachers sabotage this order, some of them are wildly fanatic in this respect. In 1959 it happened that a schoolmistress in a third class brought an icon into the classroom and, in the presence of all pupils, threw it out of the window.

148

The time religious students spend at an institute becomes a time of torment. They are compelled to present their work from the so-called Marxist-Leninist anti-religious point of view. If it is found out that a student is religious, he will be immediately excluded from the institute for "unproficiency." This is done in the following way: The teacher, who is a CPSU member, is summoned to the Partkom[3] and is given the task of insuring that a certain student fails his examination. In accordance with party discipline, the teacher must obey the order. This leads to absolutely incredible incidents.

Thus, a young man, Alexander Ogorodnikov, who lives in Moscow, has a certificate that says that for 3 years he had been studying at Moscow's Cinema Institute, and had received the mark "excellent" in all his subjects, and was excluded on account of . . . unproficiency.

Alevtina Filatova was first dismissed from the Institute of Rocket Construction and then from the Moscow Conservatory because she used to sing in a church choir.

Alexander Men, now an archpriest, was excluded from the institute in Irkutsk. There were thousands of such young people. When it turns out that a person who has finished a higher educational institution is religious, criticism is levelled against the institute's administration by higher officialdom and the press. Therefore the administration, as a precaution, endeavors to get rid of students who are believers.

As regards people of mature age, their position is even more difficult.

For one thing, they cannot hold an administrative post, because to do so they have to be a member of the CPSU, which of course is impossible for a religious person. Thus every religious person has to write off any career. Secondly, religious persons cannot hold any position connected with ideological work (teaching in school or at an institute, or working in a humanitarian profession) . . .

Persons who protest against this attitude towards the believers are subjected to barbarous repressions. Thus, Boris Vladimirovich Talantov was put in a camp because of his works in which he portrayed the true position of religion in the U.S.S.R. He was 66 years old at that time and seriously ill, and he died in the camp on January 4, 1971. Likewise, on May 19, 1971, I was sentenced by the Moscow Town Court to 3 years' imprisonment pursuant to Article 190.1—calumny of the Soviet socio-political system—only because I had shown in my article the actual position of the faithful in the U.S.S.R.

The hunting down of the courageous clergyman, Father Dimitri Dudko, is generally known. Father Dudko had protested from the pulpit against the persecution of religion in the U.S.S.R.

I have here stated the facts concerning the position of the Russian Orthodox Church in the U.S.S.R.

The position of the other religious denominations is literally horrifying. The persecution of these reminds one of the times of Nero and Diocletian . . .

---

1) Kulaks—wealthy peasants, prime targets during the collectivization of Soviet agriculture in the late 1920's and early 1930's.
2) Rayispolkom—district executive committee
3) Partkom—party committee

DAVID KLASSEN

*" . . . police and KGB troops . . . broke up the gatherings
(of Christians) like vandals . . . "*

KLASSEN, David

Volga-German. Born April 14, 1927 in the village of Volodymyrivka in Zaporizhzhya region, Ukraine, into a Baptist family.

On August 18, 1941 his village was occupied by the German forces. As the German army withdrew, Klassen was forcibly evacuated by the Germans to Poland. On February 23, 1945, when the Soviet army occupied Poland, Klassen, together with other Volga-Germans, was led away by Polish soldiers to be executed. He managed to survive the massacre that followed.

In 1946, while awaiting repatriation to his native land, he was instead deported to Siberia and placed under police surveillance.

Having become a presbyter of the Novosibirsk Church, Klassen was subjected to continuous repressions. He was arrested five times and spent almost 10 years in various Siberian concentration camps and Moscow prisons.

On May 31, 1974, Klassen was granted permission to emigrate as a result of the agreement on family reunions signed between the Soviet Union and West Germany.

152

ON THE SUFFERING OF EVANGELICAL CHRISTIANS AND BAPTISTS

. . . Allow me to express my gratitude to my Creator and Saviour that on the invitation of the Common Committee of East Exiles I am granted the opportunity to speak as a witness of the situation of Christians in Russia [U.S.S.R.]. And if I am allowed to speak about the persecuted church in Russia, then I shall do it according to the order of the last words spoken by Jesus Christ on the Mount of Olives, on the day of His Ascension: "You shall be my witnesses in Jerusalem and in all Judaea and Samaria and to the end of the earth." (Acts 1:9)

There was a time when my witness, like the witness of my brothers and sisters, found expression in prison cells among criminals, in investigation offices and court rooms, in mental hospitals, in distant camps, and in exile. Now we have been allowed to witness in Jerusalem and Samaria and Judaea, in distant Africa, in the U.S.A., in England and France, the Netherlands and Belgium, Finland and Austria, Switzerland and Sweden, in Rome and in Berlin and in various countries of the world, to the end of the earth.

But first of all, before I speak of the severe sufferings of the Russian Christians, let me express my feelings of gratitude towards my fatherland. My fatherland is for me not the country in which I feel free and where I am surrounded by friendliness and love. My fatherland will remain forever the piece of earth where I was born, even though I have been persecuted and abhorred there. And just as an animal leaves its lair, enjoying

153

nature, and will return to its lair to die, I wish to be buried back home.

While saying this, I can on no account forget the mean, abominable things done there, the cunning provocations of arbitrary rule, the wicked deceit and terrible violence under the yoke of which the Russian brethren groan. Never did I think that the country about which I sang from the bottom of my heart as a child: " . . . my land, my Moscow, most beloved . . . "—that it should swallow me up in its thick prison walls, for years on end, as if in the belly of a whale of reinforced concrete. Never did I expect that the words I used to sing: "I know of no other country, where man breathes so freely," would in my lifetime become the opposite; and it was those very officers who in the military group taught me, a 14-year-old lad, to handle a gas mask, to bandage wounds, and to save people, it was those same officers who poisoned us with gas, as was the case on January 22, 1972, in camp P/Ya 243/2-2 in the Komi A.S.S.R. Who would have thought that after studying the most democratic constitution, an investigator could have said: "I am sending you to the polar bears, to the borders of the world," and that a camp boss could say: "Take into consideration that here in the north the taiga is the law, the bear is the boss, and if the cock goes barefoot in the winter—in what way are you his better?"

Still ringing in my ears is the threatening voice of warning which spoke before over 400 delegates on May 17, 1966, at the parade entrance of the government building. It was the voice of KGB boss Semichastny. Over 400 delegates [of the non-registered Evangelical Christians and Baptists] heard Minister of the Interior Shcholokov's threat: "I am going to set Moscow police and druzhinniky on you."

It was frightening to look on when at two weddings in Frunze, in March 1974, police and KGB troops plus two lorries full of soldiers of the interior armies broke up the gatherings like vandals, wrenched and broke arms, and scattered the Christians.

In Ukraine (Luhansk region) a school director armed pioneers and Komsomol youth with saws and axes and attacked the Evangelical Christians' and Baptists' prayer house. The pioneers with their red scarves, the Komsomol youths with their badges rushed to the cellar, carried up a whole battery of jam jars and threw them against the walls of the prayer room . . .

154

In the Altai region, the local organs of authority decided to persecute the believers by depriving them of the possibility of buying fodder for their cattle. Thus, in the Soviet Union it is not only the Christians who suffer, but also its entire population, innocent children, animals . . .

Soviet humanism is capable of mercilessly tearing a child from its mother's arms, to sever this bond only because children were educated in the evangelical spirit.

In the miners' village of Pridolinki, 45 kilometers from Karaganda, going towards Shakhtinsky, is a child's grave, where a young Christian, Yelena Klassen, lies buried. After several girls had disappeared, the Soviet press dared slander the believers as "those who offer sacrifices." Our God, to Whom we submitted this sorrow in prayer, our God about Whom it is said: "He will bring forth your vindication as the light, and your right as the noonday" (Psalm 37:6)—this God heard our prayers and fulfilled His promise. There came the day and the hour when the corpse of a girl who had been raped, strangled, weighted with a concrete block, and thrown in the lake, was discovered—a corpse of which only bones and hair had remained. Thus it was made clear that it was not the Christians who offered sacrifices, but a Communist, the communications chief of Pridolinki. A similar provocation took place in the town of Dzhezkazgan in Karaganda region. Two girls who were under age were brutally raped, carpenter's nails were driven through their skulls, and then they were thrown onto the threshold of the prayer house—upon which the authorities closed the prayer house.

The Soviet state is the largest in the whole world, it stretches from sunrise, the Pacific, to sunset, the Baltic Sea, and from the mountain range of the Tanshet to the Arctic Ocean. It is impossible to tell all in ten or fifteen minutes. . . Thousands of Christians were buried in the depths of the White Sea Channel, under the railway sleepers, in the deserts, in the death valley on Kolyma, in the mountains of the Urals, and in the swampy tundra of Vorkuta. Thousands of wives were made widows in the Yezhov era, and millions of children were condemned to be orphans. In bonds and handcuffs, in prison cars and prisoners' trucks, in the holds of boats, and in airplanes the Russian brethren were transported to the most distant and ghastly places. From the Central Asian desert where temperature reaches +50°

to +60°C, to cold Yakutia where it gets as much as 60° or 70°C below zero—everywhere our brothers and sisters are suffering. Prison life in the Soviet Union has become so habitual that the saying has been coined: "He who has not been inside isn't a human being."

In prisons and camps I happened to meet various believers, from the illiterate Nenetz from the Far North to the [Ukrainian] Cardinal Joseph Slipyj. In one experimental zone of camp P/Ya 385/1 alone, situated 450 kilometers southeast of Moscow, representatives of over forty denominations were detained. If one were to put together all the prison and camp terms spent there by Christians during the reign of the Soviets, one would get millennia upon millennia. And if one were to calculate the material losses caused by confiscation and fines, the sum would be equal to thousands of millions of rubles. In Ukraine alone, over 70 prayer houses were closed down between 1959 and 1961. In Novosibirsk one church was turned into a training center for tanks, another into a coal warehouse, and two churches were pulled down. The Militant Atheist Union adopts the tactics of the Trojan War in its fight against the Christians, such as provocations and national as well as racial hostilities.

N. V. Odintsovo was torn to pieces by dogs, Osypenko was strangled, Moiseyev was drowned, Khmara was tortured to death —this does not astonish us. It is in the tradition of Red terror.

Finally I wish to note that, knowing all this, you still have merely the faintest idea of what is happening to the persecuted brethren in Russia. I am grateful to you for listening to me. . . .

EVGENI BRESENDEN

"... the court will pay close attention to a preacher's religious activity and will sentence him accordingly ..."

BRESENDEN, Evgeni

Born 1941 in Barnaul, R.S.F.S.R. Because his father had died at the front and his mother was sentenced to 10 years in prison for her religious convictions, Bresenden, as an 8-year-old, was placed in a children's home. In 1954—after the death of Stalin—Bresenden's mother was released and he was returned to her care. He became a believer and was baptized in 1957.

In 1962, Bresenden was arrested for his religious convictions and sentenced to 3 years' deprivation of freedom. After release in 1965 he became actively involved in religious work.

Numerous repressive measures—such as summonses by official authorities, insults, dismissal from work because of his religious beliefs, threats to take away his children and incarcerate him in a psychiatric hospital—led Bresenden to believe that he was a "stranger in his own land." Fearing that the fate that had befallen him, and earlier his parents, might also be that of his children, Bresenden applied for an emigration visa.

On September 11, 1975, Bresenden and his family left the U.S.S.R.

158

THE PERSECUTION OF PENTECOSTAL EVANGELICAL CHRISTIANS

The Pentecostal movement spread out in the U.S.S.R. in 1924, when a preacher, Ivan Efimovich Voronayev, arrived from the United States and subsequently became the head of the Union of Christian Evangelic Pentecostals. A large net of communities was formed in Central Russia, in Ukraine, and in Central Asia. They published a magazine called *Evangelist*. The movement then spread out to Siberia and to the Far East.

Voronayev was arrested and jailed in 1928. During one of his daily walks in the [prison] courtyard, watchdogs were let into the yard and mauled him so badly that he died of the wounds in his cell. His relatives and friends were told that he had been killed by watchdogs in an attempt to escape. All his closest assistants were jailed, but some decided to cooperate with the authorities and joined the official Union of Christian Evangelic Baptists most of the true believers, however, later broke away from this Union and formed an Initiative Group. This was the end of the Pentecostal Movement's freedom. Their magazine ceased to exist. The leaders of Pentecostal communities in Central Asia, Ukraine, and Central Russia were arrested; some of them were shot, others sentenced to 10 years.

Most of them never returned. They perished in the camps. Subsequently, the Pentecostal Movement was headed by Bidash, who was arrested many times and sentenced to different terms of jail or house arrest; he is under house arrest to our days.

159

A second wave of jailings swept the country in 1939. Again the preachers and community leaders were arrested, and most of them were shot. (In the city of Svobodny, Amur region, they arrested the head of the community, Afanasi Georgiyevich Raylan, and his three brothers. All were sentenced to death. The brothers were shot immediately; Afanasi spent 72 days in the death cell but was then sent to camp, and his sentence was commuted to 10 years.)

The same proportion was maintained in all other towns. In 1941, they jailed not only the preachers and community leaders, but all the members of the church and all men from the age of 18 to 50. Those who would not accept to serve in the army because of their religious beliefs were either shot (Arbuzov Nikolai, city of Svobodny, Amur region) or sent to camp for 10 years (Arbuzov's father, Tikhon). I am quoting from the testimony of Nikolai's mother, Alexandra Arbuzova.

The same thing happened in other cities. In 1946, on Stalin's personal initiative, there was an attempt to unite Baptists and Pentecostals; the so-called August Agreement was worked out, according to which Pentecostal communities were to exist and work, while their rights were to be fully respected. This agreement was broken, however, by both the authorities and by the senior priests of the All-Union Council of Christian Baptists. The representatives of the Pentecostal Movement protested, and as a consequence, authorities ordered that Bidash, Belykh, Levchuk, and many other leaders of the so-called "clandestine" Pentecostal union be jailed.

In 1949, most community members throughout the country were arrested—women and men, girls and boys. It happened that they would carry to court 80-year-old women and men (in the city of Barnaul). They were all processed as "American spies," and sentenced to 10 or 25 years. The accusation was based on the fact that the Pentecostal preacher Voronayev had come from the United States, and therefore whoever belonged to this religion was an American spy.

In 1961, after Khrushchev launched his slogan "Death to religion," community heads and preachers were tried again for "belonging to a sect whose rites are harmful to the citizens' health" (Art. 227 of the Penal Code). The harm consists in the fact that people allegedly gather in rooms which are too small, with scarce ventilation and light. But this is no fault of the preachers; the responsibility lies with the officials in charge of religious matters at the Council of Ministers of the U.S.S.R., hence with the government itself, which will not grant free and normal celebration of religious rites.

Those who were tried under Article 227 were sentenced to 5 years of jail or of camps, and 5 years of deportation (exile).

It is very difficult nowadays to find a Pentecostal who was an eyewitness of the founding of the Voronayev community, in spite of the fact that there are Pentecostals old enough to have seen it. The majority of the participants were either shot or perished in camps which Solzhenitsyn rightfully called "camps of extermination by work." There are very few people who managed to survive. They now are all in very bad physical condition, and they have spent at least 10 years in jail, some of them 19 years, as did Afanasi Raylyan, in Nakhodka.

As I said, Bidash is still under house arrest. I cannot indicate the exact number of those who died. But I can quote the official at the Council of Ministers of the U.S.S.R. who is in charge of religious matters for the Primorsky region, A. Shlandakov, who on April 19, 1974 said: "The Soviet government is strong, it does not fear world public opinion. Thousands of you died, and if it will be necessary, thousands will die again."

We quite believe that what he said of the past is true; but we would like to avoid that this should happen in the future.

I also want to say something about the so-called "personal trials." Our faith forbids us to kill, to seek revenge, and to swear. But since the Soviet legislation does not admit a right to religious beliefs, it is compulsory to obey the law on general military service and to let oneself be drafted, to swear that one will fight the enemy with arms and until the last drop of blood—that is, that one will kill other people. As soon as a young Pentecostal reaches the age of 18, he is faced with the dilemma: if he acts according to his conscience, he will be tried and sentenced to 3, or 5, or 7 years (it is for the courts to decide); otherwise he may act against his conscience and accept to be drafted. The law on military conscription can be applied even if the Christian who is to be drafted simply can't serve because of his health condition (this was my case), or if he is actually already too old for service (now, for instance, there is an attempt to draft, and hence try and sentence, our Bishop Vashchenko Grigori, from Nakhodka, though he is 48 years old).

There are cases where a person's family situation is such that he would be entitled to be exempted from service, but it does not happen; such is the case of Daniil Grigoryevich Vashchenko.

A preacher may be summoned to the military authorities at any time and told to serve in the army, no matter what his age, or his family situation, or his health may be. But the court will pay close attention to his religious activity, and will sentence him accordingly. The more active he is, the longer his term will be.

Thus we are always under the threat of being prosecuted for a criminal offense, and the authorities have only to decide: "Shall we put him into jail now, or a little bit later?"

Methods of Persecution:

The absence of a real law on freedom of conscience. Since the law does not allow us to exist, we are outlaws and criminals.

No right to education.

No right to work, to rest, to tourism.

No right to correspondence, to secrecy of correspondence.

No right to travel even within one's own country.

Until 1941, shootings.

Jail, psychiatric homes, deportations. Parents are deprived of the right to educate their children; children are actually taken away from them.

Fines. People are dismissed from work and are subsequently sentenced to forced work.

It is forbidden to meet for prayer, though the meetings are peaceful.

It is forbidden to practice charity.

It is forbidden to educate one's children in a religious spirit, to teach them religion, or to study religion.

It is forbidden to form unions or associations.

There are still Pentecostals in camps and prisons.

The lack of support by world public opinion has very negative consequences.

The prosecutor of the city of Nakhodka, one Bokhan, told me: "We spit on world public opinion and on international laws on human rights. We've got instructions and we are enforcing them."

162

Consequence of persecutions:

In view of the religious intolerance in the U.S.S.R., the majority of Christian Pentecostals wait for a chance to leave the country and to emigrate to any non-communist country. They would rather go to Israel than to any other place because according to the Bible and Gospel, when justice and peace will be re-established after the present turmoil, the beginning of everything will be in Israel. Therefore we would be prepared to share all the Israeli people's difficulties and hardships.

CHAPTER III

The Abuse of Psychiatry

MARINA FAINBERG

*" . . . I realized that people who were healthy were being
sent to psychiatric asylums . . ."*

FAINBERG, Marina

Marina Fainberg, nee Voikhanskaya, is a graduate of Leningrad's First Medical Institute. She was a practicing psychiatrist for 13 years, mostly in the Psychiatric Hospital No. 3 in Leningrad. There she met Victor Fainberg, a patient whom she would later marry. She saved his life by making sure that he was not administered any drugs. They were married after his release from the hospital. Victor Fainberg emigrated from the U.S.S.R. in 1974. In April 1975 Marina Fainberg was given permission to leave the U.S.S.R. and joined her husband in England.

ON THE SANE IN
INSANE ASYLUMS

I graduated from the Leningrad Medical Institute in 1960. From 1962 until April 1975 I worked as a psychiatrist in Leningrad. For the last 8 years I worked at Psychiatric Ward No. 3 of the Skortzov-Stepanov Clinic in Leningrad.

I was proud of my profession, believing that its task was to help people. We know that people in psychiatric asylums are sick and need affection and love.

I was not involved in politics. After the invasion of Czechoslovakia I used to listen to the Western radio, particularly in the summer, because in the winter it's much more difficult—there's more jamming.

I heard on the radio that in the Soviet Union normal people were sent to psychiatric wards, but I considered this to be the usual Western provocations. But when case histories of healthy people were submitted to the World Congress of Psychiatrists in Mexico in December 1972, I slowly began to have my doubts. But I did not harbor those doubts for a very long time; I appeased myself by thinking that if there were indeed such people in the Soviet Union, then they were probably in special prison hospitals. Certainly this would not occur in the hospital where I worked.

But soon I learned that one Vladimir Borisov was in my hospital, and he was not sick, nor did he have any neurotic symptoms.

Then I remembered the history of a patient, a woman in her

60's, her name was Kondakova. Her husband was a well-known director of a Leningrad factory. Because of his prestige, she could permit herself to criticize her colleagues. She thought that all had the same freedom to criticize others as she had. But her husband died, and she forgot that she was no longer protected by his position. She wanted to discuss in her office violations of party discipline. She turned to one of her superiors who, however, did not want to meet with her. She then went to the post office and sent a telegram to Brezhnev in which she requested a meeting with him. But when she returned home from the post office she was arrested at her doorstep by several helpers from a psychiatric institution. She was brought to a psychiatric hospital. She believed, of course, that it was all a misunderstanding.

In December 1973 I had a patient who was perhaps somewhat strange in his behavior but who certainly did not have any neurotic symptoms. His name was Yevgeni Komarov. He spent 2 days in our hospital under observation, and I determined that he was mentally sound. He only suffered from high blood pressure.

This case left no illusions; I realized that people who were healthy were being sent to psychiatric asylums.

In January 1974, my friends told me there was a patient by the name of Ivanov in my hospital. They asked me to examine him to find out whether he was ill or healthy. I called the chief of the ward, a young woman psychiatrist, and asked her about the patient. But she became suspicious, and told me: "Don't you get involved. But to you I will tell that he is well, but don't tell this to those who asked about him." I then visited him and looked after him while he was in our hospital. He was a painter and had spent 15 years in prison for anti-Soviet propaganda, but his real offense was the fact that he had exhibited his paintings in Paris. He had been released and rehabilitated in 1971, and had received the right to return to his native Leningrad. But the authorities in Leningrad did not want him to come back. He had to settle in Smolensk, and was forced to work in a ceramic factory . . .

In 1973, he appealed to the KGB in Leningrad, Smolensk, and Moscow for permission to return to Leningrad. He was told that of course he could do so; all he had to do was to report to a house on Litejny Boulevard to pick up his permit. When he showed up, an ambulance was waiting for him—I don't know whether there was a doctor or a nurse. In any case, he was sent to a psychiatric asylum and diagnosed as schizophrenic.

At first Ivanov was sent to a psychiatric hospital in a suburb of Leningrad, where the doctors were young and courageous. They apparently did not yet know the realities of Soviet life, and decided that he did not need any treatment because he was healthy. He was then transferred to our hospital. When he came to us he did not even have a toothbrush, no soap; he had nothing, really. I visited him daily and I must say that the doctors did not even try to treat him because they realized he was healthy.

They permitted me to visit him, but I was generally ostracized. Six months later there was a change in the directorship of that ward. The new ward chief was on good terms with the KGB. My visits were reported to the head physician, and subsequently I became subjected to petty harassments and was no longer allowed to visit Ivanov.

He was eventually transferred to other psychiatric hospitals in Leningrad. He was released in April 1975, and was issued a certificate that he had spent two years under observation.

In April 1974 one of my patients was Anatoli Dimitriyevich Ponomarev. He was a very mild, fine, and somewhat intimidated person. He had been transferred to my ward from the notorious ward No. 8. He was treated with tremendous doses of drugs, which usually are given only to mentally very sick persons. He did not want to answer my questions, saying only that he was not ill. This was the first such case I had, and I did not know what to do. I was at a loss, and told him that if he was well I would not treat him, and if he stayed calm, I would not administer any drugs.

He was an engineer and had a degree. He was born in 1931. In 1970 he had been arrested under Article 193. The KGB had not forgotten that in 1968 he had been the only person at his place of work to openly speak out against the invasion of Czechoslovakia. . . . When he became my patient I observed him carefully. His case history said that he was a schizophrenic, but there were absolutely no corresponding symptoms to be found in him, and his case history also made no mention of any symptoms. He was a very quiet person . . .

In recent years it has become common in the Soviet Union to send to psychiatric hospitals all socially unreliable persons, including alcoholics, dissidents, and people who constantly change their opinions. Such admissions (to mental institutions) frequently occur before visits of heads of state to the Soviet Union. Ponomarev's admission coincided with the May 1st celebrations and Nixon's visit to the Soviet Union . . .

In September 1974 he was again sent to a psychiatric institution because he had sent Brezhnev a telegram inquiring about a job. After his initial release from the hospital he had been unable to find a job although he mastered all European languages. Ponomarev sent the telegram in the morning, and in the afternoon he was arrested and sent to a psychiatric institution where he spent many months. The London Society of Psychiatrists sent a telegram to the Soviet Union in which Ponomarev was mentioned. A commission was immediately convoked and Ponomarev was released as a result of this intervention.

Two years ago we had a very fine man in our hospital, Vasili Tchubarov. He did not drink and was a very quiet person. His neighbors thought his behavior very strange and suspicious. This was enough to have him sent to the psychiatric institution. . . . After he was discharged he would come by on Sundays to get a meal. I don't know what has happened to him because he has since disappeared.

Now I would like to tell you about my friends. Vladimir Borisov has spent 9 years in psychiatric hospitals. He was in the hospital not only because he was the leader of a small group of dissidents, but also because he simulated mental disorders.

He simulated illness because there were minors in this group, and he knew that they would not be arrested if their leader turned out to be mentally sick. He was together with Victor Fainberg. Both fought for their rights in the hospital.

Another fine person is Yuri Shikhanovich, a mathematician. Some years ago he was arrested because they found samizdat publications in his apartment. Since he did not say a word throughout a whole year, he was brought to a psychiatric institution. Because French mathematicians spoke up in his defense —there were many protests—he spent only one year in a psychiatric hospital, and only in a regular institution. He was then unable to find a job. Three years ago he started posting posters all around Moscow and so was arrested. He spent a year in Lefortovo Prison and the investigators wrangled with him for a whole year because he would not say a word. He was then sent to Kazan, where in a psychiatric institution he was treated with various drugs and injections. . . .

From December 1974 on, I frequently encountered Pyotr Grigorenko. I suppose all of you know of his case. Still I would like to say something about him. The first time Grigorenko was arrested was in 1964 for distributing leaflets. I should point out that he was a General, and a professor at the Military Academy of Cybernetics. He was asked: "How is it that you are now against Khrushchev?" And he answered: "Well, what can one say about a man who soon will be toppled?" This answer was recorded by a nurse in his "case history," who added: "Disloyal development of a person with a fixed idea of being able to predict the future."

Grigorenko was admitted to a special psychiatric clinic in Leningrad, where he spent a month and a half. In the meantime Khrushchev did indeed disappear from the political scene. His wife was called and told: "Your husband is a General. We did not know that." In any case, he was released. But he was again arrested in 1968 in Tashkent when Crimean Tatars invited him to the Crimea. He was sent to a psychiatric institution in Tashkent on orders of the KGB. But the Tashkent psychiatrists . . . concluded that he was perfectly sane. Grigorenko was then sent to Moscow's Serbsky Institute. Here, of course, psychiatry was of "a higher caliber," and so Grigorenko was found to be mentally disturbed after all.

He was sent back to Tashkent, and from there to the Chernikhovsk special institute. He then spent a year and a half in a place called Byelyye Stolby, a public hospital outside Moscow. His wife attempted to have him released because he was weak and of advanced age. But during a hearing on her request, a psychiatrist said: "He can't be discharged from the hospital. Though he does not have to take drugs, he needs chemotherapy." This happens often [in other cases] . . .

I'd like to say a few words about Vladimir Bukovsky. His name is well known. He did what we psychiatrists should have done. For this he received a 12-year sentence. He was the first person to document that psychiatry in the Soviet Union has become a shameful profession. He showed that healthy people, on orders of the KGB, spent years, as much as 10 years, in psychiatric "hospitals."

There's also another man, whom I don't know personally, but about whom I would like to speak. His name is Semen Gluzman. He is a young psychiatrist, one of the few psychiatrists in the U.S.S.R. who dared to tell the truth about Grigorenko and the latter's samizdat case. For this he was sent to prison, for 10 years all told, particularly since his appeal was published in the Western press and threw light on what is going on in Soviet psychiatric clinics.

Many of you are aware of all these facts. I can only assure you that I have not made anything up, and that I have only spoken the truth about the conditions in the U.S.S.R. In Russia they already thought that it would be enough for me to appear here and to speak to make everyone in the West understand the situation. But it seems to me that this is not at all the case. The West is not at all aware of the threat from the U.S.S.R. Since I am of the opinion that it is necessary to repeat the warning if we want to master the situation, I am repeating the lesson: black is black, and white is white.

VICTOR FAINBERG

" . . . what is taking place in the Soviet Union . . . is a threat to all mankind . . . "

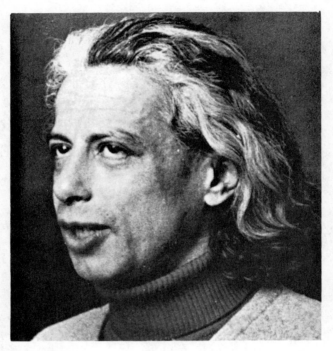

FAINBERG, Victor

Born 1933. A philologist, Fainberg participated on August 25, 1968 in a demonstration in Moscow's Red Square protesting the invasion of Czechoslovakia. For this he was arrested and charged with "slandering the Soviet state." He was judged to be of "unsound mind," and sent for compulsory treatment to a psychiatric hospital. He spent the next 5 years in psychiatric hospitals, including 4 years in the Leningrad Special Psychiatric Hospital.

During his confinement Fainberg regularly defended the rights of hospital prisoners, issuing protest statements and participating in hunger strikes. His open letter of 1972, addressed to U.N. Secretary-General Kurt Waldheim, which discusses the conditions of patients in a special psychiatric hospital, was widely publicized in the West.

Fainberg was released in 1973, but on April 30, 1974, after having published a statement in defense of V. Bukovsky, he was again forcibly taken to a psychiatric prison-hospital.

He was released the same year and permitted to emigrate.

176

CONDITIONS IN
PSYCHIATRIC HOSPITALS

First of all, I would like to apologize that I'm taking the floor here; because according to the laws of the Soviet Union I have no right to take the floor, since I was diagnosed to be schizophrenic with symptoms of paranoia, which showed itself in my wish to freely express my political thoughts. The courts placed my father in charge of me, and I am in fact still under his guardianship.

My wife has told you of the fate of political prisoners in psychiatric hospitals. She has also spoken about the kind of treatment these people receive. She has also told you about how the fate of these political prisoners depends on the stand the West takes, and how Western interventions can have positive effects.

I believe that much more should be said about the prison regime in psychiatric wards, about the life of prisoners in the wards, and how an indifferent Western attitude affects the fate of political prisoners who are being held in psychiatric hospitals.

I was arrested on August 26, 1968, in connection with a protest against the intervention in Czechoslovakia. I was arrested in [Moscow's] Red Square. At that time I was already under investigation in connection with the case of Kwatchevsky, who is here today, and other persons who were being tried in Leningrad. I had been told to give state's evidence in these cases, but I had refused to do so. In fact, the Colonel who was in charge of that investigation on behalf of the Leningrad KGB had warned me that if I refused to give evidence I would be sent to prison or to a psychiatric hospital. That opportunity arose very shortly when a few weeks later I was seized in Red Square.

I was beaten up rather badly and a few of my teeth were knocked out. It would not have been very good for the KGB were I to appear in an open court, and this is why I was sent from Lefortovo Prison to the Serbsky Institute. I was declared a schizophrenic rather quickly, and was thereupon committed to the Leningrad psychiatric hospital.

I would like to tell you about the people I met in the Serbsky Institute, particularly about the so-called doctors who can be found there. To classify these doctors as "human beings" would hardly be appropriate.

Psychiatric prison hospitals have the same type of prison cells that one finds in other prisons. These psychiatric prisons hold "abnormal offenders"—as they say in England—and these "abnormal offenders" are people who have committed crimes for which they are not held responsible, because they are considered mentally abnormal. In our prison there were 750 such patients; on the average, seven to ten of all such "patients" were political prisoners . . .

The hospital can be distinguished from a regular prison in that part of the staff are doctors who wear prison officers' uniforms. These special hospitals are not under the Ministry of Health, but are regulated by the Department of Internal Affairs. The "medical personnel" sent to such hospitals are usually selected from among criminals serving their sentences in prisons. They then serve as the "nursing staff," for which they get about six rubles a month. They don't get enough food, and so they frequently steal food from patients.

It is important to note that the whole "treatment" has but one purpose: to enforce absolute order. And that means, absolute silence. Patients are forced to obedience and silence with all methods, including beatings.

Political prisoners are often held in other sections, where the regime is even more severe. They are generally deprived of those few rights which prisoners in camps usually have. They have no right to receive any literature, and are allowed to read only what is available in the psychiatric hospital. Political prisoners are not allowed to receive visitors, except the closest relatives, and they cannot ask help from defense lawyers. To qualify for release from such a psychiatric hospital, one has to observe three rules: recant, promise absolute silence, and thank the hospital for your treatment . . .

I would now like to cite a few examples which show how events abroad, events across the ocean, can influence events in prison.

In 1971, my friend and fellow prisoner, Vladimir Borisov, and I began a hunger strike demanding an end to all treatment of healthy people, of healthy "patients" in psychiatric hospitals. We also demanded that the label "psychiatric patient" be removed from us. In addition, we demanded to be able to write letters and to obtain lawyers for our defense. A commission was formed during our hunger strike. It consisted of Nadzharov, Professor Serebryakova, an expert from the Ministry of Health, and Belyayev, the chief psychiatrist of Leningrad. They wanted to convince us to end the hunger strike because it was receiving considerable attention in the West. Our appeal, which we had directed to the West, was therefore having a certain effect. We were told that we should have confidence in an authority in psychiatry such as Nadzharov, whose name they said was well-known in the West. They tried to convince us that our hunger strike was nothing but a symptom of our schizophrenia. I took notes about this discussion and was able to smuggle them out of the institution.

Borisov and I were then again called for a discussion. This time they spoke differently with us. We were not asked about our convictions. Professor Lunts told us our opinions were of no interest to them. But they were interested to know what we would do if we were freed. Would we continue our activities?

And then Nadzharov ceased to be a gentleman any longer. . . . He became rather hysterical. He shouted . . .

I'd like to return to our hunger strike. I want to describe the way the events in the West had an impact on our fate. At that time we won a little success, because Bukovsky had been able to send many documents to the West. Because of their impact, a number of political prisoners who were being held in our psychiatric hospitals were almost freed. Academy of Sciences member Snezhnevsky declined to attend the World Congress of Psychiatrists in Mexico City that was being held in December 1972. At the same time our "treatment" eased up a bit. But when the Congress began, the Eastern block delegations stated through the Czechoslovakian spokesman that they would leave the Congress and the International Association of Psychiatrists if there would be any discussion of Soviet psychiatry. On the suggestion of Dennis Allen, the chairman, a majority vote was cast in favor of not discussing this subject. After that the atmosphere at the Congress improved, but our conditions remained the same. And so we were again cheated out of the previously granted improvements, and we again began receiving injections and various medicines . . .

I have to say that our conditions improved every time before an international, or even national, congress of psychiatrists was convened. But every time the topic of Soviet psychiatry was not allowed to surface we could feel the effects, as if someone was trying to take revenge on us.

I was released without any conditions, presumably only because an international congress of psychiatrists was to convene in autumn 1973 in Tiflis. I would probably not have been released had the authorities known that the subject of Soviet psychiatry would not come up . . .

After the conditions [in psychiatric hospitals] had become public knowledge, new regulations for the institutions went into effect in February 1973. But this is how they were implemented: Because peepholes for patient observation were now not permitted, small windows were installed in the doors. Visits that were now allowed—in the presence of supervisors—were not announced beforehand.

The new guidelines were not fully implemented because campaigns in the West began to ebb. And this is very dangerous for Soviet political prisoners. It is better not to start a campaign at all unless it is meant to be conducted seriously. The lot of political prisoners can only be improved if the campaign continues on an escalating scale, or by threatening a break in relations between Soviet and Western psychiatrists.

I would like to say a few words about Krasivsky. He is a talented Ukrainian poet who was arrested in 1967 for publishing samizdat articles about the Ukrainian National Front.[1] He received a sentence of 5 years in Vladimir Prison, 7 years in labor camps and 5 years' exile. He is a very strong and powerful man in every respect. Even the prison authorities thought him a man of iron, and did not think it would be a good idea to transfer him to a camp. And so he was transferred to the Serbsky Institute instead.

This is where I met him during his second observation period.

He was once asked during an interrogation: "Why are you such a nice man during the day, but during the night you write such tragic poetry?" This was deemed a symptom of schizophrenia. Now he is in a psychiatric institution in Smolensk, without any hope of ever being permitted to leave the asylum and to be free.

Once more I would like to remind you, as my friends have said before me, that what is taking place in the Soviet Union is in no way a local phenomenon. It is a threat to all mankind. . . .

---

1) Ukrainian National Front—an underground organization (1965-1967) which espoused the cause of an independent Ukraine. The U.N.F. reprinted and disseminated samvydav (Ukrainian for samizdate) and nationalist literature and published its own monthly journal *Batkivshchyna i volya* (Fatherland and Freedom). The U.N.F. was broken up in 1967 with the arrest of its members by the KGB.

LUBA MARKISH

" . . . the true purpose of experimentation is to create different levels of human capability . . ."

MARKISH, Luba

Born in Moscow in 1946 into the family of a musician.

In 1960 Luba Markish graduated from the Department of Chemistry at Moscow University, and in 1972 she received a degree from Moscow's Institute of Journalism.

She emigrated from the U.S.S.R. and settled in the U.S. in 1974.

ON EXPERIMENTATION ON
HUMAN BEINGS IN THE U.S.S.R.

In February 1965, more than 20 pregnant women were working in the experimental chemical plant in the suburbs of Kalinin. Because this plant produces extremely poisonous organic compounds for military purposes, the pregnant women were isolated from the main production and kept together in a separate wing of the plant so as to work under better and easier conditions. This, however, was only the official reason for keeping them separate. After several days the women detected the smell of some unfamiliar gas and, naturally, they tried to leave. But for some reason unknown to them the door was locked. In spite of their loud screams the door remained locked. After some time the military guards standing at the exit permitted three women to leave. Thereafter, the rest of the women were allowed to leave in groups of two or three during fixed intervals of time. Each time the door was again locked. All the women were immediately evacuated to various hospitals.

I met one of them, Nina Bakova, in Moscow in the special hospital in Perovo. She was worried about the possible damage to her unborn child and wished to terminate her pregnancy. There was absolutely no reason not to abort. Furthermore, exposure to the gas could make childbirth difficult. However, this woman was forced to remain in the hospital for 6 months where she was carefully observed. The child was born with some defects and they kept the baby from her, sending it to another hospital. During the following year Nina Bakova applied to various organizations and departments with regard to the child. She wished to at least claim the dead body, but she got no results.

During this period she met a number of other women who had worked with her in the plant near Kalinin. The fate of some of them was similar. They too had never been permitted to see their children who had been born alive; some of the children were stillborn; and some of the women themselves died. Undoubtedly, those who perished were those who remained longest in the contaminated conditions. None of these victims received any explanation or compensation. There were some rumors that the chemical plant in which they had worked was conducting experiments on human beings; but these rumors did not spread further than the neighborhood of the plant because officials harshly warned all concerned that such rumors must be squashed.

The above story is no more than a single episode. The hospital in Perovo is but one of some hospitals in which people arrive suffering from the ill effects of toxic chemical substances. It must be emphasized that the victims of which I speak were not victims of accidents. The one thing that all these people had in common was the fact that they were called by the odd nickname "moles," which is synonymous with "guinea pigs." I discovered the meaning of this "innocuous" word in October 1968 in Moscow in another hospital, the Institute for Occupational Diseases. At this time, I came to understand that the choice of the word "mole" was by no means accidental or inappropriate. Just like the little animal that is blind in the daylight, there is a whole invisible army of people who are named "moles." "Moles" are workers, lab assistants, and sometimes even students—all those who work blindly on chemical warfare. With the use of these "moles," that power which screams louder than any other about disarmament increases its military potential from day to day in subtle ways that are possible only under the Soviet regime. "Moles" are an extremely cheap labor force. By their hands, experiments for purely military purposes are being performed. But they are being carried out in civilian scientific centers. It is possible to do this because some Soviet civilian chemists are also engaged in military research; but since this is their secondary field, they do military work under the cloak of secrecy.

"Moles" are useful because they are not paid extra for their hazardous work; nor is it always necessary to provide them with expensive protective equipment. Moreover, "moles" do not need to go through bureaucratic clearance, so the state saves money by not having to pay administrative clerks. What's more, another great advantage of using "moles" is that those who are aware of military secrets can be kept to a minimum. In addition, the use of civilian "moles" falsifies the statistics regarding military personnel, for it keeps the number down. But "moles" not only provide the state with labor for experimentation, they also sometimes become the subjects of experimentation themselves. Often these experiments result in death—which, of course, removes them from the labor force. But this loss is more than compensated for by the unique scientific information which the military gains from these victims.

In the 1974 edition of the *American Reference Book of Super Toxic Substances* it says: "It is understandable that it would be most important to know the precise effect of poisons on human beings, but for obvious reasons we can only indicate the results of each poison with regard to animals." For Soviet scientists this kind of imprecision is quite unsatisfactory. In the same reference book I found the substance from which I myself suffered —chlorethylmercaptan—an analogue of mustard gas. Lethal dosage was indicated in milligrams per one kilogram of weight. A cat was the chosen animal for this determination. But, of course, I am not a cat—and thus I ended up in several Soviet hospitals with other "moles" like myself.

I planned to tell in my book not only about my personal experience, but also about the experiences of those who were in a similar position. To support my claims I have a number of documents from Russia. The book was almost ready; I kept the documents and the first part of the manuscript in a bank vault. I was in the process of editing the second part in preparation for publication. On September 3, 1975, the second part of my manuscript as well as all my other papers were stolen from my apartment; hence the publication of my book is now delayed. But I feel an urgent responsibility to expose the phenomenon of the "mole" in the Soviet Union, at least superficially at this time, for this problem is extremely dangerous for mankind and should be exposed as soon as possible. Experimentation on "moles" is not simply for the purpose of mass extermination, because hydrogen bombs would easily accomplish this. The true purpose of such experimentation is to create different levels of human capability, such as those physically strong but mentally disabled; mentally acute but physically restricted; physically and mentally normal but incapable of reproducing.

We must keep a close watch on the political activty of the Soviet Union, for it will use any method to establish worldwide rule of communism. And, hence, we must not underestimate the role of chemical experimentation in the service of transforming human nature. Nazi doctors were working on similar objectives in their times; it is difficult to determine who can claim priority for this type of work. But from my point of view, some Soviet specialists have left the Germans far behind. I am talking only about doctors and military scientists with whom I met personally.

I myself might never have believed that Russians would experiment on human beings—especially not at Moscow University, which I regarded with great reverence. And, in fact, were it not for a case of mistaken identity, today I would probably be a submissive pro-Soviet practicing chemist. In 1968 I was a fourth year student at Moscow University. I went under the name of my first husband, Ryabova. But there were two Ryabovs in the fourth year, and my supervisor did not know me personally very well. And, as the officials later discovered, a "monstrous" mistake was made, and I was chosen instead of the other Ryabova. Only because of my well-placed relatives did I survive. My first husband was the son of the notable Admiral Ryabov, and all members of his family were in high military positions. My mother's brother, A. Plate, and her nephew, N. Plate, are well-known Russian chemists.

My supervisor asked me to synthesize chlorethylmercaptan, which is very toxic and which students in all parts of the world are prohibited from working with. Moreover, fully trained chemists who work with this substance must be protected by masks and special outfits. and one must only work on this poison gas under a double system of ventilation.

Let me give you some quotations from official reports which I have brought from the Soviet Union. I have numbered them documents 1 through 10. In document 1, it says: "There was no journal of instructions . . . Work was performed in an ordinary exhaust hood . . . The student did not use any individual shielding devices." —In document 2, my supervisor Pzezhetsky wrote: "In instructing L. B. Ryabova I did not indicate the toxicity of chlorethylmercaptan." Thus it is clear that I did not understand the toxicity of the substance. Moreover the ventilation system stopped working. And as it is recorded in document No. 1: "Pzezhetsky was present during the assembly of the apparatus, the beginning of the synthesis, and also during the distillation of the reactive mixture." The supervisor left only for a period of time when the ventilation was off. And in the list of injured in document 1, there is only one person named—me. If there were only one person injured, it suggests that I was alone during the period of the ventilation failure. We might conclude that it was only coincidence that the supervisor left at this critical moment, but as it is written in the same document, "At the moment of synthesis a cutting off of the exhaust was noticed. This was noted by the student herself and by coworkers of the laboratory." Therefore, the supervisor clearly was aware that the ventilation system had shut down and that I was without protection. And even if the failure was accidental, the supervisor was still more than responsible for getting me out of the room, especially knowing that I had no mask or special outfit. But this was no accidental breakdown of the exhaust system, for as it plainly says in document No. 1, "It was established that on October 14, 1968, no shutdown of the exhaust in Room 422 occurred." But later in the document it states that Pzezhetsky himself "restarted the unexpectedly shut off ventilaion."

Moreover, the truth of the matter is that he did not restart it for 40 minutes. We might believe then that this was a crime to be charged against one person—my supervisor. In such a case, under Soviet law—Criminal Code 108—the guilty person must be sentenced to prison for 8 years. But what was the fate of Pzezhetsky? Academician Kargin requested in document No. 4 that Pzezhetsky be given a reprimand. A reprimand, you understand, is the most minor form of prosecution. Moreover, after this case, junior scientific worker Pzezhetsky became senior scientific worker Pzezhetsky.

Furthermore it is important to remember that the regulations for instructors at Moscow University are quite rigid. A teacher is usually prosecuted for the slightest injury to students. And in document No. 6 it is made quite clear that 5 years after this case I suffered very severe consequences. It indicates that I had a 60 per cent loss of general and 70 per cent loss of professional working ability. The October district People's Court of Moscow established in a decision in the name of the R.S.F.S.R.: "The plaintiff in 1968, during her studies at the chemical faculty of Moscow State University, suffered the onset of professional illness by fault of the administration." For more complete proof I would need to read at least 20 pages of documents. However, it is more important to tell about the other victims.

At the hospital I discovered that I was Exhibit No. 4 with respect to this substance. Three were men; two of them died; one survived. Is it not curious that each of us synthesized this substance without any precautionary measures and with ventilation failure? Moreover, this kind of synthesis seems quite senseless because there are large military plants devoted to the synthesis of this substance. Finally, I would like to mention the reaction of two famous Russian chemists to my case, Kargin and Kabanov: "It is a vexation that such a thing happened to a relative of Plate." Usually this kind of thing happens to students who do not have high-placed relatives. Incidentally, I do not place the largest share of blame on Pzezhetsky, for he is only a cog in the machine . . .

I would also like to point out here that these monstrous crimes are perpetrated not only by professional executioners—that is, by the military—but also by scientists and doctors. Among those Soviet scientists who are respected in the West not a few are criminals. You may have met them at international conferences, but they really belong in a court of justice. Those whom I personally know will be precisely identified in my book. In this work I will try to describe the character and the scale of their crimes.

How many students are threatened with becoming "moles" in the future? I can only say that in one hospital room in October 1968, besides myself, there was one student from Moscow University and one student from the Moscow Institute of Chemical Technology.

The most terrifying thing that I have ever witnessed were those who had been rendered psychotic by artificial means. This procedure was the subject of wide research in several Soviet hospitals. In this report it is impossible to describe even a small part of those subjects which cry out to be heard. But the majority of witnesses to such things have perished, and those who have survived are afraid to testify.

Even now, in the free world, I am unable to work on my book in peace and tranquility. During our first year in America, my husband and I have been the objects of purposeful and serious harassment. We have both been hospitalized as a result of two different attempts to frighten us. Everything is being done to prevent me from completing and publishing my book. I was forced to keep silent for 7 years; and here in Copenhagen I can tell you only a small fraction of what I feel must be revealed to the world. It would be naive to believe that this report will stop the Soviet military from committing crimes against humanity, but if the number of victims is diminished by even one, I will feel that I have fulfilled an obligation.

DAVID S. AZBEL

" ... experiments on human beings are made with no peace-ful purpose in mind ... "

AZBEL, David

Born January 26, 1917 in Chernihiv, Ukrainian S.S.R. Azbel graduated from the Mendeleyev Institute of Chemical Technology in Moscow in 1939. He was arrested during the Stalin purges in 1940 for dissident activities, and subsequently spent 16 years in various prisons, concentration camps, and exile, during which he was placed in charge of construction of large coal gasification plants in Siberia.

Rehabilitated after Stalin's death, Azbel returned to Moscow, where he continued post-graduate work and received his candidate of science degree in 1960. He worked as a professor at the Moscow Polytechnical Institute until 1972, when he was fired after applying for an exit visa.

On May 16, 1974 Azbel left the Soviet Union for Israel, and later came to the U.S. as Visiting Professor at the University of Minnesota's Department of Mechanical Engineering.

David Azbel has authored some sixty scientific works which were published mainly by the Academy of Sciences of the U.S.S.R. and several scientific journals.

194

POISON GAS EXPERIMENTS ON HUMANS: PARANOID FANTASIES OR REALITY?

I first heard the story of Luba Markish and her work on Radio Liberty in New York, prior to its publication in the United States press (*The New York Times, Daily News,* and the *Novoye Russkoye Slovo* [Russian Daily] of Sept. 9, 1975). Some of the commentators believed Luba's statements to be based on paranoid fantasies. Initially I, too, approached her ideas with much caution. However, after careful study and evaluation, I became convinced of the verity of her experiences.

Although I was acquainted with the fact that humans were being used in poison gas experiments in the Soviet Union, I did not believe that it would be possible to find a living witness who could bring her own experiences as testimony—such bravery and courage appeared beyond human capacity. The victims of such experiments usually die. Those who survive are generally far too terrified to speak of their experiences. They feel that they are in danger of being judged mentally ill or as anti-Soviet propagandists. The consequence of either accusation would mean incarceration in a mental hospital or prison. Even those people who have no understanding of chemical experimentation, but who have experienced life in the Soviet Union, can easily understand this situation. The death of human guinea pigs is explained in official Soviet reports as suicide, carelessness, or accident due to preoccupation with personal problems, such as unhappy love-affairs, etc. Rather than prior informed consent, signatures are forced from those who have already been subjected to experiments which resulted in disability or incipient death.

Years before leaving the Soviet Union, I visited some plants and laboratories which produced military poison gases and conducted experiments with these gases on human subjects. I was therefore interested in meeting Luba Markish in order to evaluate the press reports.

Before speaking about the basic aspects of this problem, I shall present some specific facts related to Luba's situation which I have come to know from my own direct contact and observation.

On September 3, some unknown person forcibly entered Luba's apartment in Queens, N.Y., and stole the second part of the manuscript she was writing about her experiences as a guinea pig in the Soviet Union, as well as other related documents and private correspondence with a publishing house. No money or other valuables were touched.

I arranged to meet with Mrs. Markish on Sept. 19 at 2 p.m. However, contrary to the plan arranged by telephone, I arrived at about 9 a.m., shortly after Mr. Markish had left for work. At this time I witnessed an attempt to force open the door to her apartment. Obviously the burglar believed that Mrs. Markish was alone, for he quickly disappeared when he heard me shout to Luba to call the police.

The next day, a similar attempt was witnessed by another of Luba's friends. On September 25, Mrs. Markish was visited by Isador Zysman, who attempted to convince her that the struggle against the Soviet Union was both senseless and dangerous. To continue writing her book would surely result in her death. As an alternative, Zysman suggested that she write a recantation, addressed to the KGB, and that she send this to the American press. She could then expect $500,000 in remuneration from the Soviet government. On October 5, he confirmed his proposal by phone. Mrs. Markish taped this telephone conversation. On October 7, Mrs. Markish taped a third conversation with Zysman. Upon my advice she had informed Zysman that she would accede to his proposal. He then proceeded to provide details on how to carry out this plan. On October 9, Mrs. Markish received a long distance call from Cleveland. A woman who spoke English without an accent identified herself as Margaret, an American friend of Luba's parents. Luba assumed that this was true, as she knew of a friend by this name. The woman stated that Luba's mother had been hit by a car and was critically injured. She indicated that Luba's father would telephone shortly and that she should wait for his call before making plans to fly to Cleveland. Obviously, this information, which was subsequently found to be false, put Luba in a state of extreme anxiety. It is likely that the purpose of this call was to precipitate sufficient panic to prevent Luba's trip to this conference in Copenhagen, thereby preventing her from speaking out.

On October 10, I myself heard over a telephone extension a warning in Russian from a man who identified himself as a member of the "committee," a euphemism for the KGB. He threatened that Luba's mother would be killed if Luba continued with her plan to go to Copenhagen.

Such have been the events of the past month.

What is the matter? Why all this concentrated interest in Luba Markish? Obviously, this is part of a planned chain of threats to prevent publication of a book that would expose Soviet experimentation. After the publication of Solzhenitsyn's *Gulag Archipelago* and Sakharov's works, as well as testimony of others who escaped to the West, it is surprising that so much effort should be made to prevent the publication of this book. Nevertheless, Mrs. Markish's testimony is seen as a very serious and undesirable revelation of some aspects of top-secret military chemical investigations in the U.S.S.R.

I knew for years about the existence of "moles," or human guinea pigs. "Moles" are people who work in a blind and uninformed way with extremely toxic substances. Most of these substances are intended for military purposes. The reason that they use human beings is that tests performed on animals cannot give sufficient information about the effect of these substances on people.

Since 1925, more than one hundred nations have signed the Geneva protocol abolishing the use of chemical warfare. Subsequently, nuclear weapons have occupied the attention of all nations and international bodies. Atomic warfare has been the main concern of public opinion and international agreements. Outside the Soviet Union it has been forgotten that chemical warfare can be very important in local wars.

One can notice in public libraries of the free world a proliferation of works concerning toxology. Volume after volume, peri-

197

odical after periodical has been published on the subject. Nevertheless, since 1930, there has not been a single publication on this subject in the Soviet Union. This could make one think that during a period of 45 years the Soviet Union had no interest in chemical warfare. However, a single young woman, Luba Markish, suddenly has appeared upon the scene and feels compelled to tell the truth about what is really going on in this field in the Soviet Union.

I know that in Siberia villagers were selected and used as guinea pigs in chemical experimentation. Not only was their labor exploited, but they were also unknowing participants in mass experiments. After these experiments they were put in special hospitals for observation. They were never heard from again, and their relatives never saw their bodies. Relatives were simply notified about their death, which "came as a result of an accident." It is known that even soldiers were used as guinea pigs. But all of this information was top-secret, and no one knows what became of these soldiers.

One would think that prisoners would be the ideal source of test material for experiments. However, when you consider their weakened physical state, you will realize that these people would not provide adequate information. Villagers were brought to big industrial centers such as Moscow, Leningrad, Volgograd, Chelyabinsk, Kalinin, Vladimir, Saratov, and many others. Unskilled workers were used in experiments in isolated areas, in so-called "post boxes"—areas designated off-limits.

Research was concentrated on poison gases which act on the brain and the nervous system. Of secondary concern, but no less important, was the testing of chemical mass sterilization. Perhaps the population growth in China gave rise to this interest in experimentation . . .

Similar experiments were performed near Chelyabinsk and the Sakhalin Islands. Results of these experiments have been identified. I have personally met two men who had been used as guinea pigs near Chelyabinsk. These men felt free to talk to me only after they found out that I was a former prisoner and a chemist. They told me they were used in sterilization experiments.

During the chemical warfare program the military authorities and the scientists also decided to use university students as guinea pigs—which at first thought seems to be illogical. By using students, however, it was possible to test a much greater variety of chemical formulations without the need for any explanation of resulting deaths. Chemicals which would have no place other than in a laboratory could only be tested on students. . . . Any death could be explained as an accident, and within the University it was possible to conceal the nature of the experimentation. I knew some students from the Moscow Institute of Chemical Technology who died from such experiments. It was impossible to investigate the causes of their deaths. Nicholai Derevlin from Irkutsk had the same experience as Luba Markish. In his case, however, stoppage of the ventilation system left him with a permanent physical disability.

There are many research centers around Moscow and the other big cities where scientists work with their military counterparts. My wife's friend, Antonina Kudrevtcha, was used in a chemical experiment which caused the bones in her arms to dissolve. She was placed under observation in the Moscow Hemotology Institute but was offered no help. I knew a man from Chelyabinsk who was purposely sent into a chemically infected area and then was sent to Moscow for observation at the Institute for Occupational Diseases. Actually he did not have an occupational disease—he was poisoned. It's possible to give many examples of such chemical experimentation. In most cases the victims died, and those who may have survived are generally afraid to speak of their experience.

In the case of Luba Markish everything is very clear. She was sent into a room to work with chlorethylmercaptan. The single exhaust fan failed, and Mrs. Markish was not permitted the use of a mask. Any chemist worth his salt knows that one must never be permitted to work with such dangerous poisonous substances unless there is a double system of ventilation, so that if one fails the other immediately takes over.

Having been a prisoner in the Gulag Archipelago, I know very well that in special prisons you were issued masks and special clothing when you worked with dangerous chemicals, and one also worked in laboratories with double ventilation systems. But these prisoners were valuable scientists, and the government did not want to lose them. It is a rule that no one, whether a special prisoner or a scientist, may work in a laboratory alone.

It is obvious that when a student is sent alone into an improperly ventilated room without a mask, the student is being used as a guinea pig. The gas which Luba Markish was made to synthesize has a very distinctive and noxious odor. No one will willingly stay in an atmosphere contaminated by chlorethylmercaptan. Yet this incident did take place, and it took place in Moscow University, the capital of Soviet science, where there are the best scientists, procedures, and equipment. Yet a student was improperly exposed to chemicals, against all of the University's procedures.

Why should Luba Markish have been selected for this experiment? Her first husband's family was very influential; her father-in-law was an admiral in the navy, and her uncle was a well-known Russian scientist. The only explanation can be that Luba Markish, then known as Luba Ryabov, was confused with another student by the name of Ryabov—who was an ordinary student from the provinces, with no well-known relatives. Luba was mistakenly sent into this deadly experiment because she was confused with someone else who had the same name. . . .

Now it should be clear to you why Luba Markish is being harassed. The U.S.S.R. does not want the world to know what this woman knows. What will the KGB do next? Their procedures are quite standard and almost predictable. They will call her paranoid, an agent of the CIA, a sexual maniac, and then will manufacture false documents and organize false witnesses to try to destroy her credibility. Nevertheless, the truth must be understood.

Mrs. Markish is one of the few survivors who can attest to this Soviet experimentation. She came to the West with the firm goal of alerting the world by telling what she knew—what she had heard—and what she had suffered herself. When her book will be published, the whole story will be clear to everyone. The world will then know that these experiments on human beings are made with no peaceful purpose in mind. The data on human reaction to poison gases is needed only for military purposes. The picture is now totally clear. This experimentation is being conducted for the purpose of dominating the world through the use of chemical warfare. Something must be done about this threat to humanity.

ALEXANDER VARDY

" . . . the Soviet rulers not only demand, but they compel

the people to hate . . . "

VARDY, Alexander

Born 1916 in Smolensk, R.S.F.S.R. Studied in Smolensk and Moscow. Arrested in 1936 on charges of anti-Soviet statements and sentenced to 3 years in a labor camp.

Served as an army officer during WWII. After the war, Vardy worked as an engineer until 1950, when he was arrested for a second time on the same charges. He was sentenced as a "repeater" to 10 years in labor camps, but was freed in 1955 for "outstanding inventions and record production."

Alexander Vardy emigrated to Poland in 1957, and later that same year to the West. Since 1963, he has been employed by Radio Liberty.

Vardy is author of several books and more than 200 articles on Soviet ideology, Soviet penal policy and sociology.

202

AN EDUCATION IN HATE

I am speaking for those who have no opportunity to fight for their rights—the 9.5 million children who are at present in Soviet day nurseries, kindergartens and nursery schools, in homes for children, and in special boarding schools; and for all those whose education is the result of the Soviet system. My testimony concerns principally the protection of the rights of children in the U.S.S.R. who have a natural right to obtain a human education so as to be able to develop harmoniously, to be free of having to submit to military training at an early age and of being made stupid by hate, and to be free of becoming the blind instruments of an aggressive, anti-national dictatorship which intends to conquer the world.

The Soviet leaders stir up negative emotions, especially different forms of hate: hate of non-communist ideas, cultures, societies, states, classes ...

The distortion of human souls, the growth of intolerance, hatred, ruthlessness, and aggression start in pre-school education in the communist countries, mainly in the Soviet Union.

In 1971, the Hochwacht publishing house in Bonn Bad-Godesberg published a book by Olga Pravosudovitch titled *The Germans in Soviet Magazines for Children*. Pravosudovitch reviewed and analyzed the contents of two Soviet magazines issued by the central committee of the Komsomol in the five-year period from 1966 to 1970. One of them is the magazine *Merry Pictures* (Veselyye Kartinki) for pre-school children; the other, *Murzilka*, is for 7- to 9-year-old children.

Mrs. Pravosudovitch included in her book 30 illustrations which were reprinted from the above-mentioned magazines. She has shown that even toddlers who can't yet read are educated in the spirit of hatred against the German fascists. The latter two words are used in the magazines as synonyms; their meaning is extended to all Western people. Simultaneously these magazines extol the fighting spirit, *i.e.*, aggression and ruthlessness, blind obedience, the selfless belief in leaders, and devotion to them to the last drop of blood.

Children's toys are mostly imitations of various weapons. The dolls wear uniforms and have military outfits. Children's games are mostly military ones. Books for toddlers, youths, and adults are full of cruel fables. They extol KGB-men, war, espionage and counter-espionage, hatred, and ruthlessness towards enemies. The enemies, *i.e.* the Americans and other "imperialists," "colonizers," "fascists," and similar fossil bugaboos are shown in such a way that a hysterical hatred of the West is being formed in the children's psyche.

A reader's letter characterizing the above-mentioned was published in the August 29, 1973 issue of *Literaturnaya Gazeta*. The following is the full text:

"Esteemed editorial staff!

Intending to visit a family who have a little son, I decided to buy the child the story *The Wonderful Spring*. Before giving him the book I decided to read it myself. Having done this I was horror-struck. If one wanted to raise a young sadist one would only have to give him this book to read. The story teaches how to cut off the tongue, how to prick out eyes, and cut off fingers. It is very unpleasant for a grownup to read such a book, and children take a fable for reality. How can one publish such books for children? Agafonova. Leningrad."

No commentary is necessary.

The hatred of dissenters . . . and of open democratic societies . . . is being kindled in all schools, from elementary to high school. The same takes place at meetings, obligatory courses, in seminars in political training courses for housewives, in the army, in para-military organization (Osovyakhim, Orlenok), and even in the concentration camps . . .

In the minds of the children even cats and dogs become enemies unworthy of mercy because they "spread dirt," the sparrows because they "steal corn from the fields, so scarce in the U.S.S.R."

The sadism of KGB-men of all ranks and services, and also of members of the militia, procurator's offices, and courts, is in a great measure the consequence of the long-lasting compulsory education of Soviet citizens. From childhood on they are educated in a spirit of inflamed hatred against all people whom they are ordered to hate and liquidate.

Certainly the pathologic ruthlessness of the KGB-men and other Soviet officials has stirred up and is stirring up reciprocal hatred from the dictatorship's victims against the tormentors, official murderers and torturers . . .

One can find the confirmation of these statements in thousands of testimonies of former Soviet citizens, as well as of those who remain slaves in Soviet society. Look particularly at the works of Shalamov, Solzhenitsyn, Vardy, Ginzburg, Marchenko, and at *Archiv Samizdata Radio Svoboda*, particularly AC No. 2220 of August 1, 1975 titled "MVD and KGB Apply Torture: Confessions of an Agent."

It's no wonder that the Soviet society lives in a state of permanent shock and stress, when all it sees and hears is extreme ruthlessness. The Soviet press writes about this a lot. Occasionally one can find complaints in the press that children, even during recesses between classes, hang dogs, burn cats alive after pouring gas over them, prick out the eyes of birds, and injure one another. If it were not a mass phenomenon, the newspapers wouldn't drop a word about these facts. The so-called "unmotivated" crimes, including murder, are committed more and more often.

The hatred of the West and of those with different beliefs is also incited in Soviet movies, television and radio, in theatres, books, and in the periodical press. The following examples serve as an illustration:

Here is a quotation from Lenin's works. These works are still topical in the Soviet Union. Lenin wrote in 1922 in a letter . . .

"The court must not eliminate terror—to promise this would be a self-deceit. The courts must rather legalize terror, frankly, unadorned, and without hypocrisy. This has to be formulated as broadly as possible because the revolutionary interpretation of law and the revolutionary conscience can set up conditions which demand the use of terror in greater or lesser form."

It is known that official state terror is a display not of the sound, civilized understanding of law, but a realization of hatred. Soviet rules not only demand, but they compel people to hate.

In a March 11, 1969 editorial in *Soviet Russia,* the organ of the CPSU, the Supreme Council and the Council of Ministers of the R.S.F.S.R., one can read:

"The Soviet people have to be educated in hatred, burning hatred of everything which hinders our progress."

Isn't this the same practice described by Orwell in *1984?*

As in Oceania, the Soviet rulers incite hatred of dissenters and of other countries. In particular, they show a large number of anti-American, anti-democratic, and anti-Western films . . .

Soviet theatres show spectacles inciting hatred of the U.S.A., West Germany, and other developed industrial countries.

The Soviet mass media started a propaganda campaign in March and April in connection with the murder of King Faisal of Saudi Arabia. Its purpose was to make people believe that Faisal's murder had been organized by the CIA. This provoked an official protest from the U.S. State Department.

On August 24, 1975, an article by Mikhaylov, *The Fascist Werewolves,* was published in *Izvestia,* the organ of the Supreme Soviet. Mikhaylov tried to convince Soviet readers that in England four fascist parties had started to show extraordinary militancy. Here are the alleged parties: "Union of General Walker," "Troops of Colonel Stirling," "National Association of Taxpayer Groups" and "National Front." Mikhaylov tries to convince the readers that if England isn't yet wholly in the hands of the "rabids," it will become their victim in the nearest future.

Mikhaylov invokes as usual the bugaboo of the world Zionist danger. He writes particularly about some "Zionist assault detachments" in the U.S.A. and in West European countries . . .

By the way, the Soviet officials' anti-Jewish chauvinism, showing itself now in the form of hysterical anti-Zionism, is one of the most severe and disgraceful crimes of the Soviet rules, a crime against humanity and human feelings.

There are many phenomena, well-known to international society, which clearly show that the rulers incite hatred of Jews for their own imperialistic and internal political purposes. This is a means to inflame hatred of the Western countries and also a propagandistic preparation for possible direct aggression in the Middle East . . .

Preparation for a war or wars determines the whole life of the Soviet society. Inciting hatred of the West is one of the main components of this preparation. Many people know about the Soviet armaments race and the export of Soviet arms. Few know about the totality of the military training of the population. For example, every high-school student has to pass an examination after participating in a course called "Ready for Work and Defense." At military preparation courses the children learn to shoot army guns. Read, for example, the articles by Chaykorskaya in *Literaturnaya Gazeta* of May 21 and 28, 1975. She writes how a schoolgirl killed a schoolboy in her class at the military shooting range because of jealousy.

The first page of *Komsomolskaya Pravda* of July 31, 1975 is devoted to the all-union maneuvers of the children's military organization Orlenok. The pictures show how school children in uniforms with automatic rifles, grenades, and other arms overcome obstacles on the "battle grounds."

Look through the Soviet newspapers. Read the headlines. You'll see how militarized the Soviet language has become. Everything is "front," "frontal attack," "battle reconnaissance." Even weeding on collective farm fields is called "battle on the weed front."

Look at photomontages showing American soldiers. You'll see the faces of degenerates. Moscow has not forgotten the lessons of Goebbels and Streicher . . .

Roy Medvedev wrote in his artice, *Once more about Democratization and Detente,* published by Radio Liberty (No. 1688), as reported by UPI of April 28, 1974, *The New York Times* and *Washington Post,* April 29, 1974: "The man in the street in our country, as a rule, believed the version spread by the Soviet mass media of the preparation for the invasion into Czechoslovakia by the West German and NATO armies."

Similar misinformation was spread by Soviet rulers at the time of the invasion into Hungary in November 1956, and on the eve of the preparation for the landing of Soviet troops in Sinai in October 1973. Washington put the U.S. Army on combat alert, and this prevented the Soviet aggression.

Here is how the Soviet rulers define peaceful coexistence in textbooks for universities: *Marxist-Leninist Philosophy: Dialectical Materialism,* Moscow, Mysl Publishing House. This is for internal use, not for export. On page 171 one can read:

"Peaceful coexistence doesn't mean the rejection of the revolutionary transformation of society nor the passive waiting for the automatic crash of imperialism. Peaceful coexistence under contemporary conditions is the most concentrated expression of class fight on the international scale."

It is clear, therefore, that it is not for true peaceful coexistence, but rather for an aggressive war, that the rulers incite in the Soviet people hatred of other ideas, cultures, peoples, and countries. The Soviet rulers use this in order to transform the Soviet society into an isolated, closed society, or, as Solzhenitsyn wrote, into a "deafened zone." In his Nobel Prize lecture Solzhenitsyn wrote:

"Inside the deafened zone there lives a people as if it were not of the Earth, but instead a troop of Martians; they don't know anything about the other places on the earth and are ready to trample them down in a holy belief that they are liberating them." . . .

As you see, the Soviet rulers' propaganda of hatred against dissenters is not only the internal business of the Soviet Union. History shows that the kindling of hatred is the most important precondition of the realization of aggression. Those people who aren't poisoned by hatred can't be thrown into the fire of wars, can't be compelled to die in the name of victory of the Orwellian world . . .

The Soviet rulers' misanthropic practice of inciting hatred against others is a threat to all mankind.

CHAPTER IV

The Oppression of Non-Russian
Nationalities in the Soviet Union

JONAS JURASHAS

" . . . The Soviet regime . . . has now for 35 years endeavored to conceal from the world's conscience the seizure by brute force of the Baltic states . . . "

JURASHAS, Jonas

Born June 19, 1936 in Lithuania into the family of an army officer. Theater director by profession.

In 1963, Jurashas graduated with distinction from the Lunacharsky Institute for Theater Art in Moscow. From 1963 to 1967, he worked as theater director in various theaters in Moscow, Chelyabinsk (in the Urals), and Vilnius. From 1967 to 1972, Jurashas was the chief director of the State Drama Theater of Kaunas in Lithuania.

Because of arbitrary censorship to which his plays were subjected, harassment by official authorities, and continuous mutilation of his art, Jurashas wrote an open letter of protest in August 1972, which led to his dismissal from work. Being unable to find further employment in his profession or in any other field for two years—despite the fact that his work had been highly acclaimed by critics—Jurashas applied for an exit visa.

He was granted permission to emigrate in December 1974, and settled in the U.S.

ON THE OPPRESSION OF
THE LITHUANIAN PEOPLE

Today, on the occasion of the Sakharov Hearing, and in a spirit of fairness and equity, let my personal testimony concerning the persecution of an entire nation be placed on the scale of Justice. This deposition contains only a fraction of the whole bitter truth about the decades of continuous destruction, occupation, and genocide of a nation of three million people.

The Soviet regime—with the aid of its powerful propaganda machine—has now for 35 years endeavored to conceal from the world's conscience the seizure by brute force of the Baltic states: Lithuania, Latvia, and Estonia . . .

Let us hope that today, from this chair, the voice of Truth will not be lost in the wilderness.

It is fitting to recall that already on August 23, 1939, the grave for the independence of Lithuania, Latvia, and Estonia had been dug. That was the date of the secret agreement between Ribbentrop and Molotov, by which the spheres of influence were defined between Nazi Germany and the U.S.S.R. This agreement immediately broke to pieces the non-aggression pact signed between Lithuania and Soviet Russia on October 28, 1926, and which was in force on paper until 1945.

But already in October 1939, Moscow demanded to send 20,000 of its troops into Lithuania and to establish military bases there under the pretext of wishing to protect the country's security.

213

On June 14, 1940, Molotov issued his ultimatum following the alleged death of two Soviet soldiers. The ultimatum demanded that members of the Lithuanian government surrender for trial, that the entire government be reorganized, and that Soviet military units be given access to the most strategic points. Moscow however refused to approve the nominees for a new government, and sent a vice-commissar by the name of Dekanozov to Lithuania.

On June 15, 1940, twelve divisions—250,000 men—crossed Lithuania's border.

Dekanozov appointed his protege Yustas Paletskis as prime-minister, dissolved all political parties, closed all newspapers, and banned all cultural, religious, and public associations. The Communist Party, which until then had consisted of less than 700 members—and these being of their own rather than Lithuanian nationality—was henceforth declared the only legal party.

On July 14 elections for the national assembly were carried out in the manner of Soviet election farces. Nine days were spent on preparations. There were exactly as many candidates as there were voting districts. Three days before the election, mass arrests and deportations of the nation's leading politicians began. A foreign national, Felix Baltishis-Zhemaytis, was appointed commander-in-chief of the Lithuanian army.

On July 21, 1940, the puppet National Assembly of Lithuania proclaimed the country a Soviet Socialist Republic. Its Decree No. 2 was a petition addressed to Moscow for the integration of Lithuania into the U.S.S.R.

Similar events took place in those days in Latvia and Estonia.

A spontaneous will of resistance arose throughout the country. Leaflets urging a boycott of the elections were distributed . . .

The "Lithuanian Action Front" was formed. The Front united all resistance units and originated in the two university centers, Vilnius and Kaunas.

On June 23, 1941, a nationwide insurrection broke out, in itself evidence that the annexation of Lithuania had been carried out by a mighty power in an act of force and aggression on a peaceful Western neighbor . . .

The Lithuanian partisan movement of 1945 to 1952 might serve as an unprecedented example of a struggle for freedom in this century. Lithuanians put their losses in this unequal fight at more than 30,000 partisans, who gave their lives for the future of their country . . .

Although 1952 is considered the final year of active resistance, it is difficult to assess how long it continued, since the spirit of resistance itself changed in character and assumed new forms as it penetrated into ever deeper layers of national life. In 1958, Soviet authorities proclaimed am amnesty, knowing only too well that the movement's main forces had been destroyed in this unequal fight through the infiltration of secret agents, informers, and traitors. They knew the nation had grown tired. They knew it was deprived of all help and all hope. The sleepless nights and troubled days, the smoldering sites of conflagrations, the gunshots in the woods, the corpses lying in city squares as a warning to those who still refused to be enslaved—all this had had its effect. Even when some participants in the partisan movement broke through to the West in 1948, they did not succeed in awakening the Western world from the shock created by the victorious U.S.S.R. What, the Western world asked, could possibly be the objective of such a senseless struggle? Better to applaud the strong, victorious conqueror lest he attack us!

The following deserves mention: In 1970, in the township of Shemoulyai, Shirvintai district, a unit of the secret police discovered Henrik Kayota, who had been hiding for 26 years in a bunker he had built under his mother's house. This did not happen in a jungle, as was the case recently with a Japanese soldier, but in the midst of Eastern Europe.

This excursion in my deposition into a recent past has been made with one single objective, which is to testify how and to what purpose Lithuania, or rather all three Baltic states, were "voluntarily" united with the U.S.S.R. . . .

In March of this year it has been 3 years since the first copy of the Lithuanian underground periodical *The Chronicle of the Lithuanian Catholic Church* appeared. This underground publication has in its 3 years of existence become a supremely impartial document on contemporary life, giving expression to that spirit of independence and character-building of a nation that was about to be devoured by a totalitarian regime.

The *Chronicle* came into existence as a successor to the *Chronicle of Current Events* and after the alarm for truth had been sounded in Solzhenitsyn's books. Together with these it gives expression to the revival of faith in the final triumph of truth and justice. The *Chronicle of the Lithuanian Catholic Church* is being published despite efforts by authorities . . . to discredit it from within. . . .

Issue XV of the *Chronicle of the Lithuanian Catholic Church* contains the following circular: "The Soviet authorities intend, by means of the Criminal Code and through the Committee on Public Safety, to destroy not only the *Chronicle of the Lithuanian Catholic Church,* but also the Lithuanian Catholic Church itself. We, the Lithuanian Catholics, however, are fully resolved to fight with Divine help for our rights. We still cherish the hope that the Soviet authorities will understand that they are making a great mistake in supporting atheists who are in a minority, while arousing against themselves the Catholic masses. The Catholics of Lithuania beseech our brothers who have emigrated, and all friends of Lithuania all over the world, to inform a wide general public as well as governments about the repression of human rights in Lithuania."

The *Chronicle* publishes letters from its readers. One of the letters contains the following account:

"Recently we learned through the *Chronicle of the Lithuanian Church* about the arrest of Sergei Kovalev, who has a doctorate in biology. We Lithuanian Catholics pray to God that He will endow this scientist with all spiritual and physical strength. What the world needs most urgently today is love. Jesus Christ said: 'There is no greater love than in giving one's life for one's friends.' We are confident that the sacrifice of Sergei Kovalev and others will not be in vain.

We bow in reverence before Andrei Sakharov, this brave champion of human rights in the U.S.S.R., and in doing so we revere all Russian intellectuals of goodwill. By their daring and their spirit of self-sacrifice they have again caused us Lithuanian Catholics to look to the Russian people. Their self-sacrifice is necessary for all Russians who are persecuted—it is also necessary for the Catholics of Lithuania.

We are deeply grateful to the great Russian writer A. Solzhenitsyn for his warm words addressed to the Lithuanians in defense of their country. Thousands of us, especially former prisoners of the Gulag Archipelago, pray to the Almighty on his behalf."

The *Chronicle of the Lithuanian Catholic Church* constantly publishes lists of victims of persecution and of persons interrogated—not only for their religious convictions—by the KGB. Through its underground periodical, the Catholic church has become the only reliable source of information that is available. It's therefore only natural that the KGB is trying with such desperate hate to destroy the *Chronicle*. . . . There are waves of arrests. There are actions of almost epidemic proportions that are aimed at breaking up this type of resistance from within through collaborators and informers. Punishment for distributing the periodical is draconic. . . . But so far, fortunately, without any noticeable results. It may be hard to understand why, but the obvious reasons are above all truthfulness and faith.

The *Chronicle* collects testimonies from the most remote corners of Lithuania and informs its readers about injustices committed by certain authorities. It defines the limits of the authorities' rights in legalistic terms and so acts strictly in accordance with the rights guaranteed by Soviet legislation and the Soviet constitution.

The *Chronicle* has bravely acted in defense of the Roman Catholic priests A. Sheshkevichyus, Y. Zdebskis, and P. Bubnis, who were sentenced to various terms of imprisonment for having provided religious education for children and for their catechization. But in the eyes of the general public it was not the servants of religion, as the authorities wished, but rather the brutal persecutors of the church who were guilty, since these priests were forced to "break the law" because of their conscience and the entreaties of parents.

In Lithuania priests are forbidden to go about their most urgent duties. They cannot instruct or confirm children. They are forbidden to attend the sick and the dying or to read funeral masses. All these duties are strictly prohibited, but the freedom of conscience, which the constitution guarantees, forces them to carry out these duties in secret. Thus it is that the Lithuanian Catholic Church, the traditional bulwark of national identity, has been brought into the same situation as that of the early Christians who had to assemble in catacombs. Our persecutors do not realize that in this country faith is irradicable, and that persecution will only strengthen it.

In Lithuania it is not possible to enter a seminary without the approbation and consent of the Communist party and the

KGB. This was attested by Virgilius Yaugelis as he spoke in his defense at his trial in connection with case No. 345. In his defiant address to the court V. Yaugelis, among other things, confessed to his deep belief and pleaded not guilty to the indictment. He was sentenced to a forced labor camp for hardened criminals. The criminals beat him severely. He fell seriously ill, then contracted cancer, but he still refused to let prison doctors operate on him. Rumors from camp say that V. Yaugelis will not live to see the end of his term in 1976.

In Lithuania it is prohibited to publish, print, or distribute books, booklets, or newspapers dealing with religious matters. The few official publications with a ridiculously small circulation can in no way satisfy the needs of the believers. A large part of the prints of the Holy Scripture and of the prayer book is sent to the West for propaganda purposes. Some believers, trying to make amends for this shortage by taking matters into their own hands, were severly punished. On September 3, 1974, sentence was passed in case No. 345 on persons who had prepared and distributed prayer books and religious literature. P. Plumpa-Plyuiras was sentenced to 8 years, P. Petronis to 4 years, V. Yaugelis to 2 years, and I. Stashaitis to 1 year of imprisonment.

I myself have seen people fired from their jobs on the basis of merely a phone call from the KGB, which did not even attempt to prove their "guilt." These people made photocopies of old prayer books.

In Lithuania it's forbidden to repair Roman Catholic churches or to build new ones. Many old churches have been closed or are being used as storage halls, museums of atheism, or "palaces of culture." After many years of efforts by believers from the town of Klaipeda, Moscow authorities permitted that a church be built with funds collected by the parishioners. But municipal authorities appropriated the church—built at the cost of incredible efforts—the day before it was scheduled to be consecrated, and turned it into a concert hall. To this day the town population has refused to enter this "cultural institution."

Monuments and national relics of a religious character, and even those of an artistic value, are being systematically destroyed in Lithuania. In the past there was an immense number of crosses in the country that were decorated with sculptures of a unique character . . . The story of the Hill of Crosses at Shyaulai is remarkable. Following the 1861-1864 insurrection against the czarist regime, Cossacks [Czarist police] drove the insurgents into a chapel on a hill in Shyaulai and buried them alive by covering the chapel with earth. Since then, people for a century have carried beautiful crosses to that hill to commemorate a bloodstained chapter in their country's history. But in the summer of 1961, Soviet soldiers who had arrived only a short while before destroyed several thousand crosses in one night. Orders for this destruction were given by the representative of the minister of the Supreme Soviet, comrade Dirzhinskaite-Plyush-chenko. Nevertheless, new crosses were erected every time old ones were destroyed, and every year the hill is laid waste again. In the course of this year people brought new crosses to the hill three times to replace those that had been destroyed . . .

Edward Kuznetsov in his *Prison Diaries* has included a document that is horrifying in its intensity and strength. It is a letter from the political prisoner Lyudvikas Simutis. The letter includes some stark figures. Seven Lithuanians in his camp accounted for approximately six per cent of all prisoners. Compare this to the percentage of Lithuanians in the entire population of the U.S.S.R., which amounts to one per cent of a population of 240 million. The seven prisoners are serving sentences totaling 182 years—an average of 26 years per prisoner. On the average, each prisoner has already served 18 years. Their average age is 46 years. They are all Catholics. "The impression is created," writes Edward Kuznetsov, "that in relation to the citizens from the Baltic states and western Ukraine—and surely it is in these regions that the Soviets most openly demonstrate their true character—the Soviets are acting most harshly in keeping with their merciless and revengeful laws, which prescribe that anyone who is not prepared to crawl on his knees will end up in prison. Correspondingly harsh will be the hatred for those who have caused these dire sufferings."

In Lithuania, a 25-year sentence is still called "the Lithuanian term."

Today there are still hundreds of innocent Lithuanians imprisoned in the concentration camps of the wide land of the Soviets. . . . Upon completion of their astronomically long sentences, former prisoners are not permitted to return to their country. In 1971 a secret decree of the Supreme Soviet of Lithuania was disclosed, according to which no former prisoners, or those persons who might be termed "bourgeois nationalists," soldiers of the liberation movement, and members of the former Lithuanian government, are to be permitted to register in Lithuania. All of these were forced to find a place of residence outside their country. . . .

Persons who fall into this category of outcasts do not even have the right to emigrate from the U.S.S.R. I know of instances where persons were quietly confined to psychiatric hospitals upon the merest expression of such a desire to emigrate. My personal friend Kestutis Yakubins, who served two 10-year sentences and who was being endlessly harassed with interrogations, visits by police to his home, and threats, applied for an emigration permit, but in July of this year was refused permission without being given any reason.

At present the KGB is searching all over Lithuania for evidence in case No. 345. Criminal charges were brought against the following persons, who were then sentenced to various terms of confinement in prison camps: P. Plumpa-Plyuiras, P. Petronis, I. Stashaitis, B. Yaugelis, Y. Grazhis, B. Kulikauskas, and I. Ivanauskas. The poet Mindaugas Tamonis was forcibly confined to the psychiatric hospital on Vasaros St. in Vilnius, where white-coated torturers subjected him to experiments which broke his health.

Case No. 345 assumed all-Union dimensions. The investigations and interrogations were undertaken with the aim of destroying the *Chronicle of the Lithuanian Catholic Church*. It is especially disquieting that the KGB, without any evidence, is prosecuting persons who have nothing whatsoever to do with the *Chronicle*. Sergei Kovalev has already been interrogated for half a year by the KGB in his solitary confinement cell in Vilnius. Others who are being prosecuted include his wife L. Boytsova, Andrei Tverdokhlebov, A. Plyusin, Galya Solova, Malva Landa, and Irina Korsunskaya. Their participation in the *Chronicle* has not been proven. The best evidence of this is the fact that even after their arrests, new editions of the *Chronicle* continue to appear in Lithuania and in the West. Not long ago, issue XVI appeared. . . . The *Chronicle* is operating strictly within the limits of Soviet law. It does not print any unconfirmed information, and it defends the freedom of conscience, which is guaranteed by the constitution . . .

Lithuania has been shattered from within as a result of the efforts of the occupants who in three decades have changed the very essence of Lithuanian identity into an utterly false concept of "homo sovieticus." Formerly, in Stalin's days, they acted more directly by destroying lives. At present they destroy the spiritual concept of national identity. This concept, as we understand it in the genuine sense, has been changed by the horror-phantom of "class struggle." . . .

There are people who love their homeland more than their lives. The following are at present real martyrs for freedom:

Pyatras Paulaitis, who has been suffering the "Lithuanian term of imprisonment" since 1947.

Pyatras Paltarokes, suffering the same term since 1950.

Klemensas Shirvias—since 1952.

Lyudvikas Simutis—since 1955.

The biography of each one of these might serve as subject matter for a literary, moral, or political analysis. Take the example of Lyudvikas Simutis, a member of the national underground movement, who as a mere boy participated in the unit of the "Forest Brothers." Confined to his bed during a serious illness (tuberculosis of the spinal column), he was brought to a hospital. There he was arrested, brought to court . . . and sentenced to death. This sentence was then commuted to 25 years' imprisonment in a camp. In 1958, a medical commission established that his illness was incurable, and proposed that he be set free at once. And yet he is a prisoner to this very day. There are still 6 years left until he has served his sentence. He is an invalid, and yet the administration forces him to work.

Pyatras Paulaitis, born in 1904, studied philosophy in Italy, then worked in Germany and Portugal until 1938. He then returned to Lithuania where he taught Latin. With the arrival of the Reds in 1940, he went to Germany, returned in 1941 to Lithuania, then occupied by the Germans, and joined the underground anti-Nazi movement. He co-edited the illegal newspaper "For Freedom," writing articles against crimes perpetrated by the Nazi administration. For this he was arrested by the Gestapo, but managed to escape during a prisoner transport and went into hiding. After 1944, when Lithuania fell into the hands of Soviet administration, Paulaitis stayed on in the national underground movement and edited the newspaper *The Voice of Freedom*. In 1947 he fell into the hands of the secret police. The investigation lasted 9 months, during which Lieutenant Colonel Zakharov used his basic persuasive power: torture. Paulaitis received the traditional 25-year sentence. Just recently, he was brought back to the 19th district for strict regimentation. In 1963, a major Svyatkin of the MVD proposed to Paulaitis that he write an article in a paper on "The Resistance against the Liars from the South," for which he would be granted a reprieve. "You'll never gain your freedom, just you believe me!" The prisoner is now 70 years old and he has 9 years left of his term.

According to most recent statistical data, Lithuania at present has 3.3 million inhabitants.

Had there been no genocide, the population by 1959 would have been 5.5 million . . .

As a result of genocide, Lithuania's population was cut in half. Over a period of 20 years Lithuania has lost 1,239,000 citizens.

During the 1941-1959 period of Soviet occupation alone, the losses amounted to 1,090,000 persons.

Of these:

1941: Deportations to the Soviet Union—5,000
1941: Evacuated to the Soviet Union—1,200
1941: Killed by the Soviets—1,200
1942-1945: Killed during the war—25,000
1945-1958: Deportations to the Soviet Union—260,000
1944-1953: Partisans killed in fighting against the Soviets—30,000-40,000
1945-1959: Transferred to other republics—30,000

In all, 400,000 Lithuanians were sent to Russia in 1948 and 1949. In Germany, which lost the war, the population from 1939 to 1959 increased by 4.3 percent, in the Netherlands by 29.9 percent, in the U.S.S.R. by 10.1 percent. Not only did the population in Lithuania not increase, it actually decreased by 13.7 percent!

After long years of darkness and, as it appears, shameful subservience, the nearly-extinguished flame of freedom is suddenly blazing again with unexpected brightness. The dark night of despair was suddenly illuminated by a torch: Romas Kalanta.

222

He burned himself, his 19-year-old life, to illuminate the way for his young contemporaries who were born under conditions of serfdom. In the spring of 1972, thousands of young demonstrators, surrounded by soldiers who were beating them with clubs, shouted "Freedom for Lithuania!"

The 1970's ushered in a new epoch of Lithuanian resistance. Its banners are dignity and faith.

In 1971, a speech the sailor Simas Kudirka made at his trial was passed from mouth to mouth. In his speech, which attained the force of an indictment against the regime, he refuted the accusation that he had betrayed his country, because, he said, his country was Lithuania. The (Lithuanian) Soviet Socialist Republic, like the creation of an empire loaded down with guilt, was a lie and an injustice. The fate of this daring man became known to the whole world.

In 1973, the organs of the KGB brought to trial the Lithuanian Student Society of National Lore, a trial which in its dimensions was comparable to the action against the *Chronicle of the Lithuanian Catholic Church*. On March 27, 1973, at 8 o'clock in the morning, more than 100 persons were arrested in Vilnius, Kaunas and Riga—all of them members of the Society. The investigation dragged on for 11 months, the whole Society was destroyed, and in the end five persons were sentenced to various terms. They are:

— S. Zhukauskas, born 1950, a former medical student—6 years of severe labor.
— A. Sakalauskas, born 1938, a teacher at the Polytechnic Institute—5 years.
— V. Povilonis, born 1947, a technical engineer, 2 years of hard labor.
— A. Matskevichyus, born 1949, a student at the Institute of the Communist Party—2 years in prison camp.
— I. Rudaitis, born 1911, a physician, member of the underground anti-Nazi movement, who had saved hundreds of Jewish children in his clinic during the German occupation and provided medicines and other medical aid to Soviet soldiers—3 years' strict regime prison camp.

They are serving their sentences in Solikamsk in the Perm region.

Zhukauskas, during his trial, made a speech similar to that made by Simas Kudirka. He explained to the merciless court the history and origins of Lithuania's colonization declaring that Russia to this very day remains a prison of nations.

He said that all nations fight for their freedom and that all progressive forces support them. In which way, he asked, were the Lithuanians worse than others? He characterized the trial as a farce and concluded his statement with the poet's words: "The enemy forces us with iron hands, but there is no dearer word than 'freedom'" . . .

In the summer of 1972, after Kalanta had burned himself to death, 10 Lithuanians of various ages killed themselves in the same manner. The aim of such self-sacrifice was to focus the world's conscience on the oppression of the Lithuanian people. The sources of this information are unofficial, since they are careful to stay out of view. But this information was confirmed to me by an official at the Central Committee of the Lithuanian Soviet Socialist Republic who took part in the inquiry into the series of self-immolations. In all these cases the official conclusion was the stereotype "psychic illness," and the funerals were held in total secrecy . . .

The Lithuanians are uniting their not always very strong, but sincere voices with the voices of all nations of goodwill . . . we beg you to intercede on our behalf, on the behalf of the oppressed, and perhaps on your own behalf . . .

EDWARD OGANESSYAN

" . . . the best representatives of the [Armenian] nation have been systematically liquidated . . ."

OGANESSYAN, Edward

Born in 1932 in Yerevan, Armenian S.S.R.

In 1956 Oganessyan graduated from the Moscow Industrial Institute and in 1961 from the Leningrad Electro-Technical Institute. In 1967 he received the candidate of sciences degree, having successfully defended a thesis in the field of cybernetics.

Oganessyan was laboratory chief at the Armenian Academy of Sciences and chairman of the Armenian Committee for Cybernetics. Since 1959 he was a member of the Communist Party of the Soviet Union and was an elected deputy of the City Council.

In December 1972 Oganessyan visited France as a tourist and decided not to return to the Soviet Union.

226

ON THE OPPRESSION
OF THE ARMENIAN PEOPLE

I consider it a great honor to be given the opportunity to testify at the International Sakharov Hearing. My testimony will concern violations of the rights of my nation as well as of the rights of individual citizens in Soviet Armenia.

The following facts, in my opinion, are incompatible with norms of morality and right common to all mankind:

The forcible establishment of Soviet power in Armenia.

The independent Armenian Democratic Republic was overthrown by the Soviet Army on December 2, 1920. The leaders of the republic were killed with an axe in Yerevan prison (I submit photos).

The destruction of the nation's elite.

The best representatives of the nation—prominent military leaders, scientists, poets, writers, politicians, and workers in the field of art—have been systematically liquidated by the Cheka since 1934. To give a complete list of the victims of this genocide one would require much more time than we have at our disposal. As a result of this genocide, the nation was deprived of its intellectual elite and irreparable damage was done to all spheres of national life.

The violation of constitutional guarantees concerning the sovereignty of the republic.

The republic lacks such institutions as a ministry of foreign trade, its own army, ministry of defense, foreign ministry, etc. This deprives the republic of the right to be considered sovereign, as the constitution states. Not one of the republic's newspapers has its own correspondents abroad. Yet two and a half million Armenians are living abroad; that is exactly as many as in Armenia itself. And the life of Armenians abroad has a clearly expressed national character, both socially and politically. Still, there is nobody who could inform the citizens of the Armenian Soviet Socialist Republic about life of their countrymen abroad. Radio Liberty broadcasts are the only source for such an information.

Violating its own constitution, which includes the right of a Union republic to secede from the U.S.S.R., the Supreme Court of the Armenian S.S.R. in 1974 sentenced the following to terms of imprisonment ranging from 2 to 7 years, with subsequent deportation: Ashot Navasardyan, Anait Martirossyan, Kadjik Arakelyan, Levon Badalyan, Azat Arakelyan, Rasmik Markossyan, Samved and Norik Martirossyan, Gagik Arakelyan, Konstan Karapetyan, and Rasmik Zagrabyan. These young people were accused of organizing the "National Unity" party which defended the right of the republic to secede from the U.S.S.R. But if this right is included in the constitution, does it not also mean the right to propagate this idea? And earlier, in 1965, seven young patriots were sentenced to 5 years imprisonment for organizing a demonstration in commemoration of the 50th anniversary of the Turkish genocide.

The absence of a national economy.
Armenia is completely deprived of its own national economy, that is, an economy on which the economic well-being of a nation is based. The living standard of the people does not at all depend on the level of productivity of Armenian enterprises or on the natural resources of Armenia. Aside from this, the natural resources of Armenia are mercilessly exploited. Although Armenia has four times less land per each inhabitant than the Soviet Union as a whole, several huge concerns have been built in Armenia, such as a group of chemical enterprises, aluminum enterprises, the enterprises of Kadyaran, Kafan, Alavery, and many other huge plants which pollute "tiny" Armenia but give her nothing in return.

The policy of Russification.
The policy of identifying "Soviet" with "Russian" created a situa-

tion where priority is given to the Russian language, Russian schools, Russian culture, etc. . . . This policy gives rise to hostility of Armenians towards Russians—from my point of view this is a crime because the sympathy of Armenians towards Russians has always been quite natural, as the Russians were defenders of Christian interests in the times of the Ottoman empire.

The lack of freedom to travel and to information.

The lack of these freedoms is felt acutely in Armenia. As already stated, two and a half million Armenians are living abroad; they want to meet their relatives and often they want to reunite families. But this is prevented by all kinds of obstacles. I can mention my own example—I left my wife and three children in Yerevan. My mother, father, and two sisters are also there. Normal contacts with them are broken. Letters do not reach them, things sent through tourists are confiscated at the border. I have sent my wife through the Red Cross an application for permission to join me, but she still has not received it although more than a year has passed. I submit to this Hearing the Red Cross letter and the postal receipt for this document.

ANDREW ZWARUN

" . . . Soviet authorities are prepared to destroy the civili-
zation, the culture, and . . . the physical being of over forty
million Ukrainians . . . "

ZWARUN, *Andrew Alexander*

Andrew Alexander Zwarun was born in 1943 in Pidvolochyska, Ukraine and spent his early years in German refugee camps. He emigrated to the United States in 1950 where he completed his education. In 1970 he received the Doctor of Philosophy degree in the field of soil microbiology and chemistry at the University of Kentucky. Currently, he is the research director for an industrial firm in New York. Zwarun is also vice-president of the Baltimore, U.S.A.-based SMOLOSKYP Ukrainian Information Service.

ON THE OPPRESSION
OF THE UKRAINIAN PEOPLE

The details and descriptions of violations of individual human rights will not be emphasized in this presentation. This will be adequately done by others. Our purpose is to present data on the premeditated destruction of every facet of ethnic identity of the Ukrainian nation. Although this has been Russia's aim since czarist times, this process has been greatly intensified in the last few years, especially since the Twenty-Fourth Communist Party Congress in March 1971.

Everything that is non-Russian is willfully destroyed or eliminated, while everything that is Russian is exalted as beneficial, with the justification that it strengthens internationalism, the goal of Soviet internal policy. The implications of this policy for non-Russian nationalities in the U.S.S.R. are disastrous.

A. Persecution of Ukrainian Language, Culture, and the Educated Class

Especially hard hit was the Ukrainian language. After the November 1971 meeting of the Presidium of the Central Committee of the Communist Party, a letter was circulated which stated that Ukrainian bourgeois nationalists were using the Ukrainian language to further their aims. Consequently, the use of Ukrainian in governmental, educational, and productional institutions should be regarded as a manifestation of Ukrainian bourgeois nationalism. Therefore, Russian should be the language used by Ukrainians in Ukraine. As can be seen, the Ukrainian language is classified as nationalistic, a dirty word in the U.S.S.R., but the Russian language is not classified as nationalistic. Somehow it is internationalistic, even if it is forced on others. None of these party resolutions or decisions appear in the Soviet press since they are in contradiction to the constitution. In reality, Ukrainian as well as every other non-Russian language is being destroyed. Some examples:

Recently, many ministries of individual, sovereign republics (Article 15, Soviet Constitution) have been changed into all-Union ministries. This act forces these ministries to use only Russian for record-keeping and forces all subordinate institutions to do the same. This type of trickery is also practiced in Ukrainian universities.

In 1971, at the State Institute in western Ukraine, that area of Ukraine which has had the least Russian influence, only 25 per cent of all lectures were in Ukrainian. By 1974, only 15 per cent of all lectures were in Ukrainian. In the entire Ukrainian S.S.R., where Russification has been very intense, the percentage of instruction using the Ukrainian language is lower.

In the University of Dnipropetrovsk, lectures on Ukrainian literature for Ukrainian students are given in Russian.

At the Kiev Polytechnic Institute, only Professor Voytko of the philosophy department gave lectures in Ukrainian. Within one year he was removed.

If a student asks a lecturer to make his presentation in Ukrainian, the student is immediately marked by the KGB, who attend most lectures, and he is frequently dismissed from the university or is placed under surveillance. Should the lecturer agree, he is dismissed from his position.

All doctoral dissertations by Ukrainian students must be submitted for approval to an accreditation committee in Moscow. not in Kiev. Consequently, they must be in the Russian language.

During one of the 1973 meetings of the Politburo of the Ukrainian Communist Party, it was decided that most scientific journals that appear in Ukrainian, or in both Ukrainian and Russian, must be published only in Russian.

This strangulation of the Ukrainian language also encompasses Ukrainian literature, art, and culture.

The Writers Union of Ukraine has become an organ of the KGB. It is, in fact, run by Soldatenko, a colonel in the KGB.

234

The Union has expelled many of its best writers. To be expelled means to be unable to publish your material anywhere.

There now exists a blacklist of Ukrainian writers who not only cannot publish (many are now in concentration camps), but whose works cannot be cited by others nor reference made to them. Only a fragment of this blacklist, approximately 50 names, is currently known.

Most of the literature of the 1960's by noted Ukrainian writers has been given the library classification of "not recommended." This means that should foreign visitors visit a library, they will find these books on the shelves. However, these books are not allowed to be read or borrowed by the general public.

In the spring of 1973, Academician Babiy notified the Ukrainian Communist Party that all manuscripts from the social sciences sector were returned by the publishers to party officials for revision. Among them was Volume III of *Archaeology of the Ukrainian S.S.R.*, returned because there were too many references to M. Braychevsky, a noted archaeologist who was blacklisted. Babiy also complained to party officials that the journal *Ethnic Creativity and Ethnography* idealized the past; *i.e.*, he criticized the journal for mentioning Ukrainian ethnic songs, folk stories, sayings, and adages.

The Ukrainian educated class is currently being repressed because it is a potential vector of Ukrainian identity. Thousands of educators, scientists, and students have been dismissed from their positions and schools in the last 5 years. For example:

At the Institute of Polymer Chemistry, four scientists (Kolotylo, H. Minaylo, Nosorih, and Skarychenko) were dismissed because on May 22, 1972, the KGB photographed them standing by the statue of Taras Shevchenko, Ukraine's greatest poet.

From March to May of 1973, the KGB carried out a pogrom at the University of Lviv. It began when students were forbidden to hold their traditional "Shevchenko Evenings," gatherings in honor of Shevchenko during which his works and works about him are read and discussed. The students organized this Evening on their own initiative, but they were physically scattered by party activists. Then began massive arrests of students. The arrested were subjected to torture (*e.g.* rubber sacks tied around the head till the person fainted,

235

and beatings). Many students were also expelled, primarily from the departments of Ukrainian philology, the physical science, and history. One student, Volodymyr Udovychenko, was expelled because he refused to become a KGB informer. Also dismissed were at least 20 professors and lecturers.

In December 1973, another group of history students was expelled for reading the Bible.

In 1974, again at Lviv University, the "Shevchenko Evening" was sponsored by the authorities, and only student leaders were given written invitations. It was forbidden to stand during the singing of Shevchenko's "Testament," as is customarily done. Most of the Evening was spent singing party and Komsomol songs with little mention of Shevchenko.

In January 1974, M. Melnyk was expelled from the Medical Institute for taking flowers to the graves of Ukrainian soldiers killed in the 1914-1922 independence movement. The KGB ordered his lecturers to fail him during his final exams.

Similar harassment of students and professors has taken place at Kiev University.

The common factor in all these episodes is not the violation of certain laws, but the direct or indirect acknowledgment by Ukrainians that they are Ukrainian and are aware of their present and past. Although the right to a national identity is guaranteed by the Soviet Constitution (Articles 123 and 125), these people were hunted down and punished for exercising their right.

B. Destruction of the Historical Past

There is special emphasis placed by Soviet authorities on the destruction of the Ukrainian historical past.

Old churches, some dating back several centuries such as the Church of St. Paraskeviya in the village of Kosmach, are forbidden to be restored or even kept up.

All the crosses in Yanivsky cemetery, where Ukrainian soldiers from the 1914-1922 independence struggle are buried, have been destroyed. This is also true for cemeteries in Ivano-Frankivsk, Ternopil, Zolochiv, Horodok, and other cities.

In 1972, on orders from the KGB, the Ukrainian Museum of I. Honchar was closed in Kiev. Honchar himself is constantly hounded by authorities.

In December 1972, in the city of Zboriv, the statue of Khmelnytsky, who re-established an independent Ukraine in 1648, was removed and replaced by a statue of Lenin.

Spontaneous fires frequently occur in libraries, primarily in those sections which house ancient Ukrainian archives (never in Russian sections).

There is never any funding available for the upkeep or building of Ukrainian museums. The Franko Museum in Kryyorivna was restored only when, in 1971, a visiting student fell through the second floor and the entire floor subsequently collapsed.

No new memorial to Shevchenko is allowed to be opened. There isn't even a marker in the Leningrad cemetery where this giant of Ukrainian literature was originally buried.

When archaeological or historical objects from Ukraine are displayed in foreign museums or exhibits, they are rarely labeled as Ukrainian or coming from Ukraine. Most frequently, they are described as originating from southern Russia. The most recent example of this forgery of origins has been the Scythian exhibit from the U.S.S.R. displayed at the New York Metropolitan Museum of Art. Many of the Scythian objects, excavated in central Ukraine (not even near the border between the Ukrainian S.S.R. and the Russian S.F.S.R.), were identified as originating from southern Russia and not from Ukraine, nor even from the southern U.S.S.R.

The persecution of the Ukrainian past has stooped to such low levels that in 1973, Y. Hoysak of the village of Dashava was imprisoned for 3 days, fined, and subsequently harassed for painting his yard gate blue and yellow. Blue and yellow are the colors of the pre-Soviet Ukrainian flag.

Even old Ukrainian songs which touch on historical themes are forbidden. Songs permitted at concerts and on broadcasts are those which deal only with contemporary topics. Some can be sung in Ukrainian only if the majority of a repertoire is in Russian.

The Ukrainian past is even used by the KGB. During the last few years, it has become a common practice for the KGB to order a delegation from the Writers Union to place a wreath on a memorial to Shevchenko. KGB agents then photograph those who follow this delegation or those who also bring flowers. If they are students, they are expelled from school. If they are adults, they are dismissed from their jobs.

C. Religious Persecution

Religious persecution has also been intensified since, in many instances, religion and national identity are closely linked. Religious freedom, of course, is guaranteed by the Soviet Constitution (Article 124).

Whereas each village at one time had at least one church, most villages in eastern Ukraine now have none. The Lviv district, which came under Soviet rule only during World War II, had over 1200 churches at the end of the War. In 1961, there were only 528 churches. With every subsequent year, there are fewer churches.

The building of new churches is strictly prohibited.

Many churches are destroyed outright. In 1972, in the city of Lviv, the church on Artem Street was willfully destroyed with a tank. The parishioners threw themselves before the tank to block its way, but the militia dragged them away.

In 1971, the church on the main road between Kiev and Lviv in the village of Pidlisky was destroyed. On its site was built a teahouse.

During the night of December 19, 1973, along the roads of the villages of Babukhiv, Verbylivtsi, and Zaluzhya, all the roadside crosses were smashed; some had been erected over a century ago to commemorate the abolishment of serfdom.

Father Sava of the Church of St. Volodymyr in Kiev disappeared after he gave a sermon in Ukrainian instead of in Russian.

Just before Christmas 1973, all school principals in the Lviv oblast were called and warned that if any of their students were seen in church during Christmas, the principals would be dismissed from their posts.

School teachers are commanded to forbid their students to go caroling or to perform any other ethno-religious rites.

During Christmas and Easter, local Communist Party authorities send activists to church to observe if party members, teachers, supervisors, or other white-collar workers are present. These are then in danger of losing their party membership or employment.

Bus drivers are warned, under penalty of being fired, not to take on passengers who are carrying Easter baskets.

Militiamen are frequently stationed near churches to deny entry to parents with children.

In 1972, in the village of Zaluzhya, party activists forcefully evicted people from the church. A fight broke out. The church was sprayed with chemicals and the interior destroyed. When the parishioners refused to hand over the keys to authorities, the church doors were electro-welded shut.

In the village of Smilna, in 1972, the church was covered with chemicals. The parishioners cleaned the church and continued to come there. The church doors were then welded shut. The villagers sent a delegation to Kiev and to Moscow, but to no avail.

In the summer of 1972, in the village of Volsvyn, party thugs broke into the church, stole all church treasures, tore the cloth embroidery, and slashed the icons. For several days thereafter, a Jewish junk dealer, named Broder, was commanded to take the destroyed church property in order to incite anti-Semitic feelings among the villagers. Broder steadfastly refused to do this. He was beaten until he needed hospitalization. Broder took the thugs to court, but the case was dismissed.

It is amazing that Filaret, the Exarch of the Russian Orthodox Church in Ukraine (the Ukrainian Orthodox Church and the Ukrainian Catholic Church have been destroyed), could come to the United States and state that he knows of no violations of religious rights in the Ukrainian S.S.R.

D.   Official Anti-Semitism

The previous mention of attempts by Soviet authorities to incite anti-Semitic feelings among Ukrainians is not an isolated incident. Nor is the reverse, anti-Ukrainian feeling among Jews, ignored. It is official, although covert, policy for Soviet authorities to set both these nationalities against each. For example, when Petro Shelest was being removed from his position as First Secretary of the Ukrainian Communist Party for being pro-Ukrainian, the faction supporting Shcherbytsky, current First Secretary and vehement "internationalist," tried to label Shelest as an anti-Semite. The two pogroms near the synagogue in Kiev, organized by the KGB in March and May of 1972, were used as provocations. Rumors were spread among Jews that these pogroms were initiated by Shelest, while among Ukrainians the story was spread that the Jews were demanding an autonomous republic in Ukraine. Although this attempt at antagonizing both sides failed, it clearly shows that anti-Semitism is a means which Soviet authorities use to defame Ukrainian identity.

An example which shows how anti-Semitic policy is used for anti-Ukrainianism, and how it succeeds, is the case of the book *Judaism Without Embellishment*. This book was written by Trofim Kichko and was published in 1963 by the Ukrainian Academy of Sciences in Lviv, the city where Ukrainian consciousness is probably strongest. It is important to note that 1963 was the year that the Ukrainian Academy of Sciences ceased being an independent academy equal to other academies in the Soviet Union, but was forced to become a subsidiary of the Academy of Sciences of the U.S.S.R. in Moscow (note again Article 15 of the Constitution and its guarantee of sovereignty). The book was written in the Ukrainian language and was virulently anti-Semitic, complete with vulgar caricatures worthy of the Nazi Julius Streicher.

The book was widely condemned in the West, and *Literaturnaya Gazeta* (Feb. 10, 1963) condemned it also. The article even called Kichko a scoundrel who collaborated with the Nazis during World War II. However, Soviet authorities did nothing to stop the spread of this book, nor was any punishment prescribed for Kichko. The point becomes quite obvious: the book was purposely written to degrade Ukrainians in the eyes of world opinion. Few books are permitted to be published in Ukrainian. This one was. It had the outward sanction of the Ukrainian Academy of Sciences (even though the Academy was now run by Moscow). Obviously, one was to conclude that the Ukrainian Academy of Sciences must be full of Jew-haters. It was published in Lviv because this city is closely identified with Ukrainianism. Obviously, one was to conclude that Ukrainianism is closely linked to anti-Semitism. *Literaturnaya Gazeta* condemned the book publicly to disassociate the Kremlin from official anti-Semitism and to make it appear as if Ukraine enjoys a certain degree of autonomy which it uses, in spite of Kremlin disapproval, to further its hatred of the Jews.

Although these maneuvers are obvious to those who understand the situation, this ruse produced the desired effects. In 1971, the Macmillan Company of New York published a book entitled *Soviet Jewry Today and Tomorrow,* by Boris Smolar who was born in Ukraine, but who has lived in the United States since 1919. In Chapter 5, "Anti-Semitism and the Secession Movement in the Ukraine," he draws exactly those conclusions which Soviet authorities want the world to draw: that Ukrainians are *a priori* fascistic Jew-haters who collaborated with the Nazis, who are so dangerous even to the Kremlin that they are reluctantly given a certain degree of autonomy. This freedom they use to further their hateful objectives through their nationalistic institutions. And although the Moscow government has made anti-Semitism illegal and has condemned Kichko and his book, it is powerless to fight this disease in fascistic, autonomous Ukraine.

The types of questions which Boris Smolar should have asked Soviet authorities, when he was researching for his book, are obvious. If the Ukrainian S.S.R. is so autonomous, why was P. Shelest removed by Brezhnev instead of by the Politburo of the Ukrainian Communist Party? Why, for example, was Mykola Rudenko, a member of Amnesty International who resides in Kiev, the capital of an autonomous and sovereign Ukraine (Article 15), arrested and searched on orders from a Moscow prosecutor? Moscow is not in autonomous Ukraine. Why was the Ukrainian Academy of Sciences forced to lose its autonomy and become part of the Moscow Academy? Why must most scientific works in journals of the Ukrainian Academy of Sciences be written in Russian? If fascistic nationalists run Ukraine, why is the Ukrainian language not used in that republic's schools, universities, and other institutions? Why is a priest in the nationalistic capital arrested for preaching sermons in Ukrainian? Why are statues of the nationalist Taras Shevchenko forbidden to be visited? Why are crosses in nationalistic cemeteries smashed? Why are nationalistic children forbidden to sing "fascistic" Christmas carols?

But more important—why was Kichko, a Nazi collaborator according to official newspapers, allowed to live and to write more anti-Semitic diatribes (he wrote another one in 1968) when all other Soviet citizens even suspected of Nazi collaboration are executed or imprisoned? Why is Kichko walking the streets of the U.S.S.R. after his condemnation by *Literaturnaya Gazeta,* when Leonid Plyushch, a Ukrainian mathematician who provoked *Komsomolskaya Pravda* by writing a letter to the editor, is in the Dnipropetrovsk psychiatric prison undergoing chemical poisoning? His letter was not even published. Why are thousands of Ukrainians serving long sentences in concentration camps for violating the nebulous Article 62 of the Penal Code ("anti-Soviet agitation and propaganda"), when Kichko obviously violated a definite, official ban on anti-Semitism and is still free?

The answers are self-evident to those who analyze this whole affair and understand what goals the Soviet government wants to achieve in Ukraine through Kichko and official anti-Semitism.

Through the few examples presented above, it becomes very clear what Leonid Brezhnev meant when he recently stated ". . . that the nationality question . . . has been settled completely, settled decidedly, and settled irreversibly." To Ukraine it means the destruction of everything that is Ukrainian. This includes language, history, literature, education, traditions, religion, art, and even thought. Under Stalin, this objective was to be accomplished by the policy of genocide—the physical destruction of Ukrainians and the physical manifestations of their nationality. Under Brezhnev, the policy has become one of ethnocide—the secretive destruction of the soul of Ukrainianism, for without this spiritual entity, no physical manifestations can survive. In the Soviet Union this ethnocide is not called Russian chauvinism, it is called internationalism. For this goal, Soviet authorities are prepared to destroy the civilization, the culture, and, if necessary, the physical being of over forty million Ukrainians.

Due to the time limit imposed by the panel, the following points were not covered in Dr. Zwarun's prepared statement. They were, however, delivered to the panel in the form of an appendix and are here included for the benefit of the reader.

Petition of S. Ya. Karavansky to the attorney-general of the Ukr.S.S.R. that Yu.M.Dadenkov, Minister of Higher Secondary Special Education be arraigned on charges of promoting Russification.
To the attorney-general of the Ukrainian S.S.R.
From citizen Karavansky, Svyatoslav Yosypovych, who resides in the city of Odessa, at 59 Chornomorsky Road, Apartment 47.

PETITION

I request you to arraign on criminal charges the Minister of Higher and Special Secondary Education of the Ukrainian S.S.R., Dadenkov, Yuri Mikolayevich, under sections of the Criminal Code of the Ukrainian S.S.R. which provide penalties for:

1. Violation of national and racial equality. (Sec. 6, CC Ukr.S.S.R.)
2. Opposition to the restoration of Leninist principles in the practical organization of higher education of the Ukrainian S.S.R. (Sec. 167, CC Ukr.S.S.R.)
3. Failure to implement the resolutions of the Twentieth Congress of the CPSU regarding the liquidation of the consequences of the cult of the individual and impeding the restoration of normal conditions of development of the Ukrainian socialist nation. (Sec. 66, CC Ukr.S.S.R.)
4. Training of unqualified personnel and disorganization of the pedagogical process in the system of higher and specialized education. (Sec. 167, CC Ukr.S.S.R.)

In accordance with the rules of admission to higher and specialized secondary educational institutions, Russian language and literature are among the subjects of the entrance examinations. Graduates of Russian schools are more successful in this examination than graduates of Ukrainian schools. In addition to this, entrance examinations in specialized subjects are conducted in Russian; this also makes it more difficult for graduates of Ukrainian schools to write these subject examinations. Therefore they achieve fewer points on these competitive examinations.

Of the total number of those who study in the higher educational institutions, Ukrainians make up a significantly lower percentage than they do in the sphere of production of material goods on the territory of the Ukrainian S.S.R. Thus, among those who entered the Odessa Polytechnical Institute in the school year 1964-65, Ukrainians made up 43 per cent. Of 1126 Ukrainians who made entrance applications, 453 were accepted, *i.e.*, 40 per cent. But of 1,002 Russians who applied, 477 were accepted, or 46 per cent. This procedure of admittance to higher and specialized secondary educational institutions of the republic now in force is anti-Leninist and a direct restriction of the rights of citizens as regards their nationality. Acts of this nature are subject to penalty under Sec. 66, CC Ukrainian S.S.R.

> Sec. 66. Violation of national and racial equality. Propaganda or agitation with the view of inciting to racial or national animosity as a direct or indirect limitation of rights, or the establishment of direct or indirect privileges of citizens as regards their racial or national affiliation. — Punishable by imprisonment for a term of from 6 months to 3 years, or by banishment for a period from 3 to 5 years.

In the overwhelming majority of higher and specialized secondary educational institutions in Kiev, Kharkiv, Odessa, Dnipropetrovsk, and others, instruction is not in the Ukrainian language.

The teaching personnel in higher educational institutions of the Ukrainian S.S.R. "do not understand the Ukrainian language." Thus in the Odessa Pedagogical Institute which trains teachers for secondary schools, lectures are in Russian because the lecturers "do not know" the Ukrainian language. In the Odessa State University, even in the Ukrainian department of the philological faculty which trains the Ukrainian philologists, the majority of the subjects (history of the CPSU, foreign languages, logic, psychology, foreign literature, Marxist philosophy) are not taught in Ukrainian. This is the direct result of the negligent attitude of the minister of higher education to his responsibilities:

a) failure to have published a whole series of textbooks for higher educational institutions, *e.g.*, foreign language, logic, foreign literature;

b) failure to train national (*i.e.*, Ukrainian) personnel as lecturers.

Such conditions in higher education in Ukraine destroy the normal conditions for the development of the Ukrainian Socialist nation.

As a result of relegating the Ukrainian language to second place, graduates of Odessa University and the Odessa Pedagogical Institute refuse to teach in Ukrainian schools, giving as their reason ignorance of the language.

I beg you to study the above facts and to determine the degree of guilt of Yuri Mikolayevich Dadenkov.

An Excerpt from Vyacheslav Chornovil's Statement to The Presidium of the Supreme Soviet, CC CPU and The Council of Ministers of the Ukrainian S.S.R.

It is difficult to imagine anything more barbarous, inhuman, and dreadful than contempt for the dead. Perhaps it is more "humane" to execute a person by firing squad than to demolish his grave and scatter his remains.

That which is taking place in Yaniv Cemetery in Lviv may be described in terms of medieval Asiatic savagery. Under supervision of specially appointed individuals, soldiers' graves are bulldozed while workers shovel out the remains. They say that all this is sanctioned by Telishevsky, head of the Lviv Regional Executive Committee.

Consider for a moment what is being done.

First, desecrating the graves of the enemy is a profanity repudiated by the civilized world. Death equalizes all opinions and ideologies. Death demands reverence. Article 212 of the Criminal Code of the Ukrainian S.S.R. prescribes penalties for the dishonoring of burial grounds.

Second, are the youths of western Ukraine, who perished in the struggle to rid their land of Polish colonial repression, to be regarded as enemies of the Soviet State? Why are reprisals being carried out against those who died over fifty years ago? For defending western Ukraine from Polish oppression?

We—who censure Pilsudski, condemn the "pacification" and decry Bereza Kartuzka—see that even the Polish occupiers, whose enemy these soldiers had been, did not disturb their graves. Even during Stalin's reign such destruction was unheard of . . .

. . . I restrained myself from appealing to individual party and Soviet authorities after the events of 1967—when I was imprisoned for honestly questioning the violations of Soviet legality.

Today I cannot remain silent. In the name of humanity, I urge

245

you to interrupt the actions of these self-satisfied provincial auto-crats and restore a portion of the ruined gravesites. In this way, disassociate yourselves from the crime that is presently taking

Excerpts from a Memorandum
on
THE PRESERVATION AND SUPPORT OF THE IVAN HONCHAR MUSEUM-ARCHIVES IN KIEV, UKRAINIAN S.S.R.
submitted to
The United Nations Educational, Scientific and Cultural Organization (UNESCO)

The Ivan Honchar Museum-Archives occupies a narrow, crumbling, two-story building. With objects dated from the tenth century to the eighteenth century, it is a unique and priceless collection. The elderly Ivan Honchar realizes the acute necessity to move his possessions to a well-protected museum. But—the government refuses to provide accommodations for the collection; permission for constructing or purchasing a building cannot be obtained.

Such a government policy indicates that the museum is on the "black list" and is doomed for destruction. Many intellectuals in Ukraine and abroad feel that the government of the U.S.S.R. has embarked on an outright policy of cultural genocide. Numerous incidents in recent years indicate that there is an attempt to destroy the cultural heritage of the people of Ukraine. On May 14, 1964, fire destroyed the library-archives of the Ukrainian Academy of Sciences in Kiev; on November 26, 1968, fire destroyed more rare documents, books, and archives in St. George's Church of Vydubetsky Monastery in Kiev; the same night fire destroyed the library and documents of the Great Synagogue in Odessa. All of the above incidents were witnessed by tourists and reported by *The New York Times* on February 20, 1969.

Intervention by the U.N. is imperative. For to know that one's history is being erased is frightening; to do nothing to prevent it is inexcusable and unforgivable. Only a body such as the United Nations Educational, Scientific and Cultural Organization, internationally recognized and respected, can stop the insane annihilation of a people's culture. It is therefore suggested and earnestly hoped that the United Nations Educational, Scientific and Cultural Organization [will]:

1) Appoint and dispatch a committee to investigate the possibilities of preserving the Ivan Honchar Museum-Archives in Kiev, Ukrainian S.S.R., and

2) Assume guardianship and active support of the Ivan Honchar Museum-Archives, allocating sufficient funds for this purpose.

Justice demands that, despite any difficulties which might arise, the Ivan Honchar Museum-Archives must be saved. If it is not, libraries, will continue to burn, churches and monasteries will continue to be razed, museums will continue to disappear. And gradually, the forty-five million population of Ukraine will lose its cultural identity.

RELIGIOUS PERSECUTION IN UKRAINE

Article 18 of the Universal Declaration of Human Rights reads:

Everyone has the right to freedom of thought, conscience and religion; this right includes freedom to change his religion or belief, and freedom, either alone or in community with others and in public or private, to manifest his religion or belief in teaching, practice, worship and observance.

Following the revolutionary period in Ukraine a new wave of national reawakening swept the country. One of the many areas to experience this cultural renaissance was the church. In 1921, a conference of Orthodox clergy and laymen gathered in St. Sophia's Cathedral in Kiev and unanimously agreed to break ties with the Russian Church. They formed the Ukrainian Autocephalous Orthodox Church.

In western Ukraine, a portion of the Ukrainian Orthodox Church had accepted a union with Rome in 1596. This church was called the Uniate, or Byzantine Catholic Church.

Fearing the loss of central authority, both the Soviet state and the state-controlled Russian Orthodox Church initiated a campaign to halt both Ukrainian autonomy and cultural development. Metropolitan Lypkivsky was removed from the leadership of the Ukrainian Church in 1927.

A fierce atheistic campaign was initiated during the 1930's. During this period over 30 bishops and several thousand clergy and monks were executed or exiled. Hundreds of ancient church monuments were dismantled or blown up.

With the establishment of the Soviet state in western Ukraine a similarly ruthless campaign was carried out. Eleven bishops and over 2,000 priests of the Ukrainian Catholic Church were arrested and sentenced during and after World War II. The Ukrainian Catholic Church was formally dissolved and the faithful were forced to join the Russian Orthodox Church.

Letter to the editor of
Komsomolskaya Pravda
March 1968

" . . . It (the Soviet Press) is a deluge of lies, both exposed and unexposed: tyrants and flunkeys are lauded and our finest people are covered with filth; history is falsified (for example, the 'miraculous' transformation of Bohdan Khmelnytsky from a traitor to the Ukrainian people—see the prewar edition of the *Great Soviet Encyclopedia*—into a hero of the same people); and so on.

Leonid Plyushch

Note: Because of these remarks Plyushch, a highly trained specialist, was fired from his job at the Cybernetics Institute in Kiev. He was arrested in January 1972 and sent a year later to a "special" psychiatric hospital in Dnipropetrovsk, Ukrainian S.S.R. for indefinite confinement.

INGRIDA LEVITS

" ... the final objective is to destroy the Latvian people as an ethnically distinct nation ... "

LEVITS, Ingrida

Ingrida Levits, nee Barg, was born on March 31, 1926 in Latvia. After completing her secondary education, she worked as a nurse in Germany from 1943 to 1945. Following Germany's surrender she found herself in the Soviet occupation zone from where she was forcibly repatriated to Latvia. Shortly thereafter Ingrida, her parents and sisters were arrested and sent into exile in Russia. Ingrida, however, was able to elude the militia and lived illegally in Latvia for five years. She finally obtained her residency papers and worked in Riga first as a nurse and then, from 1958, with various publishing houses. She emigrated to West Germany in 1972, where she now works as a journalist.

THE RUSSIFICATION
OF THE LATVIAN PEOPLE

I will testify about how the Soviet Union with its destructive policy is gradually russifying Latvia in order to completely absorb the Latvian people into the Russian people.

The destructive policies include many components. The first, chronologically speaking, was the mass deportation of the civilian population in 1940-1941 and in the first 5 postwar years. A large part of the deportees died.

Another important component is indifference, a lack of interest in reforms needed to restore the natural growth rate and to safeguard the survival of the nation.

The most topical question today is the Russification of Latvia. A person who does not know the circumstances may think Russification means that the Soviet authorities are forcing the Latvians to become Russians through various compulsory measures. This is, however, not yet the case. Compulsory measures cannot succeed as long as the people stick together and can resist pressure.

At present, Russian immigrants are systematically brought into Latvia and the other Baltic republics. These immigrants are recruited by Soviet agencies in various parts of European Russia.

Since we know that the final objective is to destroy the Latvian people as an ethnically distinct nation, we have reason to maintain that the Soviet regime is guilty of genocide, although at the moment it is a genocide without bloodshed.

One might ask how we can be sure about the final objective when we are actually experiencing an intermediate stage of the process. The answer is to be found in Russian history. About a dozen small nations in Russia's neighborhood have in the past few centuries met the fate that now threatens the Baltic nations. The transition from czarism to communism did not change anything in this respect. Russian communism has developed a theory of the merging together of all nations under communism. This theory serves as a cover for Russification. . . .

I shall testify here how Russians treat Latvians unjustly. But I want to underline that I do not intend to condemn the Russian people or incite hate. The real culprit is the communist regime, which exploits nations for its own purposes. I am aware that Latvians have been exploited in the same way to the detriment of other nations. . .

Though my testimony concerns Latvia, everything I say also applies to Estonia. The situation is basically the same in Lithuania, though things there may be somewhat different.

The Baltic area is not part of Russia. Our case has nothing to do with the merging of ethnically related nations. None of the Baltic peoples—the Estonians, the Latvians and the Lithuanians —are Slavs. The Latvians and the Lithuanians are the last surviving Balts. The Estonians are Finno-Ugrians. All three nations have clearly marked ethnic frontiers. . .

Not only are the Baltic peoples ethnically different from the Russians, but their history and culture are also different. It is said that the Baltic area belongs historically to Russia. This statement only demonstrates an ignorance of the facts. The different parts of the Baltic area were merged with the Russian empire at different times in the eighteenth century. The latest Russian acquisition was the province of Courland in south-west Latvia, in 1795. But up to the last decades of the nineteenth century the Baltic provinces lived their own life administratively, culturally, and legally. It was only in the last decades of the nineteenth century that the Russian administration started to link the Baltic provinces more closely with the empire, and launched a policy of Russification.

All three Baltic nations have languages of their own and use the Latin alphabet. They have their own literature, folklore, and a way of life that is different from the Russian. This has given rise to a strong awareness of their national integrity. The Estonians and most of the Latvians are Lutherans, the Lithuanians and the inhabitants of Latvia's eastern province are Roman Catholics. The Russians were Greek Orthodox before the advent of the communist regime. The Baltic nations have always been Western-oriented in their culture. . . .

The influx of Russian settlers constitutes the gravest element of the Soviet policy of destruction. The number of immigrants to Latvia averages 15,000-18,000 annually. The number for Estonia is 7,000-10,000. These figures may seem very small to the big nations in the West, but are very much felt in the Baltic states. Their significance is underscored by the following circumstances:

a) The immigration has gone on unceasingly for 3 years since the end of the War.

b) At the same time, Latvians and Estonians have been decimated through deportations and various recruitment drives for settlers for Asia.

c) The birthrate among Latvians and Estonians is relatively low as a result of harmful demographic policies.

According to the 1959 census, Latvians constituted 62 per cent of the 2.1 million inhabitants of Latvia. By 1970, only 56.8 per cent out of a population of 2.4 million were Latvian. Of the 1.2 million population of Estonia in 1959, Estonians constituted 74.6 per cent, but of the 1.4 million population in 1970 Estonians accounted for only 68.2 per cent. The Russification process has continued unabated since 1970.

The degree of Russification can also be deduced from data on the ethnic composition of the five largest Latvian cities. In 1959, non-Latvians already accounted for 55 per cent of the 580,000 inhabitants of Riga. By 1974, the number of inhabitants had increased to an estimated 776,000, but the share of Latvians decreased to about 37 per cent. In Dangavpils, Latvia's second largest city (109,000 inhabitants in 1974), Latvians constituted only 15 per cent, in Liepaja (population 98,000) about 42 per cent, in Ventspils also about 42 per cent, and in Jelgava (Mitau), the old center of Courland, Latvians were estimated at about 40 per cent in 1974. In other words, the Latvians are already a minority in all the larger cities of their country, and in smaller towns the immigrants will become a majority within the next few years.

253

The large-scale Russian immigration is made possible only under three conditions:
   a) Work must be procured for the immigrants.
   b) Housing must be provided.
   c) Administrative support for them must be safeguarded.

Jobs are made available by establishing new industrial enterprises or expanding existing ones. This is done irrespective of economic conditions or profit motivation; the primary consideration is to provide a number of jobs for immigrants.

Immigration has caused a heavy housing shortage in all post-war years. The housing shortage has considerably hampered the establishment of new families, and has been one of the causes of the low birthrate among Estonians and Latvians. New housing is being constructed at a fast pace, but the supply has never been able to catch up with demand. The immigrants have priority when new flats and homes are made available. Last but not least, administrative support is safeguarded because all leading posts are held ·by members of the Communist Party who blindly obey directives from Moscow. The CPSU is mainly responsible for the Russification policy in the Baltic area.

The Latvians are formally regarded as the native majority population, and their country is called the Latvian S.S.R., but in reality it is the Russians who have all the rights. The Russians themselves are convinced that the future of Latvia is theirs.

All political activities are conducted in the Russian language, although even Latvians take part in them. Russian is spoken at meetings of the Latvian Supreme Soviet, at party and trade union congresses, and at official celebrations. Laws are compiled in Russian and often come ready-made from Moscow. Later they are translated into Latvian. The courts conduct their business in both lanuages: cases are tried either by a Latvian or by a Russian judge, depending on the nationality of the parties.

Both Russian and Latvian is spoken in factories and other places of work. There are factories where Russians are in the majority. Foremen, if they are Latvians, must be able to issue their directives in Russian, because Russian workers are not willing to learn Latvian. The management of enterprises uses Russian only. Managers can be of either Russian or Latvian nationality.

Russian is mandatory in Latvian schools starting with the

second year of elementary school. Russian children have schools of their own and can, if they so wish, study Latvian, but usually they are not interested. Schools with parallel classes are fairly common—some classes are for Russian children and other classes for Latvian children. The Russian language predominates in joint meetings and activities of the entire school.

Industrialized Western countries also have foreign labor, and its presence there has occasionally caused unfavorable reactions among the population. But there are several circumstances which make it virtually impossible to compare these two kinds of immigration.

1. The concentration of immigrants in the Baltic states is much higher and growing steadily.

2. Immigrants in the West come from various countries and cultures; this means their presence is not as oppressive as it is in the Baltic states, where virtually all immigrants are Russians, or at least adherents of the Russian way of life.

3. Immigrants in the West try to adapt to conditions in the host country and learn its language, but in the Baltic states they force on the native population their own language, culture, and way of life.

4. An immigrant to a Western country cannot take an active part in its political life before he becomes a naturalized citizen. In the Baltic States, immigrants have all the rights from the first moment of their arrival and are quite frequently appointed to high political or economic posts on the second day of their arrival. This is so because they are actually nominated in Moscow, although formally the appointments are made in Riga.

5. The most important difference is that the Western countries are sovereign and adapt immigration for their own interests. The Baltic peoples, on the other hand, cannot do this; they are forced to bow to decisions that are made in Moscow.

The Russification of the Baltic peoples is an international problem. I called Russification a genocide without bloodshed. Unfortunately, the International Convention on Genocide does not deal with this kind of crime.

There are several international agreements which contain provisions to protect ethnic minorities. Such protection is accorded in one form or another, e.g., to the Tyroleans in Italy, to Yugoslavs in Austria, to Italians in Yugoslavia, to Swedes in Finland, etc. These ethnic minorities shall not be destroyed through an influx of an ethnic majority into their territory. Other states also respect similar principles without being directly bound by agreements or treaties.

In view of this, it is inexplicable why Moscow should be given a free hand to colonize the Baltic countries.

The U.N. General Assembly and its subordinate agencies have approved a number of resolutions concerning decolonization, and have condemned attempts of the colonial powers to send settlers to their colonies in order to change the ethnic composition of the population. A few years ago such resolutions were aimed, e.g., at Portugal. Even today, South Africa is warned not to colonize Namibia. If this is not permitted in colonies, why should the Soviet Union be permitted to Russify its small non-Russian constituent republics?

The Soviet Union is carrying out this genocide without bloodshed by referring to its sovereignty and to the principle of non-interference in the domestic affairs of other countries.

Soviet diplomats at the United Nations have stated that there is one important difference between the Soviet Union and the colonial powers: under the Soviet constitution, the Soviet constituent republics have the right to secede from the Union, while the colonies lack this right.

I can bear witness that the nations in the Soviet Union also lack this right. Those members of the United Nations who cherish human rights and international law have every reason to initiate an objective inquiry into this matter within the framework of the United Nations. It would be of great service to mankind.

REIZA PALATNIK

" . . . anti-Semitism has a long history in the Soviet Union, and its end is not yet in sight . . ."

PALATNIK, Reiza

Reiza Palatnik was born in 1936 and is a librarian by profession. She was arrested on December 1, 1970 in Odessa after expressing her desire to emigrate to Israel, and was charged with "circulating fabrications known to be false which defame the Soviet state and social system." Her trial took place June 22-24, 1971. She was sentenced to two years' imprisonment in ordinary-regime camps.

After her release Reiza Palatnik emigrated to Israel.

ON THE DESTRUCTION
OF JEWISH CULTURE

Anti-Semitism has a long history in the U.S.S.R. and its end is not yet in sight. Since time immemorial, all governments have used Jews as safety-valves to draw their people's anger away from the confusion reigning in their countries. The U.S.S.R. is no exception to this rule. On the contrary: although Jewish culture flourished in czarist Russia despite pogroms, discrimination, and the harsh living conditions imposed on Jews, it has been completely destroyed in the last 30 years of Soviet rule.

After all the pogroms, restrictions, and interference with their rights which Jews had been subjected to in czarist Russia, Russian Jews joyfully welcomed the October Revolution, which proclaimed equality for all nationalities.

Jewish culture and education in pre-revolutionary Russia are described in the *Large Soviet Encyclopedia,* Edition I, Volume 24.

According to the census of 1926, the Jewish population came first in literacy: 69 per cent for women, 76 per cent for men.

In 1928, there were 1,075 Jewish schools in the U.SS.R., where 160,000 children studied. Seven-tenths of the Jewish population considered Yiddish its mother tongue.

At the time of the sweeping cultural revolution of 1930-1931, the number of Jewish cultural institutions increased considerably.

At that time, three daily newspapers were published in Yiddish: *Der Emess* (Moscow), *October* (Minsk), and *Stern* (Kharkiv). Monthly publications were *Royte Welt* (Kharkiv), *Prolit*

(Kharkiv), and *Stern* (Minsk). Many local newspapers were published in Odessa, Kiev, Berdychiv, and other cities. The children's magazine *Zei Gereit* [Be Ready] was also issued in Kharkiv. Finally, many wall-poster newspapers were printed in the Jewish language in almost every factory employing Jewish workers, as well as in clubs, reading rooms, and kolkhozes.

The number of books, magazines, and newspapers published in the Jewish language were:

	titles	*number of copies*
1923	11	155,000
1924	83	320,000
1925	211	798,000
1926	213	781,000
1927	298	1,136,000

The Byelorussian Academy had a Jewish section for the study of Jewish culture. This section collected material and did research on matters related to Jewish history and to the participation of Jews in the Revolution, and engaged in the scientific study of the Jewish language, literature, and folklore.

The professorship of Jewish language and literature originally established at the Ukrainian Academy of Sciences was transformed into an Institute for Jewish Culture in 1929.

In some pedagogical institutions of higher learning (Moscow), special Jewish departments were established to train qualified personnel for Jewish schools and other educational institutions.

Jewish literature was represented by the following names:
Poets: Harik, Gofstein, P. Markish, L. Kvitko, L. Reznik, M. Kulbach, S. Galkin, N. Oislender, etc.
Prose writers: E. Gordon, Noah Lurie, Noteh Lurie, Itzik Kipniss, Bergelson, Godiner, Daniel, H. Tietch, etc.
Critics: Nussinov, Dobrushkin, Gurstein, M. Litvakov, Vinner, etc.

The "great indestructible friendship of peoples" led to the creation in 1934 of an autonomous Jewish region named Birobidzhan. Located in the Khabarovsk region, this province has an area of 35,800 square kilometers. Two newspapers were published, one in Russian and one in Yiddish.

In 1959, the population of Birobidzhan was 163,000, of which 14,200, or 8.8 per cent, were Jewish, 78.2 per cent Russian and 8.9 per cent Ukrainian.

During the pre-war years the government's policy shifted radically in the direction of forced Russification, anti-Semitism, and outright terror.

Between 1936 and 1939, a large majority of Yiddish secondary, technical, and trade union schools and institutions of higher learning were closed. All Jewish newspapers were discontinued except the *Birobidzhan Stern*. All but 4 (Moscow, Kiev, Minsk, Birobidzhan) of the 11 Jewish theaters were shut down.

Between 1937 and 1939, the following prominent Jewish writers were arrested and died in concentration camps: Izi Harik, Zelik Akselrod, Moshe Kulbach, Max Eric, Haim Gildin, Moshe Litvakov, and many other writers and representatives of Jewish culture.

But then the war broke out and this process was arrested. A Jewish anti-fascist committee was created (which incidentally is not referred to in any Soviet publication at present), Jewish cultural activity was allowed to flourish openly, there were some improvements in religious life, and attempts were made to establish ties with Jewish communities elsewhere in the world. For this purpose Michaels and Itzik Fefer were sent to the U.S.A. in 1943. They established ties with the American Jewish community, from which they obtained considerable material assistance for the U.S.S.R.'s military potential.

Jews, along with the other peoples of the U.S.S.R., engaged in mortal combat with fascism. But in 1943 a new wave of anti-Semitism swept the country, far exceeding anything known under the czarist regime. Anti-Semitism spread from the occupied territories in the ranks of the partisan movement, the Red Army, and the rear guard.

Discrimination against Jews was felt more and more in the army. Thousands of Jews who had performed heroic acts during the war were left without awards because of their nationality. At the same time, rumors spread persistently that "Jews do not fight, but lie low behind the front."

The catastrophic annihilation of European Jewry by the Nazis was passed over in silence. Throughout the war years, Stalin only once mentioned the Nazi policy of extermination of Jews.

The end of the war was accompanied by growing anti-Semitism among the population. At this time Jews were almost completely excluded from positions of political and military importance in the party and the government.

After the war, the few remaining Jewish schools were closed. The last schools in the Bukovyna territory were closed in 1948.

In 1946, an active campaign was resumed against nationalism. It soon became apparent that this campaign was directed against the most prominent representatives of Jewish culture and art. At first they were accused of nationalism and lack of political commitment. Later they were charged with Zionism and hostility towards socialism and the Soviet people.

In 1947-1948, the campaign was broadened considerably. The press and the radio endlessly repeated words like "rootless cosmopolitan," "unpatriotic" and "decadent cosmopolitans" coupled with the names of Nussinov, A. Guritch, Boyadziyev, Galkin, Sutzkever, P. Markish, Kipniss, and many others. The circle of accusations and the accused widened.

Among the charges made were the following:

1. Jewish writers and poets use the word "Jew" too often in their works.

2. They use words borrowed from Hebrew needlessly in an exaggerated way.

3. Their works contain too many national-historical and biblical legendary themes.

4. The subject of the Jewish wartime holocaust is particularly dangerous.

5. Nationalism and Zionism reached their apex in the works of Itzik Kipniss.

It is easy to see that these accusations were made in pursuance of a far-reaching objective. And that objective was obtained. Now, nearly 30 years later, we can justifiably affirm that the purpose of the campaign against "rootless cosmopolitans," begun in 1946, was the destruction of Jewish culture and its foremost representatives in the U.S.S.R.

But this was only the first part of the program.

On April 13, 1948, the president of the Jewish anti-fascist committee, Solomon Michaels, artistic director of Moscow's Jewish theater, was brutally murdered. Two months later, financial support was withdrawn from all four Jewish theaters. All were ordered to substitute guest artists for their regular programs. Everything possible was done to disrupt the work of these theaters, and the Jewish population was asked to refrain from attending performances. All these measures resulted in reduced audiences, which enabled the authorities to say that the theaters were unprofitable. At the end of 1948, almost all of these theaters and artistic groups were disbanded.

On November 20, 1948, it was announced that the Jewish anti-fascist committe was dissolved, its main journal, *Einikeit*, closed, its publishing house, *Der Emess*, shut down, and the publication of literary-political almanacs in Yiddish discontinued.

In December, a wave of arrests began among prominent Jews engaged in cultural activities. David Bergelson, David Gofstein, Leib Kvitko, Peretz Markish, Itzik Fefer, Benjamin Zuskin, Schmuel Persov, Nussinov, Dobrushkin, Galkin, and many others were arrested.

But even after the first arrests, the anti-Jewish campaign continued. The expression "rootless cosmopolitan," which had first appeared in a newspaper article, became a byword on the pages of the Soviet press. In this connection the 19th century Russian critic Belinsky's definition of cosmopolitan was often quoted:

"A cosmopolitan is a false, senseless, strange and incomprehensible phenomenon, a sort of pale, nebulous ghost, an immoral being, soulless, unworthy of the sacred name 'human being'."

At the beginning of 1949, a loud, massive, and meticulously prepared campaign began, using all the mass media: the press, the radio, the cinema, as well as lectures and above all countless meetings where Jews accused of cosmopolitanism criticized and condemned themselves in every way.

Jewish surnames were singled out and identified, and, as though this were not enough, Jewish names and patronymics as well. Pseudonyms were exposed. Cosmopolitans accused themselves of hating the Soviet people.

An analysis of newspaper articles published at that time shows that of the people attacked more than three times, 80 per cent were Jews.

What conclusions were drawn from this campaign?
1. The mildest punishment for those accused of cosmopolitanism was a reprimand or a stern reprimand.
2. Harsher sanctions were: dismissal from jobs, expulsion from creative unions.

3. The strictest punishment was expulsion from the party, often followed by arrest and trial.

It should be noted that whereas there were massive arrests of Jewish writers writing in Yiddish and Jewish actors performing in that language, there were no massive arrests of those accused of cosmopolitanism. This is additional proof that the main aim of the first stage of Stalin's anti-Jewish policy was the destruction of Jewish culture and of its best representatives.

At the end of 1949 and the beginning of 1950, a second wave of arrests of Jews began. The charges were nationalism and Zionist activities. Most of those arrested were condemned to 10 or more years of imprisonment in Soviet concentration camps. The principal trial of prominent Jews engaged in cultural activities was held in secret in July, 1952. The accused were charged with the following offenses:

1. Preparing an armed uprising which was to seize the Crimea from the U.S.S.R. and establish a bourgeois-Zionist republic on its territory.

2. Espionage for foreign states.

3. Bourgeois-nationalistic activities and anti-Soviet propaganda.

4. Organized actions and activities forbidden by Soviet law.

Twenty-three of the 24 defendants were sentenced to death and executed on August 12, 1952. Although all of those executed were fully rehabilitated after Stalin's death, their place of burial is still unknown and the authorities refuse to reveal it.

The worst period for Jews began on January 13, 1953, with the publication of the announcement of the doctors' conspiracy— "the murderers in white coats." This provocation was invented so as to definitively solve "the Jewish problem" in the U.S.S.R., following Hitler's example: hang the "doctors-murderers" in Red Square, provoke a wave of Jewish pogroms, and then, rescuing the Jews from the "wrath of the people," throw some of them in concentration camps and jails and move the rest from the western part of the country and resettle them in Siberia or the Far East.

The January 13, 1953 edition of the newspaper *Izvestia,* in an article entitled *Spies and Murderers in the Guise of Doctors-Scientists,* said:

"Today we are publishing TASS's chronicle about the exposure and arrest by state security forces of terrorist groups of doctors whose goal is to kill the Soviet Union's most active citizens by treacherously administering harmful treatment to them.

Among the members of this vile band of murdering professors-doctors are : Vovsky, Vinogradov, M. Kogan, B. Kogan, Yegorov, Feldman, Ettinger, Greenstein, and Doctor Mayorov.

Most of the members of the terrorist group—Vovsky, B. Kogan, Feldman, Greenstein, Ettinger, and others, have sold themselves body and soul to a branch of the American Secret Service, the international Jewish bourgeois-nationalistic organization "Joint." Numerous irrefutable facts have stripped the mask of philanthropy from the repulsive face of this dirty Zionist spy ring and fully exposed it. It was from this organization, created by the American Secret Service, that the monster Vovsky, through the Moscow doctor Shimelyovitch and the well-known Jewish bourgeois nationalist Michaels, received orders for the extermination of the leadership of the U.S.S.R."

Other periodicals were not to be outdone by *Izvestia*. The newspaper *Novoye Vremya* [New Time] printed an article entitled *The Zionist Agents of the American Secret Service;* the newspaper *Trud* [Work] printed one entitled *The Zionist Agents of the Dollar,* the newspaper *Znamya* [Banner] printed one called *Watchfulness: the Soviet People a Keenest Weapon.*

The atmosphere in the country had reached the boiling point. Spontaneous scenes flared up, brawls broke out in streets, apartments, public places and schools. People refused to go to Jewish doctors. The whole country was obsessed with espionage, every Jew was considered a potential spy, murderer, poisoner. Secret denunciations rained down: many people wanted to get the Order of Lenin, like Doctor L. F. Timashuk, who "exposed" the group of Kremlin doctors.

The suddent death of Stalin—the principal director of the anti-Semitic campaign—saved the Jews of the U.S.S.R. from total annihilation.

As early as April 4, an announcement of the Ministry of Internal Affairs of the U.S.S.R. was published proclaiming the abrogation, on the grounds that it was unjustified, of the decree of January 20, 1953, which bestowed the Order of Lenin on L. F. Timashuk.

On the same day, a decision of the Presidium of the Supreme Soviet of the U.S.S.R. was published stating:

"The Ministry of Internal Affairs of the U.S.S.R. has carefully checked all of the preliminary evidence and other facts involved in the affair of the doctors accused of sabotage, espionage, and terrorist activities against the citizens of the Sovit Union. This study has shown the charges levelled against the group of doctors to be false, and the documentary data on which the investigators of the affair based their conclusions unsound. It has been established that the depositions of the accused, who allegedly confirmed the charges made against them, were obtained by the former MGB department by investigatory methods which are inadmissible and strictly prohibited by Soviet law.

On the basis of conclusions of the committee appointed by the Ministry of Internal Affairs to investigate this affair, those arrested are fully rehabilitated and released from custody.

Those responsible for the improper investigation have been arrested and brought to justice."

The April 6, 1953 edition of the newspaper *Pravda* printed an article entitled *Soviet Socialist Laws is Inviolable,* which stated, *interalia:*

"Only people who had lost their Soviet identity and human dignity could have gone so far as to illegally arrest Soviet citizens—prominent representatives of Soviet medicine—and even falsify evidence, thus criminally betraying their civic duty. . . .

The constitution of the U.S.S.R. sets forth the great rights of the citizens of the Soviet socialist state. Article 127 of the constitution of the U.S.S.R. guarantees personal inviolability to its citizens. The citizens of the great Soviet state can be sure that their rights, as guaranteed by the constitution of the U.S.S.R., will be defended and held sacred by he Soviet government."

We can hear at this Hearing how consistent such a statement is with reality. Confinement in insane asylums, prisons, and murder instead of freedom, dismissal from work and endless persecution for one careless word. This is the guarantee the Soviet government provides to all its citizens.

In the light of such statements, one might expected to see a restoration of the equal rights of the Jewish people and a rebirth of its spiritual and cultural life. But until today the position of Jews in Russia is as follows:

1. Unlike the adherents of all other religions, Russia's Jews have no central spiritual center.

2. There is not one school where teaching is conducted in Yiddish, and there are no Jewish spiritual institutes.

3. The last itinerant theatrical troupe, directed by Schwarzer, has been disbanded. The official reasons: all the actors are elderly and they have not trained any young ones to take their places.

4. A set percentage of Jews is admitted to higher and special technical institutions of learning. This percentage varies between two and five per cent. Colleges which train personnel for the defense industry do not admit Jews: they are not even allowed to take the entrance examinations.

5. Percentages are also set for employment in many state and educational institutions.

6. The slightest pretext is used for dismissal from work, especially in the case of persons who have asked for an employment reference in order to emigrate to Israel. When staffs are reduced, Jews are the first to be dismissed. Persons who have expressed a wish to emigrate to Israel (Davidovitch and Kipniss in Minsk) are deprived of military ranks and awards and war invalids' pensions.

7. One newspaper is published in Yiddish in Birobidzhan and one monthly journal in Moscow.

8. Synagogues exist only in large cities, and not in all of them. Synagogue attendance on the part of young people leads to expulsion from college, dismissal from work, and other punishments.

9. Rumors circulate persistently that Birobidzhan must have settlers and that if Jews do not go there voluntarily they will be sent there forcibly.

10. Jewish scholars who have expressed a wish to leave the U.S.S.R. are excluded from professional activity. They are not allowed to hold seminars. The attempts of professors Voronel, Zand, and Brunover are well-known.

11. Jews are the only nationality in the U.S.S.R. without its own contemporary national art, culture, and literature. Attempts

to produce any work on a Jewish subject are immediately stopped.

12. The sites of mass shootings of Jews by the Nazis have still not been memorialized. The history of the Rumbulsky Cemetery in Riga and Babyn Yar in Kiev is well-known. Furthermore, Jewish cemeteries are systematically desecrated, monuments and graves destroyed (Odessa), and no one has ever been punished.

13. The Jewish rites of Brith Milah, Bar Mitzvah, Hupa, and others are officially prohibited.

14. And to top it all off, assimilation is encouraged. Children of mixed marriages are not Jews as a rule. Edward Kuznetsov gives an example in his *Prison Diaries*. Despite all his requests to be considered Jewish because of his Jewish father, he is persistently considered Russian.

15. After the Six-Day War in Israel, a wave of national awakening stirred Jewish circles in the U.S.S.R. Heightened interest was shown in Jewish history, culture, art, and spiritual life. Since such requests could not be satisfied in the U.S.S.R. because of the total absence of literature and accurate information on Jewish matters and the State of Israel, Jewish samizdat has spread considerably. Circles began to form for the study of the Hebrew language, and many Jews expressed the wish to emigrate to Israel. The authorities' answer to this awakened consciousness among Jews of their national identity was massive repression, refusal of visas, dismissals from work, deprivation of people's means of subsistence, arrests, provocations where harassment was useless, and more arrests and convictions for hooliganism, parasitism, resisting police, speculation, etc.

In the first Leningrad trial, a group of Jews was condemned for wishing to leave the Soviet Union illegally; but previously they had repeatedly applied to the proper department (the OVIR) for exit visas, and their applications had been repeatedly rejected. All were sentenced to maximum terms of imprisonment, and two—Kuznetsov and Dymshits—were sentenced to be shot. Only the wave of indignation aroused by these cruel and senseless sentences saved their lives.

In the second Leningrad trial, a large group of Jews was condemned for studying the Hebrew language, showing interest in

Israel, and wishing to leave the U.S.S.R. Analogous trials were held in Riga, Kishinev, Odessa, Sverdlovsk, and other cities.

At the orders of the KGB, provocations were organized against Feldman (sentenced to 3½ years for hooliganism) in Kiev, and Pinhasov (sentenced to 5 years for speculation) in Derbent. Charges are now being fabricated against Lev Roitburd from Odessa for resisting police.

Isaak Shkolnik was sentenced to 7 years in a strict-regime concentration camp for espionage, although neither the nature of his activities nor the level of his development could have enabled him to engage in such work. He was originally accused of spying for England, and only when England protested energetically was the accusation changed to espionage for Israel. His lawyer nevertheless refused to appeal his case under the pretext that it would do no good anyway.

This is how "the most democratic state on earth" meets the spiritual requirements of its citizens.

It is no secret to anyone that Soviet Jews are now an object for bargaining: in exchange for certain concessions from Western countries, some Jews are permitted to leave the U.S.S.R. But this is not all. When they leave, officials often threaten them: "We'll get you in Israel too." And these words are not mere threats. The Soviet Union's policy in the Near East is directed against the existence of the State of Israel, and the U.S.S.R. is happy to furnish Arab countries and terrorist organizations with weapons with which to kill Jews. The U.S.S.R. even invites Arafat to Moscow as a symbol of the liberation movement. The goals of Arafat and the Kremlin are identical: the destruction of the Jewish people. And if we consider how much experience the Soviet leaders have in this field, we must agree that they have something to share with Mr. Arafat.

DAVID KLASSEN

" . . . (the Volga Germans) were dispersed throughout the Soviet Union . . . "

VOLGA GERMANS:
A PEOPLE DISPERSED

Before I take the floor I would like to offer my apology. I would like to beg the jury to consider that I am not very well prepared on this issue. The witness who was to have testified here is my friend and comrade from prison days who has shared my sufferings, but who for evident reasons has not come here. The documents that are in my possession by some fortunate circumstance and my own experiences make it possible for me to make a contribution as a witness.

As concerns the Volga Germans, I'd like to say a few words because I think that this issue is being mostly misunderstood. People think the Germans lived only in the Volga area and that they are still living there. This is, however, not so. The Germans were dispersed. Some were sent to Zaporizhzhya, some to the Khersov region, some to the Melitopol district, some to the lower Volga area, to the Caucasus, to Orenburg, and to western Siberia. One thing I would like to say: If there are witnesses who could have told you about the oppressions they suffered, about the extremely difficult position of that national minority, then perhaps they would have told you that some people, some minorities can invoke their constitution. But these Germans cannot do this. They were dispersed throughout the Soviet Union, from the extreme north to the south, for example to Vorkuta and along the Chinese border, from the western regions of the Baltic states to the Far East of the Soviet Union.

This was done with the purpose of silencing these people. As far as their culture is concerned this has been achieved.

I have lists here that I can submit to you. This was a document addressed to the United Nations. It exposes all the instances of discrimination. If someone is interested I am ready to give him the document. I have [also] a new document, a document which was submitted to authorities of various ranks in the Soviet Union. We have obtained the document illegally, or rather, unofficially. Four hundred thirty signatories still live in the Soviet Union. These are people who have signed this document. For example, there is Elizaveta Schmidt, a mother of 15 children, who was beaten up because she went to a prayer assembly. These people are being persecuted. It would be very difficult to understand how this can happen today. It is very difficult for us to explain that it is so. . . . When you ask a collective farmer, a member of a kolkhoz, if he understands Soviet law, he would probably tell you that the law is very difficult to understand for people who have a Western understanding of legality. Any pig farmer in the Soviet Union knows that the law is a matter of pure chance. Soviet laws are bent and twisted to fit the convenience of the authorities. . . .

I would like to say that the issue is not that the Germans wish to emigrate—it isn't only that, though of course we have have many signatures to this effect—but they're merely requesting to be granted certain freedoms; and if they cannot get them, then they request emigration. . . .

ANDREI GRIGORENKO

" . . . people who try to speak out in defense of their distinct ethnicity and civic rights are thrown into prisons, camps, and mental hospitals . . ."

GRIGORENKO, Andrei

Born September 6, 1945 in Moscow; son of army general Pyotr Grigorenko.

In 1963, Andrei Grigorenko entered the Moscow Institute of Energy Research. At that time he joined an underground Marxist organization whose aim was the revival of Leninism. In early 1964 all members of that organization were arrested. After the trial Andrei Grigorenko was expelled from the Institute and discharged from the Komsomol. Subsequently he worked briefly as a locksmith in Moscow and later as a technician in a research institute.

In 1965, Andrei Grigorenko became an active member of the movement for human rights in the U.S.S.R. Because of this and because of his writings in the samizdat Grigorenko was dismissed several times from work. He was under constant KGB surveillance until his emigration from the Soviet Union. On numerous occasions the KGB made threats against his life and threatened him with incarceration in a psychiatric institution because of what they said was his "disagreeable" heredity. Despite the repressions, Grigorenko completed a degree at the Moscow Institute of Constructional Engineering.

The KGB suggested that Grigorenko leave the U.S.S.R. as an alternative to incarceration in a psychiatric institution.

On July 20, 1975, Andrei Grigorenko and his wife left the Soviet Union.

276

CRIMEAN TATARS:
A PEOPLE WITHOUT A
HOMELAND

I shall talk about the problem of the Crimean Tatars. In order to explain the crux of the matter I shall give a brief outline of events that took place over 30 years ago.

At 4 o'clock in the morning of May 18, 1944, soldiers of the Soviet army forced their way into all buildings where Crimean Tatars were living and gave them 20 minutes to prepare for departure. Then followed the long transport in cattle trucks to the Asian part of the U.S.S.R.

On the way people died of hunger, thirst, cold, and over-crowding. . . . According to approximate estimates, about 100,-000 people died in the first 2 years after deportation, or 40 per cent of the entire Crimean Tatar nation. On June 3, 1944, the Law on the Abolishment of the Chechen-Ingush A.S.S.R. and the transformation of the Crieman A.S.S.R. into the Crimean District was decreed.[1] This ukase accused the entire population of Chechens, Ingush, and Crimean Tatars of collaboration during World War II.

A "regime of special settlements" was established in the places of exile. The inhabitants of these settlements were not allowed to go beyond the village boundaries. Moreover, these villages were located in desolate regions, and the deportees had to build their homes and work the soil with their bare hands, without any government subsidies.

Anyone who left the special settlement was either shot on the spot or sent to prison for 25 years. These restrictions applied even to children. After the war, all veterans of the deported nations—whatever their military grades and decorations—were ordered to these special settlements. The only exception was the aviator Ametkhan-Sultan, twice Hero of the Soviet Union. But even he was restricted in his movement within the Soviet Union.

The special settlements regime was discarded by the government ukase of April 28, 1956. But the ukase stated: "The abolition of the restrictions relevant to the persons indicated and to the members of their families will not entitle the return of their property confiscated at the time of the banishment, and neither do these persons have the right to return to the places from which they had been banished."

Naturally, such a solution of the problem could not satisfy the overwhelming majority of the deported nationalities.

Since 1957, the Crimean Tatars have been trying to attain the re-establishment of their national rights. It should be noted that their postulates do not include a demand to get back the property they have lost, or that the status of autonomy should be returned to Crimea. The Crimean Tatars were only asking for the right to live on their historical soil. All petitions and statements were worded in the most loyal terms, but were left without an answer and without satisfaction.

After 1964, the national movement of the Crimean Tatars became more organized. Elected representatives of the people now formed the "Initiative Groups for assisting the party and the government in solving the national problem of the Crimean Tatar people." More than 5,000 people were elected to these Groups, and permanent representatives of the Initiative Groups, armed with people's mandates—signed by all Crimean Tatars who were of age—were sent to Moscow on funds collected from among the Tatars.

Although representatives of the supreme authorities of the U.S.S.R. more than once received some of the people's representatives, the problem did not near a solution. The only "success" was the ukase of the Presidium of the Supreme Soviet of September 5, 1967: "On the citizens of Tatar nationality, formerly living in the Crimea." As a result of this ukase, the Crimean Tatar nation was abolished, and it was maintained that the Tatars had become rooted in the places of their exile. Thus the

278

problem of their resettlement in the Crimea remained open. No longer hoping to be granted an organized return to the Crimea, the people sold all their property in central Asia and tried to return to their historical homeland individually.

More than once I had occasion to witness what difficulties they encountered in the Crimea. They were not admitted to hotels, and if they bought private houses, the purchase act was considered invalid. The entrance to the building of the regional executive committee was blocked by police and by civilians . . . Once a mother of 10 children tried to enter the building . . . She was immediately surrounded by the civilians, who pushed her away and kicked the children with their boots. While doing this they shouted that the Crimean Tatars had killed Russians during the last war. This happened in 1968; the oldest of these children was 17 years old.

Being deprived of the possibility to live either in guest houses or in private homes, grownups and children alike were forced to sleep on the bare concrete floor of Simferopol airport and at the railway station. During the night the police woke people up and chased them out. Some people were forced to sleep in the parks of the town of Symferopol and in the outskirts of the town . . . I have witnessed several cases when the police arrested people without any apparent reason and had them detained for a fortnight for "petty hooliganism."

Thus, for example, on June 26, 1968, a group of Crimean Tatars went on official business to the Crimean regional executive committee. They were all admitted to the building. All doors were then closed, and reinforced police detachments began to seize the people and to dispatch them to the town's police stations where they were all accused of "petty hooliganism." Ten persons among those arrested were sent to central Asia in the night, under escort; nine were sentenced to a fortnight's detention, and one man, Mamedya Chobanov, was accused of "malicious hooliganism" and resisting authorities. On August 26, Chobanov was sentenced by the Symferopol law court to 3 years' detention.

On May 17, 1968, on the eve of the 24th anniversary of the deportation, several thousand Crimean Tatars came to Moscow to stage a peaceful demonstration in front of the building of the Central Committee of the CPSU. However, the day before this demonstration the police proceeded to arrest on the spot all persons who looked like Crimean Tatars. After their nationality had been checked at a police station, all Crimean Tatars were sent back to central Asia under escort. A number of Moscovites, people who expressed sympathy with the Crimean Tatar movement, were also planning to take part in this demonstration. Two hundred of us were approaching the building of the Central Committee of the CPSU. As we neared the Staraya Ploshchad [Old Square], where the building of the Central Committee of the CPSU is located, a number of civilians arrested those among us who were of the Eastern type. In addition, they took photographs of people of other nationalities and then arrested them. This is how I and some friends were arrested. When we arrived at the police station, there were already several hundred people of various nationalities there, including two foreign tourists. The Crimean Tatars were "picked out" and sent to the so-called special reception building of the ministry of the interior, from where they were transported to central Asia. People who were caught by chance were released after their nationality had been established. Those however who had been arrested on the basis of photographs were kept at the police station and interrogated until late in the evening.

As I have already mentioned, the Crimean authorities refuse to acknowledge the legal transaction of private houses to Crimean Tatars. In 1969, for instance, my friend Eldar Shabanov purchased a private house in the town of Belogorsk (formerly Karasubazar). Although the previous owner of the house, one Shvalyev, informed the authorities of the perfectly legal sale procedure, the Crimean authorities refused to acknowledge the purchase of the house as legal. The police detained Shvalyev for a short time in order to force him to renege on his deal with Shabanov. They also tried to force Shabanov to go back on the purchase. During the 5 years which have lapsed since he first attempted to buy that house, Eldar Shabanov has three times been sentenced to various terms of detention. And it was only quite recently that the authorities saw themselves forced to give in and to register Shabanov's family in that house, which has belonged to them for over 5 years.

But it is by far not in all cases that things work out as well as with Shabanov. Thousands of people are forced to live without being registered. And if you are not registered, you cannot find a job to earn your living. However, to buy a house one invests all of one's savings, and often also money lent by relatives and friends. Apart from all else, a person living at a place without being registered may, according to the Soviet Criminal Code, be sentenced to a term in prison.

In the summer of 1969, Shevket Beytulayev bought a house in the village of Sennoe, Belogorsk district, from one Fyodor Adamovich Luchinsky. They went to a notary's office to get an official certification of the deal. However, the notary's office refused to certify the purchase document on the grounds that Beytulayev had not been registered as a resident, and the police refused to register him on the grounds that there was no notary's certificate to the house deal. In reply to the persistent demands that the purchase act be acknowledged, the police merely threatened Beytulayev that he and his family would be "thrown out" of the Crimea altogether.

In the night of June 28, 1969, a group of 16 people, some in police uniforms, some in civilian clothes, broke into his house. . . . Beytulayev, his wife, and his daughter were dragged out of bed and—with their hands twisted behind their backs—thrown into a car that brought them to the nearest railway station. From there they were escorted as far as the Krasnodar region and made to disembark from the train at a little station.

I could quote dozens of similar cases.

The more active members of the movement have had to serve long terms of detention. It is, above all, the national intelligentsia that has to bear the brunt of reprisals.

According to KGB Major Svalov, this is to be explained by the fact that it is easier for the KGB to fight ordinary workers than intellectuals.

On July 1-5, 1969, a trial of 10 Crimean Tatars took place in the city of Tashkent. They were all found guilty of disseminating "slanderous inventions detrimental to the Soviet system." Among those sentenced was Rolan Kadiyev, a physicist, whose name is quite well-known. Kadiyev was sentenced to 3 years' imprisonment. After his release, this brilliant physicist, well-known all over the world, was forced to work at a job that does not even require general secondary education. His thesis, written before he had to serve his sentence, has not been accepted by a single Soviet university, for the sole reason that Kadiyev has been behind prison walls "for politics."

Gomer Boyev, an engineer, born in 1938, was arrested by the KGB in the summer of 1968 in Symferopol and sentenced to 2 years in prison merely because he wished to live on the soil of his ancestors. The authorities were unable to present even minimal proof of his "slanderous activity."

My friend Reshat Dzhemilev, who took part in the Crimean Tatar movement and in the international movement for human rights in the U.S.S.R., has been arrested many times. Let me outline one such event.

On August 27, 1967, a group of representatives of Crimean Tatars was received by the highest representatives of the Soviet authorities—KGB head Andropov; the Prosecutor General of the U.S.S.R., Rudenko; the Secretary of the Presidium of the Supreme Soviet of the U.S.S.R., Georgadze; and the Minister of the Interior, Shcholokov. . Reshat Dzhemilev, a member of that group later gave a report on this meeting in front of 2,000 Crimean Tatars in one of the squares of Tashkent. The people who had gathered to hear this report were assailed by the police without previous warning. The meeting was dispersed. One hundred and thirty persons were arrested, 119 of whom got a fortnight's term for "petty hooliganism." The remaining 11 persons had to appear before the court on November 28. All defendants were found guilty and were sentenced to various terms of imprisonment, some of them on probation. Rezhat Dzhemilev was sentenced to 1 year of corrective labor. . . .

On October 12, 1972, Reshat Dzhemilev was again arrested, and in April 1973 sentenced to 3 years of deprivation of freedom for "disseminating slanderous inventions detrimental to the Soviet system." It should be noted that some days before his arrest, Reshat's photograph was displayed in a number of Soviet towns, with the caption "Wanted—Dangerous Criminal," although Reshat Dzhemilev did not hide and was then arrested in his home. He is now serving his sentence in a strict regime camp in the Krasnoyarsk district. Let me list the "slanderous fabrications" he was accused of: signing appeals by the Initiative Group for the Defense of Human Rights in the U.S.S.R., making statements against the invasion by Soviet troops of Czechoslovakia, participating in the national movement of the Crimean Tatars, participating in the demonstration in protest against my father's arrest, and the like.

Another leader of the Crimean national movement is Mustafa Abduldzhemil (Dzhemilev). Thrice he was sentenced for his participation in the human rights movement and the Crimean national movement. . . .

I have listed only individual cases of persecution of Crimean Tatars with which I am personally well acquainted. But this is by no means an exhaustive list. Even according to my figures, which are far from complete, about 100 persons have been sentenced between 1963 and 1969 to terms of imprisonment ranging from 6 months to 7 years for participating in the Crimean natioal-patriotic movement; and several hundred were sentenced to various punishments not involving the deprivation of freedom, or to terms up to 6 months.

Moreover, people of other nationalities are at present serving terms in prisons or camps, or are confined in "special mental hospitals," for having supported the Crimean Tatars. Among them is Leonid Plyushch, tortured by the "criminals in white coats" in the "psykhushka" (mental hospital) in Dnipropetrovsk; there is the Ukrainian poet and philologist Ivan Svitlychny, serving his sentence in the Perm camps; there is Vladimir Bukovsky, one of the leaders of the movement for human rights in the U.S.S.R., imprisoned in Vladimir Prison; and many, many others.

In view of the limited time accorded to me in this assembly, I have been able to outline briefly just one problem—the national-patriotic movement of the Crimean Tatars. However, the Jews, the Meshki Turks, the Germans, and other national minorities are in a similar position. Even nations enjoying the formal status of Union republics are subjected to cultural and political discrimination in the U.S.S.R. People who try to speak out in defense of their distinct ethnicity and civic rights are thrown into prisons, camps, and mental hospitals—the extermination facilities of our day, the ignominy of the twentieth century.

I do hope that people all over the world will pay attention to what takes place in the so-called socialist camp—because disregard of a person's rights may easily spread far beyond one's territory, and may seize the whole world.

---

1) Crimea is now a part of the Ukrainian S.S.R.

MAHFUSE CESUR

" . . . Crimean Tatars who returned to Crimea . . . were forcibly driven back by the militia . . . "

CESUR, Mahfuse

Mahfuse Cesur, a Crimean Tatar, was born May 7, 1925 in Kerch in the Crimea.

She lived until 1943 in the Crimea, which was under German occupation from 1941 to 1943. In the fall of 1943, when the Red army was preparing to recapture the Crimea, Mahfuse Cesur lost contact with both her parents. She has not heard from them since. She fled to Germany where she stayed until 1945.

Toward the end of 1945 Cesur moved to Italy, and lived in various DP camps, where she met her future husband, also a Crimean Tatar. From 1948 to 1957 Cesur lived in Turkey. In 1957 Cesur and her family moved to Munich.

TATARS — DOOMED
TO PHYSICAL AND CULTURAL
DESTRUCTION

I am the daughter of a Crimean Tatar who was a simple peasant. Before and during WWII we lived near Kerch. Like other members of my people, I was deprived of the possibility of continuing my studies, and so I received only a secondary education at that time.

First and foremost I would like to say that by condemning the regime of the U.S.S.R. I am not condemning the Russian people. We lived in a very friendly atmosphere with the Russians and Ukrainians.

I'm sorry that my Russian is not perfect, and so I would like to read [my statement] rather than to speak off the cuff.

In accordance with the rules adopted here I must limit [my testimony] to the last 10 years of my people's fate. But it is impossible to describe the current situation without touching on the beginning of and the reasons for the tragedy that has befallen the Crimean Tatars.

The tragedy of the long-suffering Crimean Tatars, which lasts through today, started in May 1944 after the Crimea was liberated from German occupation. When the Soviet troops returned to the Crimea, a terrible period started—slaughter, rape, executions, pillage. Then the forcible expulsion of those Crimean Tatars who were still alive began. All were being expulsed: children, women, old people, disabled war and labor veterans, partisans who fought against Germans, trade-union functionaries who had been sent to Crimea for the re-establishment of Soviet power. All men who were able to carry arms were at the front in the ranks of the Soviet army. . . .

During a year and a half, 110,185 persons died in exile—that is 46.2 per cent of all who were exiled. In 3 years of German occupation only 11 per cent of the Tatars perished. From the seven Crimean districts, 52,527 men above 18 years of age fought at the front, i.e., 55 per cent of the population of these districts. Many Crimean Tatars have been rewarded with various Soviet orders. Tatars fought not only in the ranks of regular troops but also as partisans. . . .

Khalilov, defender of Leningrad, lieutenant, poet and former teacher could not work in his profession after the war ended. He was not allowed to return to the Crimea and was exiled. Muratov, leader of a Tatar partisan detachment, Hero of the Soviet Union, was exiled to Kazakhstan after the war. Some years ago, the court in Alma-Ata sentenced him to 4 years' imprisonment for demanding to have the right to return to Crimea.

It is absolutely impossible to accuse these men of collaborating with the Germans. But the Crimean Tatars have been exiled, allegedly because of their collaboration with Germans. But the above-mentioned facts and figures prove that not all Tatars were collaborating with Germans. Their only fault was that they were Tatars and Moslems. It is a fact that mosques and churches which were restored during the German occupation were again destroyed and razed to the ground in order to eliminate all traces of Tatar population.

On December 5, 1967, The Presidium of the Supreme Soviet of the U.S.S.R. finally published a decree about the rehabilitation of Crimean Tatars, according to which "Tatars who formerly lived in the Crimea from now on may live on the whole territory of the U.S.S.R." The Crimean Tatars obtained their rehabilitation after a long and risky struggle against arbitrary rule, a struggle for national rights. But the above-mentioned decree of the Supreme Soviet of the U.S.S.R. was not carried through in practice. Tatars who returned to Crimea to live there were forcibly driven back by the militia. Thus the decree became on one hand a noble gesture to calm world public opinion, but on the other, a paltry, meaningless dole for Crimean Tatars. Even today they are not allowed to return en masse to their home country. . . .

In March 1968, in order to prevent a mass return of Tatars

that was planned for the spring, and also to give a semblance of regulating this question, the authorities declared that the Crimean Tatars would be returned under the so-called "organized recruitment." But that was a new deception—under this recruitment . . . only 143 families could return. And at the same time, people of other nationalities were recruited to come to Crimea in great numbers. This campaign is very intense. Ukrainians and Russians who were brought to the Crimea are not allowed to leave it.

I'll give a few examples to show that the decree of the Presidium of the Supreme Soviet was issued not that it be carried out, but for other purposes:

Crimean Tatar M. Chobanov, in his statement addressed to General Secretary of the U.N. Kurt Waldheim, wrote: "In spring of 1968, hoping to profit by this decree, I returned to my home country after 24 years of separation. There is a great demand for labor in Crimean towns and villages. All the time new settlers are brought from Ukraine and Russia. But every time it became known that I was a Crimean Tatar, I got a refusal—I was not allowed to work and to live in the Crimea. And Pasin declared publicly at the square in front of the district party committee building: 'The decree was published not for you, but for the foreign papers so that they would not raise such a clamour about you.' Many officials were saying 'we have secret instructions not to hire Tatars, if I hire you I will lose my post.' Tatar Baytulayev in his appeal to the U.N. and to world public opinion writes: 'We heard from the chief of militia in the Belgorod district: 'Go back where you came from, go away from this district. If you don't go away, we shall simply throw you out. I will register no Tatar families.' "

Many similar examples can be given. Persecutions, assaults during prayers and meetings, court sentences against Crimean Tatars for various reasons—*i.e.*, upon false accusations—these are vivid examples of the violation of the rights of an entire people, and even of Soviet laws.

Dispersed in central Asia, in Kazakhstan, Siberia, and the Ural, Crimean Tatars are deprived of the right and possibility to keep their national traditions, to lead a cultural activity. It is already 30 years now that our nation has no national schools, no teaching in the native language.

We, a people of ancient culture, are doomed to physical and cultural destruction. . . .

Tatars appealed to the U.N., to world public opinion, to the Central Committee of the CPSU, to the Supreme Soviet of the U.S.S.R., to leaders of various countries and parties. Nobody, however, gave us effective help, nobody paid any attention to our pleas. In the U.S.S.R. such prominent persons—defenders of human rights—have come to our defense as the old Bolshevik writer, the late Kosterin, General Grigorenko, Gabai, the historian Amalrik, the Ukrainian scholar Karavansky, Andrei Grigorenko, his mother and others and, what is particularly important, Academician Sakharov.

All these persons have been persecuted because of their efforts to defend the legal rights of the Crimean Tatars.

We hope that after the Sakharov Hearing, world public opinion will pay attention to our tragedy.

SIMAS KUDIRKA

" . . . I was accused because I wanted to leave my country . . ."

KUDIRKA, Simas

Born April 9, 1930 in Lithuania into the family of a sailor. In 1948, Kudirka joined the Komsomol. But because he was a practicing Catholic, Kudirka was exposed to continuous harassment by the NKVD. To avoid this, he left his home town and applied to a seamen's school in Klaipeda, Lithuania, where he stayed until 1952. In 1952, he was mobilized into the army, and until 1955 served in the Soviet navy. In 1957 Kudirka completed his training as a radio operator and, until 1970, worked in that capacity on various Soviet fishing trawlers.

On November 23, 1970, when his trawler *Sovyetskaya Litva* was in U.S. waters, Kudirka attempted to defect to the West by jumping onto the deck of a U.S. Coast Guard ship tied up alongside the Soviet trawler, but was returned to his ship.

On May 20, 1971 Kudirka was tried on charges of "state treason" and sentenced to 10 years of imprisonment.

Following years of world-wide protest, Kudirka was released from prison on August 23, 1974, by a special decree of the Presidium of the Supreme Soviet. In November of that year he and his family emigrated to the United States.

10 YEARS FOR AN ESCAPE ATTEMPT

In the name of all those who have died in the camps, and of all those who today are still behind bars, I am grateful for everything that has been said today about what is happening over there. I would like to thank Denmark for permitting this Hearing.

I am Lithuanian. My name is Simas Kudirka. I am that sailor who so unhappily jumped ship in 1970. . . .

I was born in 1930, the son of a sailor in free Lithuania, in independent Lithuania. We had three hectares of land. . . . The money with which we bought the land was earned with our own hands in the United States.

In 1940 the Soviet Union "liberated" us by armed force, and made us Soviet citizens. But then the Germans came. In 1944, however, we again fell under Soviet domination. Forty thousand Lithuanians organized a partisan movement, and many died in battle.

After the war we received 15 hectares of land, which we bought with money earned from 3 years of work. We had to pay very high taxes, and in order to pay them, we were forced to sell off the land piece by piece. In 1949 we gave up "voluntarily," because we were given the "choice": "Either you go to Siberia, or you stay in Lithuania, but then you have to become a member of the kolkhoz." I became a member of the kolkhoz . . .

Later I served in the Soviet army . . . When I had finished my stint, I returned to Klaipeda and became a sailor in the fishing fleet. We fished in the North Sea. I could see Denmark and Sweden far in the distance. I was always looking for an opportunity to escape. But I could never make it because there was always someone around. . . .

We often stayed at sea for longer periods of time. We did not only fish in Scandivanian waters, but also navigated Canadian and American waters. We brought the Soviet spy ships the supplies they needed. And then the evening finally arrived when I jumped. It was the 23rd of November, 1970. I was, as is known, on the ship" Sovyetskaya Litva." The captain of the Soviet trawler, Popov, demanded that I be returned, saying that I had stolen something and was a criminal. I don't know whether the good American Marine believed him or not, but in any case, I was sent back. I put up as good a fight as I could, but six sailors wrestled me down, and I'm no Hercules.

Then came the trial. I was accused because I wanted to leave the country. And although we never wanted to become Soviet citizens, I was sentenced to 10 years and put in prison.

I went the way of all Soviet prisoners. And you already know the way. Therefore I want to point out only the following: The Mordovian concentration camps at that time housed about 500 persons each. I was sent to camp No. 3. Here were the labor camps and workshops that were built on top of the bones of people who had died there. There are people of all nationalities and groups in these camps. The food we received was "Soviet." We couldn't think of a better name for it—it was "Soviet" food. . . . Finally it was decided to transport me even farther to make it totally impossible to send any messages to the West.

There were about 100 people in the railroad car in which we were being transported. Those who have been to the Soviet Union know what a railroad car there looks like. In such a car there were 100 of us. All doors and windows were closed and the ventilation was shut off. Many of us lost consciousness . . . We just did not have enough air to breathe. Only later did we notice that we were being doused with cold water.

Finally we arrived at our destination—Perm. It doesn't matter where it is exactly. It is the concentration camp . . . No. 36, a special camp, a corrective labor camp. It must be noted that it was a special camp . . . In Mordovia we were permitted to wear beards, which certainly many do not know. But in this special camp we were handcuffed and then shaved. Our skull caps were taken away from us and trampled upon.

The camp's physician—I don't know what military rank he had—was Petrov. He was never in a hurry when it came to helping people who had fainted. And when we protested and reminded him of his professional oath, all he said was "Don't you tell me anything. First and foremost I am a KGB-man, and only after that a physician." There are very few honest physicians in these camps; there are a few, but not many.

What kind of work did we have to do in camp? We manufactured irons. It wasn't hard work, but very unpleasant work, because it causes lung disease from stone powder. And that is the reason why we were doing this kind of work.

I'll gladly submit to this Hearing a list of people who were sent to this camp from the Baltic states, Armenia, Ukraine, and other places. There were also Germans, Poles and Finns. They are still alive. I'll only mention a few of them. Among them are people who were sentenced to 25 years . . . M. Kybartas suffered 24 years and a few months, and then physician Petrov found out that he had cancer. He was sent to camp No. 35 for treatment. As he lay there under an oxygen tent, a KGB official came to him and said: "You see, you are as good as dead. Sign this document in which you recant your past. If you do this you can be brought to Lithuania now." Gathering what strength he had, the man answered: "Go away, Satan."

Another man, Aphanasenko, hanged himself. Still another, who had fallen seriously ill at work, was transferred from camp 36 to camp 35, which was some 60 to 80 kilometers away. But the roads there are no European or American roads . . . and he died on the way. . . .

In conclusion I want to say this: Russia must be Russia. Lithuania must again become Lithuania, Germany should be reunited, and all nations enslaved by Moscow should become free. . . .

FINDINGS OF THE
QUESTIONING PANEL

FINDINGS OF THE QUESTIONING PANEL

Following an appeal by Professor Andrei Sakharov, the International Sakharov Hearing has taken place in the Danish parliament building on October 17, 18 and 19, 1975.

An international panel consisting of people of different political and religious opinions have listened to and questioned 24 witnesses, many of whom have given accounts of violations of human rights of which they have personal knowledge.

The aim of the Hearing has been to throw light on conditions in the Soviet Union during the last 10 years.

The questioning panel comprised the following:
Professor Erling Bjol, Arhus, Denmark
Michael Bourdeaux, England
Dr. Cornelia Gerstenmaier, Germany
Eugene Ionesco, France
Dr. Frantisek Janouch, Sweden
Haakon Lie, Norway
Mme. Zinaida Schakovskoy, France
Dr. A. Shtromas, England
Victor Sparre, Norway
Professor Z. Stypulkowski, England
Professor S. Swianiewicz, Canada
Simon Wiesenthal, Austria
who were supplemented by representatives of political parties in the Danish Parliament. The Soviet authorities were invited to participate in the hearing but chose not to do so.

The Hearing dealt with the following four questions:
Treatment of political dissidents.
Treatment of religious believers.
The abuse of psychiatry.
The position of Soviet nationalities and national
minority-groups.

The panel finds that certain witnesses made statements which did not refer to the period which the Hearing aimed to cover. The majority of the witnesses, however, made plausible statements of their own personal experiences during the years 1965-1975, in most cases with exact information as to the time and place of the events mentioned. This very comprehensive material will be collected and put at the disposal of international bodies and other interested parties.

On the basis of the statements made by the witnesses, the panel finds it to have been established

that in the Soviet Union freedom of thought and expression is restricted;

that non-conformist behavior encounters harassment in vital conditions of life, such as in the field of employment, housing and educational facilities;

that freedom of movement inside the country, foreign travel as well as emigration are severely restricted;

that religious freedom is substantially restricted;

that the interests and aspirations of Soviet national minorities, such as the Jews, and of Soviet nationalities are suppressed in vital respects, particularly of those nationalities which have been deprived of their national territorial units, for instance the Crimean Tatars and the Volga Germans, and

that in the Soviet Union there are people in prisons, camps and psychiatric wards who are deprived of their liberty, often under inhuman conditions, people who must clearly be termed political prisoners. The witnesses have put forward very different estimates as to the number of these prisoners. The panel does not feel that the evidence presented has been adequate to evaluate these estimates.

The Hearing has given the panel strong reason to doubt that the Soviet Union is observing the principles laid down in the International Covenant on Civil and Political Rights, ratified by the Soviet Union in 1973, and in the Helsinki declaration of 1975,

300

also signed by the Soviet Union, especially the declaration concerning Respect for Human Rights and Fundamental Freedoms, including the Freedom of Thought, Conscience, Religion or Belief, according to which "the participating states will respect human rights and fundamental freedoms, including the freedom of thought, conscience, religion or belief, for all without distinction as to race, sex, language or religion," and which further states that the participating states "will promote and encourage the effective exercise of civil, political, economic, social, cultural and other rights and freedoms, all of which derive from the inherent dignity of the human person and are essential for his free and full development." (I, A, Art. VII).

The panel wishes to draw attention to the two sections immediately following Art. VII of the Helsinki declaration:

"Within this framework the participating states will recognize and respect the freedom of the individual to profess and practice, alone or in community with others, religion or belief acting in accordance with the dictates of his own conscience."

"The participating states on whose territory national minorities exist will respect the right of persons belonging to such minorities to equality before the law, will afford them the full opportunity for the actual enjoyment of human rights and fundamental freedoms and will, in this manner, protect their legitimate interests in this sphere."

Hoping that the Soviet government's signature of the Helsinki agreement will mean that infractions of human rights, as established during the Hearing, will not take place in the future, the panel wishes to join Nobel Peace Prize winner Andrei Sakharov in his appeal to the Soviet government for a general amnesty for political prisoners, considering this a first step towards the fulfillment of the Helsinki declaration.

The panel further finds it to have been established that the already existing conventions do not contain sufficient guarantees for political prisoners. The panel thus finds that there is a need for a special international convention for the world-wide protection of political prisoners.

Erling Bjol   Michael Bourdeaux   Cornelia Gerstenmaier
Eugene Ionesco   Frantisek Janouch   Haakon Lie
Zinaida Schakovskoy A. Shtromas   Victor Sparre
Z. Stypulkowski   S. Swianiewicz   Simon Wiesenthal

301

BIOGRAPHICAL NOTES

ANDREI SAKHAROV

Born 1921 in Moscow, the son of a physics teacher. Received Candidate of Doctor of Science Degree (roughly equivalent to an American Ph.D.) from Moscow State University in 1948. Pioneer in the field of controlled thermonuclear fission, theoretical scientist and inventor. In 1966, co-authored letter to the Supreme Soviet protesting a resurgence of Stalinism, the first time, in his own words, that he became involved with "dissenters"—a group "that was small but very weighty on the moral . . . plane." In 1968, wrote the book *Progress, Coexistence, and Intellectual Freedom,* a compilation of liberal and humanistic ideas based on his own experience. The book was widely published in the West, which he said "resulted in my being taken off secret projects and in the restructuring of my entire way of life." While working at the Physics Institute of the Academy of Sciences of the U.S.S.R., "events in society and an inner need to oppose injustice continued to urge me toward new actions," Sakharov wrote in a 1973 autobiography. Began writing open letters on the problems of democratization, protests against trials of dissidents and their confinement in psychiatric hospitals, and appeals in defense of the rights of non-Russian nationalities in the Soviet Union. Explaining his reasons for defending political prisoners, Sakharov wrote: "The era of ((Stalinist) terror . . . is now behind us. But we are still living in the spiritual atmosphere created by that era. Against those few who do not go along with the prevalent practices of compromise, the government uses repression as before."

In the autumn of 1970, V. Chalidze, A. Tverdokhlebov and Sakharov founded the Moscow-based Human Rights Committee, studying, among other things, the question of compulsory confinement in psychiatric hospitals for political reasons. In 1972, Sakharov appealed to the Supreme Soviet to grant amnesty to all political prisoners and to abolish the death penalty; later authored several appeals for freedom of emigration. Attacked by Soviet press as "slanderer" of the state, while repressions against him and his family increased. Summoned on number of occasions by police and KGB authorities; threatened with arrest. Recipient of the Award of the International League for the Rights of Man (1973) and the Nobel Peace Prize (1975).

304

AIRIKYAN, PARUIR (1949-   ): Armenian activist. In 1969, while a student at the Yerevan Polytechnical Institute, arrested with four other Armenians for founding an organization aimed at creating an independent Armenian state. Charged with forming an "anti-Soviet" group and distributing "anti-Soviet" literature, and sentenced to four years' strict-regime camp; released in summer 1973. Again arrested in December of that year on a charge of violating regulations restricting movements of released prisoners, and sentenced to 2 years' imprisonment. While in confinement, again charged with "anti-Soviet agitation and propaganda" and participating in an "anti-Soviet organization." Tried by the Armenian S.S.R. Supreme Court between October 22 and November 22, 1974; and sentenced to seven years' strict-regime camp and 3 years' exile.

ALTUNYAN, GENRIKH: Engineer from Kharkiv, Ukraine; former Major in the Soviet Army; recipient of numerous awards for his military service; member of the Soviet Communist Party since 1957; member of the Initiative Group for the Defense of Human Rights in the U.S.S.R. Outspoken critic of the violations of human rights in the Soviet Union. Expelled from the party in 1968, and subsequently dismissed from his job and discharged from the army. Arrested July 11, 1969 on a charge of "circulating fabrications which defame the Soviet state" (Art. 187-1 of the Ukrainian Criminal Code). Sentenced to 3 years' general-regime labor camp.

AMALRIK, ANDREI (1938-   ): Publicist, historian, playwright; one of the most outspken critics of the totalitarian state; leading figure in the movement for human rights in the U.S.S.R. Expelled from Moscow University in 1963 for political reasons. His writings, considered unorthodox by Marxist standards, and his contacts with foreign diplomats and journalists led to his arrest in 1965 for "parasitism," a charge based on the fact that he did not have permanent employment. Although at that time he was caring for his invalid father, he was sentenced to 2½ years' exile in Siberia. His experiences there formed the basis for his bok, "Involuntary Journey to Siberia." His sentence was overturned in July 1966 and Amalrik returned to Moscow. Continued "non-conformist" activities, most notably the publication in the West of his study, "Will the Soviet Union Survive Until 1984?," precipitated his second arrest on May 21, 1970. He was charged with slandering the Soviet state and sentenced to 3 years' hard-regime camps, where he contracted meningitis and was subsequently declared an invalid. He was brought up on new charges when his term expired in May 1973 and sentenced to 3 years' strict regime colony. This sentence was later commuted to 3 years' exile following widespread protests both in the Soviet Union and abroad. Released in May 1975, but not permitted to return to Moscow, Amalrik, under pressure, left the Soviet Union with his wife Gyusel in July 1976.

ANTONYUK, ZINOVIY (1933-   ) : Ukrainian chemist from Kiev. Arrested in January 1972 for disseminating the *Ukrainian Herald* and other works of samvydav. Tried August 8-15, 1972 under Art. 62 of the Ukrainian CC ("anti-Soviet agitation and propaganda") and sentenced to 7 years' strict-regime labor camp and 3 years' exile. Has participated in numerous camp protests against the mistreatment of prisoners.

BELOV, YURI (1942-   ) : Writer, journalist; activist in the democratic movement in the U.S.S.R. In 1968, while in exile after completing a 3-year prison sentence on charges of "anti-Soviet agitation" (Art. 70 of the R.S.F.S.R. CC), re-arrested and charged under the same article for attempting to send abroad his book *Report from Darkness*. Sentenced to 5 years' imprisonment. Again charged with "anti-Soviet agitation" while in Vladimir Prison. Diagnosed to be mentally ill by a special commission of the Serbsky Institute, and in May 1972 committed for compulsory treatment to the special psychiatric hospital in Sichevka, Smolensk Region. Continued to be held in hospital despite doctors' recommendation that he be released. Transferred to the Smolensk psychiatric prison-hospital in summer 1976.

BOGORAZ, LARISSA (1929-   ) : Philologist from Moscow; activist in the human rights movement in the U.S.S.R. One of the twelve Moscow intellectuals who in Feb. 1968 signed an open letter to the Budapest Conference of Communist Workers' Parties describing violations of human rights in the Soviet Union. That same year she co-authored with P. Litvinov an appeal "To World Public Opinion" which called for an end to the Galanskov-Ginzburg trial. Arrested Aug. 25, 1968 for taking part in a protest-demonstration in Moscow's Red Square against the Soviet-led invasion of Czechoslovakia, and sentenced to 4 years' exile, which she served in the Irkutsk region. After release continued to speak out in defense of repressed human rights activists, among them A. Solzhenitsyn, the Ukrainian priest V. Romanyuk, S. Kovalev and A. Marchenko, and signed an appeal to the Supreme Soviet calling for amnesty for political prisoners in the U.S.S.R. The New York-based Freedom House awarded her its Freedom Prize in Dec. 1973.

BONDAR, MYKOLA (1939-   ) : Ukrainian philosopher; taught philosophy at Uzhhorod University in western Ukraine. Dismissed from his position for expressing critical views on Soviet government policies. Arrested November 7, 1970 for participating in a demonstration in Kiev against the Soviet invasion of Czechoslovakia. Charged with "anti-Soviet agitation and propaganda" (Art. 62 of the Ukr.S.S.R. CC), and sentenced to 7 years' strict-regime camps. In February 1975, while in one of the Perm camps, signed a statement demanding the recognition by Soviet authorities of political prisoner status, for which the camp administration punished him with several days' solitary confinement. Later transferred to Vladimir Prison.

BORISOV, VLADIMIR (1943-   ): Worker from Leningrad; member of the Initiative Group for the Defense of Human Rights in the U.S.S.R.; spent total of 9 years in psychiatric prison-hospitals. First confined in 1964 following charge of "anti-Soviet agitation and propaganda." In 1969 again forcefully taken to a prison-hospital, accused of "circulating false fabrications about the Soviet state and social system" and judged to show "residual signs of organic brain disorder." Spent most of the second confinement in the Leningrad Special Psychiatric Hospital, where he took part in various protests against the detention of political prisoners in psychiatric hospitals. Released in 1974 and settled in Moscow; continued his activities in defense of human rights in the Soviet Union. Detained on Dec. 25, 1976 and committed to the psychiatric prison-hospital in Leningrad, from which he was released in early March, 1977.

BUKOVSKY, VLADIMIR (1942-   ): Russian civil rights activist. Studied at the Department of Biophysics at Moscow University. First arrested in June 1963 and charged with "anti-Soviet agitation" for circulating Milovan Djilas' *The New Class*. Confined in the Leningrad Special Psychiatric Hospital until his release in Feb. 1965. Re-arrested Dec. 1965, for participating in a demonstration in defense of Sinyavsky and Daniel, and confined without trial to a mental asylum for 6 months. Arrested again in Jan. 1967 for organizing a demonstration in Moscow's Pushkin Square against the arrests of Galanskov, Ginzburg, and others. Sentenced to 3 years' hard labor; released in Jan. 1970. Continued his activity in defense of human rights in the Soviet Union, and collected materials documenting the uses of psychiatry for political repression in the U.S.S.R. On March 29, 1971 arrested for the fourth time, charged under Art. 70 of the R.S.F.S.R. CC with "anti-Soviet agitation," and sentenced on Jan. 5, 1972 to 7 years' prison-camps and 5 years' exile. While in one of the Perm camps, Bukovsky, together with S. Gluzman, compiled a *Manual* of advice for dissidents held in psychiatric institutions. On Dec. 18, 1976 he was flown to Zurich, Switzerland, where he was released by the Soviet authorities in exchange for the release by Chile of Chilean communist leader Luis Corvalan.

BUTMAN, GILLEL (1932-   ): Jewish activist. Engineer from Leningrad; participant in activities aimed at combatting the assimilation of Jews in the U.S.S.R. and at asserting their right to emigrate to Israel. Arrested on June 15, 1970 for attempting to leave the Soviet Union and charged with "treason" and "anti-Soviet agitation." In May 1971 sentenced to 10 years' strict-regime camps; later transferred to Vladimir Prison, where he has participated in protests against the violation of rights of political prisoners.

CHINNOV, ANATOLI (1938-   ): Russian biochemist; Christian convert. Believing it impossible to lead a Christian life in the U.S.S.R.,

Chinnov attempted to cross the border in 1968. Arrested, and later diagnosed to be a schizophrenic. Sent to Dnipropetrovsk Special Psychiatric Hospital; later also confined in the Leningrad Special Psychiatric Hospital. Continually subjected to compulsory electric shock treatment and insulin therapy, but refused to reject his religious and philosophical convictions. Released in 1974 or 1975.

CHORNOVIL, VYACHESLAV (1938-   ): Ukrainian journalist; graduate of the Department of Journalism at the University of Kiev 1960); worked as an editor of Lviv television studio, and on staffs of several publications and Kiev radio; former secretary of Komsomol in Ukraine. Covered trials of Ukrainian intellectuals in 1965-66, after which he wrote a petition to authorities protesting the violations of legality he witnessed, and compiled a collection of materials about those sentenced. Collection was published in the West under the title *The Chornovil Papers* (McGraw-Hill, 1968). Arrested and in November 1967 tried for "anti-Soviet agitation and propaganda"; served 1½ years in a labor camp in Mordovia. After release in 1969 joined in defense of other repressed Ukrainian intellectuals, especially Karavansky and Moroz; founding member of the Citizens' Committee for the Defense of Nina Strokata. Author of *Relapse into Terror or Justice?*, and a defense of Dzyuba's *Internationalism or Russification?*, titled *What B. Stenchuk Defends and How He Does It*, works which were highly popular in the samizdat. Arrested again in January 1972; tried in February 1973 under Article 62, Criminal Code of the Ukr.-S.S.R.; sentenced to 7 years' severe-regime labor camp, 5 years' exile. On December 13, 1975 the London *Sunday Times* awarded Chornovil its award for outstanding journalism in recognition of the report he wrote on the 1965-66 trials, a report the *Times* called "a classical product of investigative journalism." In March 1975 renounced his Soviet citizenship and appealed to the Canadian government for citizenship. Warned in an August 1971 letter to then President Gerald Ford that detente had led to intensified repressions in the Soviet Union.

DANIEL, YULI (1925-   ): Russian poet, short story writer and translator; author of *This Is Moscow Speaking, Hands, The Man from Minap*, and *Atonement*, which were published in the West. Daniel was arrested in September 1965 together with the writer A. Sinyavsky. Both were accused of having pseudonymously published in the West works of anti-Soviet content. Sentenced in February 1966 to 5 years' hard labor. The trial of Daniel and Sinyavsky is viewed as a key factor in the emergence of the democratic movement in the R.S.F.S.R.

DAVIDOV, GEORGI (1941-   ): Russian worker. Arrested in 1972 and charged under Art. 70 of the R.S.F.S.R. CC with "anti-Soviet agitation and propaganda." Sentenced to 5 years' imprisonment and 2 years' exile. During his confinement in Vladimir Prison appealed on behalf of the imprisoned Ukrainian historian V. Moroz. In early 1976, during the XXV Party Congress, joined other inmates of Vladimir

Prison in a hunger strike demanding an end to the mistreatment of political prisoners.

DREMLYUGA, VLADIMIR (1940-): Worker from Leningrad. Participated in the Aug. 25, 1968 demonstration in Moscow's Red Square against the Soviet invasion of Czechoslovakia; arrested, charged under Art. 190-3 of the R.S.F.S.R. CC with "violating public order" and sentenced to 3 years' corrective-labor camps. Served most of his term in the camps of Yakutia. Shortly before his release charged under Art. 190-1 of the Russian S.F.S.R. CC with "slandering the Soviet state" on the basis of conversations with fellow prisoners. Sentenced in Aug. 1971 to 3 years' strict-regime camps. Towards the end of his term "repented" his views in an article published in *Sotsialisticheskaya Yakutiya;* but continued to defend repressed human rights activists in the Soviet Union after his release.

DYMSHITS, MARK (1927-): Jewish activist; pilot. After repeated failures to receive permission to emigrate to Israel, worked out a plan in early June 1970 with 11 others to hijack a plane from Riga to Sweden. Arrested June 15, 1970, charged in Leningrad court with treason under Art. 64, R.S.F.S.R. CC, and sentenced to death by firing squad. Sentence commuted to 15 years' hard labor following widespread protests against the original sentence.

DZHEMILEV, MUSTAFA (1943-): Leading figure in the movement of the Crimean Tatars to return to their homeland; member of the Initiative Group for the Defense of Human Rights in the U.S.S.R. First arrested in 1966 and sentenced to 18 months' deprivation of freedom. Arrested for the second time in Sept. 1969 and charged with "circulating fabrications which defame the Soviet state" (Art. 190-1, R.S.F.S.R. CC); sentenced to 3 years' imprisonment. After his release subjected to continuous repressions, including arrests for periods of up to 15 days for alleged "hooliganism." Arrested again in June 1974 and sentenced to 1 year in a labor camp. Shortly before his release again charged under Art. 190-1 R.S.F.S.R. CC. Went on a 10-month hunger strike in protest against the latest charges. Tried April 14-15, 1976. Although the chief prosecution witness renounced his previous testimony, Dzhemilev was sentenced to 2½ years' imprisonment in strict-regime camps. Transferred to a concentration camp in Khabarovsky krai on June 25, 1976. Reportedly in poor health.

DZHEMILEV, RESHAT (1932-): Construction engineer; activist in the Crimean Tatar national movement. Arrested in 1967 and sentenced to 1 year of labor camps for allegedly organizing mass disturbances in Tashkent which, in fact, were meetings of Tatars in defense of their rights. On June 6, 1969 (during the World Conference of Communist and Workers' Parties) Dzhemilev and four other Crimean Tatars staged a demonstration in Moscow's Mayakovsky

Square demanding to be given back their homeland and the release of Gen. Grigorenko. On Oct. 12, 1972 Dzhemilev was arrested in Tashkent for, among other things, "disturbing public order," a charge based on his participation in the Moscow demonstration more than 3 years earlier. The Tashkent region court in April 1973 sentenced him to 3 years' strict-regime labor camp. Released on Oct. 11, 1975 after completion of sentence.

DZYUBA, IVAN (1931-   ) : Ukrainian literary critic, writer; editor and editorial assistant of a number of Soviet Ukrainian literary journals and publishing houses; leading activist of the Ukrainian literary and cultural renaissance of the 1960's. Author of approximately 100 articles published in Soviet periodicals before 1965. In September 1965 publicly called on the citizens of Kiev to protest against arrests of Ukrainian intellectuals; dismissed, as a result, from his position with the *Molod* publishing house. Wrote and signed numerous open letters and appeals to Soviet authorities, protesting against political repressions, especially in the cases of Vyacheslav Chornovil and Valentyn Moroz. In 1965 wrote *Internationalism or Russification?*, an analysis of the Russification policies of the Soviet regime, which he sent to party and government leaders. The work became the most widely read document of the *samvydav*; in 1968 it was published in the West in Ukrainian, English, and Italian, which led to increased official pressure against him; in 1969 he was forced to write an open letter condemning Ukrainian nationalism. Expelled from the Writers' Union of Ukraine in March 1972; arrested in April; tried in March 1973 on a charge of "anti-Soviet agitation and propaganda" and sentenced to 5 years' labor camp. Imprisoned until late 1973 in a KGB prison in Kiev, at which time, as a result of various KGB methods of persuasion and failing health (incurable tuberculosis) he agreed to sign a statement condemning his previous activity and was released.

FEDOROV, YURI (1943-   ) : Russian laborer from Moscow. Arrested in 1962 for belonging to the "Union for Intellectual Freedom," a Marxist group which strove for intellectual liberties in the Soviet Union. Charged with "anti-Soviet agitation" and sentenced to 6 years' imprisonment. Arrested again June 15, 1970 and charged with "treason" for conspiring to hijack an airplane out of the country. Sentenced to 15 years in a special-regime corrective labor camp, where he has participated in numerous protests against the mistreatment of political prisoners. In 1975 wrote a letter to the President of the United States in which he noted the increasing influence of communism in the world and criticized the principle of non-intervention in a country's internal affairs.

FELDMAN, ALEXANDER (1947-   ) : Ukrainian Jew from Kiev; activist in the Ukrainian Jewish movement for the right of Jews to emigrate to Israel. Served in the Soviet army, later worked as stoker in Kiev. In early 1972 applied for an emigration visa to Israel, which he was refused on the grounds that he knew "military secrets." Imprisoned in 1972 three times for a period of 15 days for protesting the refusal to grant him an emigration visa. Arrested and charged with "malicious hooliganism" for allegedly causing bodily injury to a woman and two men. Tried in closed court Nov. 23, 1973 without any witnesses being called. Sentenced to 3½ years' imprisonment in a labor colony.

GABAI, ILYA (1936-1973): Schoolteacher and poet; former editor at the Institute of Asian Peoples; one of the most active participants in the human rights movement in the U.S.S.R. in the late sixties. Arrested for the first time in January 1967 for participating in the Pushkin Square demonstration against the arrest of Galanskov and others. Released from imprisonment after 4 months because of lack of evidence against him. In 1968 co-authored with P. Yakir and Y. Kim the appeal "To Public Figures in Science, Culture and the Arts," which linked increased political repressions in the Soviet Union with the revival of Stalinism. Arrested on May 9, 1969 for the second time, charged under Art. 190-1 of the R.S.F.S.R. CC, and sentenced in Jan., 1970 to 3 years' imprisonment in an ordinary-regime camp. Returned to Moscow upon completion of his term in May, 1972. Systematically subjected to repressions and interrogations by the KGB. Committed suicide on October 20, 1973.

GALANSKOV, YURI (1939-1972): Poet, writer; one of the first compilers of the contemporary *samizdat*. Some of his books of verse were published in the West. Participated in the early sixties in poetry readings in Moscow's Mayakovsky Square. Arrested in 1961 for distributing the *samizdat* journal and confined for several months in a psychiatric hospital. In 1965 staged a one-man demonstration in front of the U.S. Embassy in Moscow against American intervention in the Dominican Republic. Arrested again on Jan. 19, 1967 for distributing *Phoenix-66*, a *samizdat* anthology he compiled, and charged with "anti-Soviet agitation" (Art. 70 R.S.F.S.R. CC) and "illicit currency transactions" (Art. 88-1). After almost one year in Moscow's Lefortovo Prison, tried on Jan. 8-12, 1968 with Ginzburg, Lashkova and Dobrovolsky. The trial sparked a wave of protests in the Soviet Union and abroad. Sentenced to 7 years' imprisonment in a strict-regime camp. Became critically ill in Mordovian camp No. 17, but continued to participate in numerous camp protests and hunger strikes. Died on Nov. 4, 1972 at the age of 33. On Dec. 4, 1973, Freedom House posthumously awarded Galanskov its Freedom Prize for his activities.

GALICH, ALEXANDER (1920-   ): Russian Jewish playwright and songwriter. Elected corresponding member of the Moscow Human Rights Committee in 1970. Expelled in 1971 from the Union of Soviet Writers and Union of Cinematographers for his human rights activities and the content of his songs. Permitted to emigrate to the West in 1974.

GINZBURG, ALEXANDER (1936-   ): Editor, journalist; well-known human rights activist; head of a special fund set up by A. Solzhenitsyn to aid families of political prisoners. Edited in 1959-1960 three issues of the poetry collections *Syntax*, for which he was arrested in 1960 and charged with distributing "anti-Soviet" literature. Charges were dropped because of lack of evidence. Was then prosecuted under Art. 196-1, R.S.F.S.R. CC, for "forgery of documents." Sentenced to 2 years' imprisonment in a corrective labor camp. Arrested for the second time in May 1964 and charged with possession of "anti-Soviet" literature. Charges were again dropped because of lack of evidence. In 1966, after the trial of Sinyavsky and Daniel, Ginzburg compiled a so-called *White Book* documenting their trial, which he sent to the Supreme Soviet of the U.S.S.R. and the KGB demanding that their case be reviewed. Arrested in Jan. 1967 and charged under Art. 70 with "anti-Soviet agitation and propaganda." Tried Jan. 8-12, 1968, sentenced to 5 years at hard labor, most of which he served in the Mordovian camps and Vladimir Prison. Released in Jan. 1972 and until April of that year held under administrative surveillance in Tarusa, Kaluga Region. In 1974 again placed under such surveillance for 6 months. In May 1976 became one of the founding members of the Moscow Public Group to Promote the Implementation of the Helsinki Accords in the U.S.S.R. Arrested Feb. 3, 1977.

GLUZMAN, SEMEN (1946-   ): Ukrainian Jewish psychiatrist; active participant of the civil rights movement. Arrested in May 1972 for dissemination of *samvydav* literature and for giving a dissenting psychiatric evaluation of Gen. Pyotr Grigorenko; October, 1972, sentenced to 7 years' labor camp, 3 years' exile on a charge of "anti-Soviet agitation and propaganda." Author of *An In-Absentia Forensic Psychiatric Examination in the Grigorenko Case*, and co-author (with Vladimir Bukovsky) of *A Dissident's Guide to Psychiatry* (dedicated to Leonid Plyushch); both works circulated in the samizdat and deal with Soviet abuses of psychiatry against dissidents. In the summer of 1974 he was the initiator of a massive hunger strike by political prisoners protesting violations of their rights.

GRAZHIS, IOUZAS (-   ): Lithuanian activist. Arrested April 24, 1974 for distributing samizdat publication *A Chronicle of the Lithuanian Catholic Church*. Tried in March 1975. Charged under Art. 68 of the Lithuanian S.S.R. CC with "anti-Soviet agitation and propaganda" and sentenced to 3 years' imprisonment in a general-regime camp. Latest sentence is third for "political" reasons.

GRIGORENKO, PYOTR (1907-   ): Military historian and former Soviet Army general. Born in Ukraine. Spent 17 years in the Frunze

312

Military Academy in Moscow, where in 1948 he earned the Master of Military Sciences degree and in 1959 was given the rank of Major-General. On Sept. 7, 1961, spoke at a party conference of the Lenin District in Moscow calling for the restoration of Leninist principles; subsequently removed from his position in Moscow and sent to the Far East; demoted. Headed in 1963 the "League of struggle for the revival of Leninism"; arrested in Feb. 1964 for "anti-Soviet agitation." Found to be "mentally non-responsible," and was confined in the Leningrad Special Psychiatric Hospital from Aug. 14 1964 to April 23, 1965. Worked as a porter after release, continuing his defense of those persecuted for political reasons; took part in protests against the occupation of Czechoslovakia and became an outspoken supporter of the cause of the Crimean Tatars. On May 7, 1969, while in Tashkent where he had come to speak in defense of ten Crimean Tatars held on trial, Grigorenko was arrested and charged with "circulating fabrications which defame the Soviet system" (Art. 190-1 of the R.S.F.S.R. CC) and with "anti-Soviet agitation" (Art. 70 of the R.S.F.S.R. CC). Judged to be of unsound mind in Oct. 1969. Tried in absentia on Feb. 26-27, 1970. Confined in a special psychiatric hospital in Chernyakhovsk until his transfer Sept. 1973, to a general psychiatric hospital; released on June 26, 1974. Awarded the Freedom Prize by the New York-based Freedom House in Dec. 1973. In May 1976 helped organize the Moscow Public Group to Promote the Implementation of the Helsinki Accords in the U.S.S.R. When a similar committee was formed in Nov. 1976 in Kiev to monitor compliance with the Helsinki Accords in Ukraine, Grigorenko became its Moscow representative.

HORBOVY, VOLODYMYR (1899-   ) : Ukrainian jurist. Practiced law in western Ukraine before WWII. Defended Ukrainian nationalists arrested for resistance to Polish occupation. During the war headed a Ukrainian organization aiding refugees and POWs, and the Ukrainian National Committee in Cracow, Poland, which in June 1941 issued a manifesto calling for an independent and sovereign Ukraine. Arrested and incarcerated in a prison in Cracow, shortly thereafter, but released a year later, for reasons of health. Lived in Czechoslovakia after the war, working as legal counsel for the agriculture ministry . Became a citizen of that country in 1947. Arrested that same year by state security organs and extradicted to Poland on charges of "treason." Handed over to Soviet authorities in 1948. Though he had never before been on Soviet territory, was sentenced by a special tribunal to 25 years in concentration camps for Ukrainian nationalism. Served the full 25-year sentence in a Mordovian labor camp reserved for foreigners. Returned in 1973 to his native village Obolonya, now in Ivano-Frankivsk Region of the Ukrainian S.S.R., and made repeated attempts to obtain permission to join his wife and son in Prague. Wrote numerous appeals to Soviet authorities during his imprisonment and after his release, claiming the case against him had been fabricated.

KALANTA, ROMAS (1953-1972): Lithuanian activist. On May 14, 1972, set himself on fire in front of a theater in Kaunas in protest against the suppression by Moscow of national and religious rights of Lithuania. Student and member of the Communist Youth Organization at the time of his self-immolation. Kalanta's death sparked mass demonstrations throughout Lithuania against Soviet rule.

KALYNETS, IHOR (1939-   ): Ukrainian poet; considered one of the brightest young literary talents in Ukraine. First collection of poetry was due to be published in 1965, but, for reasons unknown, was not; poetry collection *Kupalo's Bonfire* published in 1966, but blacklisted soon thereafter. Arrested in 1965, but released; since then, forbidden to publish, but became very popular in the samizdat. Active in defense of arrested Ukrainian inetllectuals, especially Valentyn Moroz, whose 1970 trial he attended and to whom he dedicated his collection *Summing up Silence* (1970). Arrested August 11, 1972, and sentenced to 6 years' labor camp, 3 years' exile, on a charge of "anti-Soviet agitation and propaganda." A month earlier, wife Irina Stasiv-Kalynets sentenced to similar term on identical charges. Sent to labor camp in Mordovia, later transferred to Camp VS 389/35 in Perm Region, where in May and June 1974 participated in prolonged hunger strike by political prisoners. Renounced Soviet citizenship in Setember 1975.

KARAVANSKY, SVYATOSLAV (1920-   ): Ukrainian poet, writer and translator. Sentenced in 1945 to 25 years' imprisonment for membership in the Organization of Ukrainian Nationalists; amnestied in 1960. Compiler of 1200-page *Dictionary of Rhymes in the Ukrainian Language*; translator of Byron, Shakespeare, Kipling, and Shelley into Ukrainian; author of numerous published articles on linguistics. In 1965 protested against the Russification of Ukrainian schools in two letters to Soviet authorities, and against violations of Ukrainian sovereignty and the arrests of Ukrainian intellectuals in a petition to Polish and Czechoslovak Communist leaders. Arrested November 13, 1965; returned, without trial, to serve out the remaining 9 years of his original sentence. Transferred to Vladimir Prison in 1967 for writing several petitions criticizing violations of civil rights, the Soviet nationalities policy, and the 1941 mass executions of Polish prisoners of war in Katyn Forest. In 1970, put on trial at the prison and given new sentence of 5 years in prison, 3 years in labor camp.

KHAKHAYEV, SERGEI (-   ): Chemical engineer from Leningrad. Arrested in 1965 for membership in the "Union of Communards," a Marxist group which published samizdat journal *The Bell*. Sentenced to 7 years' imprisonment and 3 years' exile. Released in early 1975 upon completion of sentence.

KHANTSIS, YANKEL (1922-   ): Jewish activist from Kishinev, Moldavian S.S.R. Arrested in the summer of 1970 near the Dutch embassy in Moscow while attempting to obtain permission to emigrate to Israel. Sentenced on August 17, 1970 by a Moscow court to 2½ years' hard-regime camps for "malicious hooliganism" (Art. 206 of the R.S.F.S.R. CC). Released on probation on April 18, 1971. Continued attempts to receive permission to emigrate to Israel; again arrested in spring 1972. Severely beaten by his jailers; suffered partial paralysis. Sentenced later that year to 2 years' strict-regime camps for "defaming the Soviet state" (Art. 190-1 of the R.S.F.S.R. CC). Permitted to emigrate to Israel on March 6, 1974 upon completion of term.

KHEIFETS, MIKHAIL (1934-   ): Historian, writer from Leningrad. Arrested on April 23, 1974 and charged with "anti-Soviet agitation and propaganda" for writing unpublished article on Joseph Brodsky. Sentenced in Sept. 1974 by a Leningrad court to 4 years' hard labor and 2 years' exile under Art. 70 of the R.S.F.S.R. CC.

KHNOKH, ARYE (LEIBA) (1944-   ): Jewish worker. Planned to hijack plane from Riga to Sweden with 11 others. Arrested on June 15, 1970 and brought to trial in Leningrad in December of that year. Charged, among other things, with "treason" and "anti-Soviet agitation" and sentenced to 10 years' strict-regime camps. In camp participated in many protests demanding the recognition of the political prisoner status. Transferred in June 1975 from one of the Perm camps to Vladimir Prison for 3 years.

KHODOROVICH, TATYANA (-   ): Russian linguist; among most active in the democratic movement in the Soviet Union. Founding member of the Initiative Group for the Defense of Human Rights in the U.S.S.R. (May 1969). Dismissed in May 1971 from her position at the Russian Institute of the Academy of Sciences, where she had worked for 18 years, because, as the institute's director put it, her views were "inconsistent with the position of a scientific worker of an academic institute." Author of numerous individual and collective appeals and essays in the area of human rights. Especially active in defense of Leonid Plyushch; compiled in 1973 two collections on his case: *Punishment by Madness (The Scientist and the State)*, and *A History of Leonid Plyushch's Illness*. Involved with the preparation and dissemination of samizdat literature.

KOCHUBIYEVSKY, BORIS (1938-   ): Jewish radio-engineer from Kiev. Spoke out at a factory meeting in 1967 against labelling Israel an aggressor during the 6-Day War. Dismissed from his job in May 1968; refused permission to emigrate. Arrested in December 1968, charged under Art. 187-1 of the Ukr.S.S.R. CC with "circulating fabrications which defame the Soviet state" and sentenced to 3 years' ordinary-regime camp. Permitted to emigrate to Israel upon completion of term.

315

KOLCHINSKY, JONAH (1952-   ) : Jewish activist from Kharkiv. Arrested on Oct. 14, 1970 and charged with disorderly conduct after applying for an exit visa to Israel. Sentenced to 20 days' imprisonment. Released at the end of December (after 6 weeks' confinement) and called up into the army. Continued to speak out for the rights of Jews to emigrate to Israel. Received permission to leave the Soviet Union in early 1974.

KOPELEV, LEV (1912-   ) : Writer, critic, and specialist in German literature. Veteran of WWII. Served 10 years in Stalin's camps. Later rehabilitated, reinstated in the party and admitted into the Union of Writers. In the 1960's defended the right of Soviet artists to develop abstract techniques, signed appeals on behalf of Sinyavsky and Daniel and on behalf of Ginzburg and Galanskov. In 1967 wrote an article for the Austrian Communist journal *Tagebuch* entitled *Why the Rehabilitation of Stalin Is Impossible.* Expelled from the party and dismissed from his job at Moscow's Institute of Art History. Some of his books were removed from publication lists. Continued to speak out in defense of civil liberties in the U.S.S.R. In 1975 addressed an appeal to the Politburo of the CC CPSU calling for amnesty for political prisoners in the Soviet Union. In April 1977 expelled from the Soviet Writers' Union.

KOSTERIN, ALEKSEI (1896-1968) : Writer; former editorial writer for *Trud, Gudok* and *Izvestia.* Member of the Communist Party since 1916. Outspoken critic of Soviet nationalities policy. Signer of numerous appeals on behalf of Soviet political prisoners. Imprisoned for 3 years during czarist times. Spent 17 years (1938-55) in imprisonment and exile under Soviet regime. Few of his stories were published officially; those that were were severely censored. Resigned from the Communist Party after the invasion of Chechoslovakia. Expelled at that time from the Writers' Union without his knowledge. Died on Nov. 10, 1968. His funeral on Nov. 14th became something of a political demonstration, with hundreds of persons attending, including Crimean Tatars, Chechens and Volga Germans who journeyed thousands of miles to pay their respects.

KOVALEV, SERGEI (1932-   ) : Russian biologist; founding member of both the Initiative Group for the Defense of Human Rights in the U.S.S.R. (in 1968) and the Soviet chapter of Amnesty International (in 1974) Dismissed in 1969 from his position as senior researcher in biology at Moscow University. Closely associated, by his own accounts, with the samizdat journal *Chronicle of Current Events.* Arrested in Moscow on Dec. 27, 1974, the day he and A. Sakharov issued an appeal for amnesty for political prisoners. Apparently because of his close involvement with another underground journal, the *Chronicle of The Lithuanian Catholic Church,* Kovalev was brought to Vilnius, the capital of Lithuania, where in December 1975 he was sentenced to 7 years' strict-regime labor camp and 3 years' exile for "anti-

316

Soviet agitation and propaganda." Sent to a labor camp in Perm Region although suffering from cancer. Taken in early 1977 to Leningrad for an operation which, according to reports, was successful.

KRASIN, VICTOR (1929-   ): Economist from Moscow; former inmate of Stalin's camps; member of the Initiative Group for the Defense of Human Rights in the U.S.S.R.; active fighter against the revival of Stalinism. Signer of numerous letters to world organizations about violations of human rights in the Soviet Union, among them an appeal in Feb. 1968 to the Budapest Conference of Communist and Workers' Parties. Arrested on Dec. 20, 1969 and charged with leading an "anti-Soviet, parasitic" way of life. Worked at that time on his Master's thesis and freelancing as technical translator. Sentenced to 5 years' exile in the Krasnoyarsk Region. Arrested again on June 21, 1972 and indicted for "anti-Soviet agitation" under Art. 70 of the R.S.F.S.R. CC. Tried between Aug. 27 and Sept. 1, 1973, together with P. Yakir. Pleaded guilty and "repented" his activities. Sentenced to 3 years' imprisonment and 3 years' exile, later reduced to 13 months' imprisonment and 3 years' exile. Officially pardoned and released on Sept. 16, 1974. Emigrated from the U.S.S.R. in Feb. 1975.

KRASIVSKY, ZINOVIY (1930-   ): Ukrainian activist, poet, writer. In 1947, deported with his family from western Ukraine to Siberia, where he served 5 years in a labor camp. Arrested again in 1967 with a group of young student activists at Lviv University; charged with organizing an underground organization, the Ukrainian National Front, and with publishing an illegal journal, *Fatherland and Freedom;* sentenced to 5 years' prison, 7 years' labor camp, and 5 years' exile on a charge of "treason." In 1969, along with other Ukrainian political prisoners in Vladimir Prison, sent an appeal to the U.N.; in 1970, participated in a hunger strike by political prisoners. A collection of his poetry written in the prison was found and confiscated during a search; this and his continued protests served as the basis for new charges against him and for his eventual transfer in 1973 to a special psychiatric hospital in Sychovka, Smolensk Region, the R.S.F.S.R., where he was subjected to forced "treatment" with heavy doses of drugs.

KUKUY, VALERI (1938-   ): Jewish engineer from Sverdlovsk. Arrested on March 20, 1971 and tried on June 15-16 of that year for "circulating deliberately false information libeling the Soviet social and political system" (Art. 190-I of the R.S.F.S.R. CC). Prior to arrest, applied for emigration to Israel and signed appeal on behalf of those convicted in the "Leningrad hijacking trial." Had samizdat literature confiscated during a search of his apartment. Sentenced to 3 years' general-regime camp, where he was subjected to numerous beatings by common criminals. Released in March 1974 upon completion of sentence. Emigrated to Israel in April 1974.

KULIKAUSKAS, BOLESLOV (-   ) : Lithuanian activist. Arrested Nov. 20, 1973 for preparing prayer books. Charged during his trial on Sept. 18, 1974 with "embezzling government property" and sentenced by a Lithuanian court to 3½ years' imprisonment in strict-regime camps and 5 years' exile.

KUZNETSOV, EDWARD (1939-   ) : Jewish activist from Leningrad; member of the Marxist "Union for Intellectual Freedom," which strove for the liberation of culture from party dogma. Served 7-year sentence (1961-1968) for "anti-Soviet agitation and propaganda," a charge stemming from his membership in the union. After several unsuccessful attempts to leave the Soviet Union legally, participated in an abortive hijacking attempt. Arrested June 15, 1970 and tried in Leningrad in December of that year for "treason." Sentenced to death by firing squad; sentence commuted to 15 years' imprisonment in a special-regime camp after widespread protests on his behalf. In 1971 his *Prison Diaries* were smuggled out of his Mordovian camp and published in several languages in the West.

LANDA, MALVA (1918-   ) : Russian geologist; one of the best-known and most outspoken of human rights activists in the U.S.S.R.; especially known for her numerous appeals on behalf of Soviet political prisoners. A number of her works have appeared in the samizdat. Though never arrested or imprisoned, she has been subjected to continuous harassment such as searches and interrogations. In May 1976 she became a founding member of the Public Group to Promote the Implementation of the Helsinki Accords in the U.S.S.R.

LITVINOV, PAVEL (1940-   ) : Russian physicist; grandson of former Soviet Foreign Minister Maxim Litvinov. Compiled records and documents relating to political trials in a collection titled *The Case of The Demonstration In Pushkin Square on January 22, 1967*. Later documented the Galanskov-Ginzburg trial in January 1968 in a book titled *The Trial of The Four*, which became popular in the samizdat and was later published in the West. Arrested on Aug. 25, 1968 after staging with six others a peaceful demonstration in Moscow's Red Square in protest against the Soviet invasion of Czechoslovakia. Charged with "disturbing public order" and "defaming the Soviet state" and sentenced to 5 years' internal exile. Served term in Chita Region in southeast Siberia, near the Manchurian border. Permitted to emigrate after return from exile and settled in New York, where he has continued activities in defense of civil rights in the U.S.S.R. Editor of *A Chronicle of Human Rights in the U.S.S.R.*, published in both Russian and English by Khronika Press.

LUKYANENKO, LEV (1927-   ) : Ukrainian lawyer. Former leading member of the so-called Jurists' Group, which in 1960 planned formation of a legal organization, to be called the Ukrainian Workers'

318

and Peasants' Union, to raise the issue of the secession of Ukraine from the U.S.S.R.—as provided for in both the Ukrainian and the Soviet constitutions—and to conduct peaceful propaganda calling for a plebiscite on this issue. All seven members of the group were arrested and tried in closed court in Lviv in May 1961 on charges of "treason" and "participation in an anti-Soviet organization." Accused of having prepared the group's platform, Lukyanenko was sentenced to death. Sentence subsequently commuted to a 15-year term in correctional labor camps. While serving in the hard-labor camps of the Mordovian A.S.S.R. and Perm Region, took part in almost every hunger strike and protest action organized by political prisoners in defense of their rights; also authored numerous statements of protest and appeals and compiled a record on his own case. Transferred to Vladimir Prison for a 3 year term after the latter document was smuggled out of the Mordovian camp and published in the West. Returned to Vladimir in June 1974 for his part in a prisoners' strike called to protest the beating of a fellow inmate. Released in January 1976 after serving full term. Settled in the city of Chernihiv where he found work as an electrical repairman. Under constant police surveillance since his release. Not allowed to resume the practice of law. In November 1976 became a founding member of the Ukrainian Public Group to Promote the Implementation of the Helsinki Accords, a Kiev-based citizens' committee monitoring compliance with the agreement in Ukraine.

LUPYNIS, ANATOLIY (1937-   ): Ukrainian poet. From 1956 to 1967, a political prisoner in Soviet labor camps on the charge of "anti-Soviet agitation and propaganda." Actively protested against violations of prisoners' rights; staged a 2-year hunger strike (kept alive by force-feeding) in order to dramatize his demands for the democratization of Soviet society. On May 27, 1971, recited one of his poems at a spontaneous meeting in honor of Taras Shevchenko, Ukraine's greatest poet; arrested a few days later; tried in Jan. 1972 in closed court on charge of "anti-Soviet agitation and propaganda" (neither his father nor Andrei Sakharov and his wife, who had flown in from Moscow, were permitted into the courtroom). Declared to be "schizophrenic" on the basis of a Serbsky Institute report, and sentenced to an indefinite term in a psychiatric prison hospital. Confined in a Dnipropetrovsk institution.

LYUBARSKY, KRONID (1934-   ): Astro-physicist; author of numerous works on space biology; former academic secretary of the Moscow section of the All-Union Society of Astronomy and Geodesy; until his arrest employed at the Chornogolovka Institute of Solid State Physics near Moscow. Arrested Jan. 17, 1972 and charged under Art. 70 of the R.S.F.S.R. CC with "anti-Soviet agitation and propaganda" for possessing and distributing *samizdat* literature. Sentenced to 5 years' strict-regime labor in Mordovian camps, where he took part in protests and hunger strikes in support of prisoners' rights. Wrote several open letters, among them to the World Federation of Scientists in London, describing camp conditions. Transferred to Vladimir Prison on Oct. 20, 1974. Awarded a prize in 1975 by the Fund for Freedom and Human Rights in Berne, Switzerland for his struggle for human rights. Released upon completion of sentence on Jan. 18, 1977. Emigrated to the West in October 1977.

MAKARENKO, MIKHAIL (1931-   ): Rumanian Jewish artist; left home in 1939 and crossed the border into Moldavia, then already under Soviet control. Spent childhood in orphanages, then served in the army and travelled throughout the U.S.S.R. Active in the arts; instrumental in organizing a number of art exhibitions and modern art galleries. His enthusiasm for modern art, especially his persistent attempts to arrange a visit and an exhibit of works of Mark Chagall, led to friction with the authorities. Arrested in 1969; tried in September 1970 in closed court in Moscow on charges of "anti-Soviet agitation and propaganda" and various "economic crimes"; sentenced to 8 years' strict-regime labor camps. Transferred in 1974 to Vladimir Prison as punishment for participating in hunger strikes and other forms of protest by political prisoners.

MALKIN, ANATOLI (1954-   ): Jewish activist from Moscow. In 1974, while a student at the Institute of Steel and Alloys, applied for emigration to Israel; subsequently expelled from school and the Communist Youth League. Granted Israeli citizenship in late summer 1974; again applied for permission to leave the U.S.S.R., but instead was drafted for active military service. Refused to comply on grounds that he was attempting to emigrate and therefore could not take the military oath. Arrested on May 28, 1975. Tried and sentenced on Aug. 26, 1975 under Art. 80-1 of the R.S.F.S.R. CC to 3 years' general-regime camp.

MARCHENKO, ANATOLI (1938-   ): Writer, publicist and human rights activist. Served 6 years (1960-66) in Mordovian labor camps and Vladimir Prison for "treason" after an unsuccessful attempt to cross the border into Iran. Author of *My Testimony* (1967), a recollection of his experiences in labor camps and prison, one of the first and among the most widely read samizdat works based on the experiences of Soviet political prisoners; also wrote numerous appeals and open letters on the treatment of political prisoners and other political topics, including an open letter criticizing the Soviet attitude toward Czechoslovakia. Arrested in July 1968 and sentenced to a 1-year prison term on a charge of internal passport violations. Brought to trial while in a labor camp in Perm Region and sentenced to a new 2-year term in strict-regime camps for "defaming the Soviet state" (Art. 190-1, R.S.F.S.R. CC). Released in July 1971 and after a period in exile returned to the Moscow area, where he became an active participant in the human rights movement. Renounced his Soviet citizenship in Dec. 1974 and declared his intention to emigrate to the U.S. His activities and insistence on emigrating to the U.S. and not to Israel, as the authorities suggested, led to his arrest in February 1975 and subsequent trial in Kaluga on charges of violating passport regulations and surveillance restrictions imposed on him. Sentenced to 4 years of internal exile at Chuna in the Irkutsk Region. While in exile, became in May 1976 a founding member of the Public Group to Promote the Implementation of the Helsinki Accords.

MARKMAN, VLADIMIR (-   ): Jewish activist from Sverdlovsk. Arrested on April 29, 1972 and charged under Art. 190-1 of the R.S.F.S.R. CC with "circulating fabrications which defame the Soviet state." Prior to arrest and conviction applied for an exit visa to Israel and spoke out in defense of V. Kukuy. Sentenced to 3 years' strict-regime camp, which he served in the Krasnoyarsk Region. Released in April 1975 upon completion of sentence.

MEDVEDEV, ROY (1925-   ): Marxist scholar and historian; twin brother of the geneticist Zhores Medvedev. Defender of human rights activists in the U.S.S.R. Authored, together with his brother, *A Question of Madness*, on the practice of compulsory psychiatric confinement of political dissidents in the Soviet Union. Dismissed from his position as senior scientist at Moscow's Institute of Professional Education in 1971. Expelled from the party for writing the book *Let History Judge*. Other well-known works include *On Socialist Democracy* and the article *The Problem of Democratization and the Problem of Detente*. Also edited several issues of the samizdat journal *Twentieth Century*.

MENDELEVICH, IOSIF (1947-   ): Jewish activist from Riga. Denied permission to emigrate to Israel, he participated in the unsuccessful hijacking attempt of 1970. Arrested on June 15, 1970 and charged under Articles 64, 70, 72 and 93 of the R.S.F.S.R. CC. Sentenced in Dec. 1970 in Leningrad to 12 years' strict-regime labor camp.

MOROZ, VALENTYN (1936-   ): Ukrainian historian, publicist. First arrested in August 1965 for possession of samizdat literature; sentenced in January 1966 to 4 years' imprisonment for "anti-Soviet agitation and propaganda"; during imprisonment, wrote *A Report from the Beria Reservation;* released in September 1969. Arrested again on June 1, 1970; tried in November 1970, again under Article 62, Criminal Code of the Ukr.S.S.R., for his authorship of the essays *A Chronicle of Resistance, Amid the Snows,* and *Moses and Dathan,* written after his release; sentenced to 6 years in prison, 3 in labor camps, 5 in exile. Sent to Vladimir Prison, where in the summer of 1974 he spent 145 days on a hunger strike in support of his demand to be transferred to a labor camp. Upon completion of prison term, sent to the Serbsky Institute of Forensic Psychiatry in Moscow, a move which for political prisoners is a prelude to indefinite confinement in a special psychiatric institution. After widespread protests in the West, Moroz was judged to be sane and in June 1976 was transferred to a labor camp in Mordovia. Valentyn Moroz has become the leading symbol of the Ukrainian movement for national and civil rights.

MURZHENKO, OLEKSIY (1942-): Ukrainian activist from Kharkiv Region; former member of the Marxist "Union for Intellectual Freedom." Arrested June 15, 1970 for his part in planning to hijack a plane in order to leave the U.S.S.R. Tried with 11 others in Leningrad in Dec. 1970; charged, among other things, with "treason," and sentenced to 14 years' special-regime labor camp.

NASHPITS, MARK (1948-): Jewish activist from Moscow; dentist; active participant in the movement of Soviet Jews to obtain permission to emigrate to Israel. Arrested on Feb. 24, 1975 for participating in a demonstration demanding the recognition of the rights of Jews in the Soviet Union. Charged under Art. 190-3 of the R.S.F.-S.R. CC with "violating public order" and in March 1975 sentenced to 5 years of internal exile.

NAVASARDYAN, ASHOT (1950-): Armenian activist; motor mechanic. Arrested in 1964, together with P. Airikyan, for membership in an organization which strove for the independence of Armenia. Charged with "anti-Soviet agitation" and forming an "anti-Soviet" organization. Sentenced in August 1974 to 7 years in strict-regime camps and 2 years' exile.

OGURTSOV, IGOR (1937-): Translator and orientalist from Leningrad; co-founder of the "All-Russian Social-Christian Union for the Liberation of the People," which aimed at establishing a democratic state system. Arrested in 1967 during a purge of the group. Charged with "betrayal of the fatherland" (Art. 64, R.S.F.S.R. CC), with "anti-Soviet agitation and propaganda" (Art. 70) and with "creating an anti-Soviet organization" (Art. 72). Sentenced to 15 years' imprisonment and 5 years' exile. Served first 7 years of the sentence in Vladimir Prison, later transferred to one of the Perm camps.

ORLOV, YURI (1924-): Physicist; corresponding member of the Academy of Sciences of the Armenian S.S.R.; advocate of the human rights movement in the Soviet Union. Authored and signed countless statements and appeals on behalf of repressed dissidents, among them Sakharov, Solzhenitsyn, Plyushch, the priest Romanyuk, Dzhemilev, Kovalev, Osipov and numerous others. One of the founding members of the U.S.S.R. chapter of Amnesty International, which was recognized by that organization in Sept. 1974. On May 12, 1976, together with other well-known activists of the Soviet human rights movement, founded the Public Group to Promote the Implementation of the Helsinki Accords in the U.S.S.R., which he chaired since its inception. Arrested on Feb. 9, 1977 in an apparent crackdown on all Helsinki monitoring groups in the U.S.S.R.

OSIPOV, VLADIMIR (1938-   ): Russian publicist. Served a 7-year sentence (1961-1968) in Mordovia following his conviction under Articles 70 and 72 of the R.S.F.S.R. CC for organizing poetry readings in Moscow's Mayakovsky Square. In 1971 began publishing openly *Veche*, a Russian patriotic journal which dealt with questions of Slavophilism, Russian history, literature and art. Left editorship of the journal in 1974 under threat of arrest on charges of anti-Soviet activity, and began to publish, also openly, *Zemlya*, another journal. Spoke out also on behalf of many repressed dissidents. Arrested Nov. 28, 1974 for "anti-Soviet agitation," tried Sept. 24-26, 1975 and sentenced to 8 years' strict-regime camps.

PAULAITIS, PYATRAS (1904-   ): Lithuanian freedom fighter who fought both the Germans and the Soviets in the Lithuanian national underground. Educated in Italy, worked for some time in Germany and Portugal. Returned to Lithuania in 1938 where he worked as a teacher of Latin. Emigrated to Germany in 1940 after the Soviet occupation of Lithuania, but returned to Lithuania in 1941 and joined the anti-German underground movement. Co-edited *For Freedom*, an illegal newspaper, which protested against the crimes of the fascists. Arrested by the Gestapo in 1942 and sent to a concentration camp, from which he managed to escape. Following Soviet occupation of Lithuania in 1944, remained in the national underground, again editing an underground journal, *The Voice of Freedom*. Arrested by Soviet secret police in 1947 and sentenced to a 25-year prison term. Sentence commuted in 1956 to 10 years. Released in 1957, again arrested in 1958 and charged with nationalist propaganda and organization activities. Sentenced to 25 years in strict-regime camps.

PAVLENKOV, VLADLEN (1929-   ): History lecturer from Gorky. Dismissed from work in 1968 after the appearance of leaflets in Gorky calling on the people to "follow the Czech example." Arrested on Oct. 3, 1969 and charged with "circulating fabrications which defame the Soviet state" (Art. 190-1 of the R.S.F.S.R. CC). Charges could not be substantiated; was then subjected to a psychiatric examination. Judged to be of sound mind, was then charged with "anti-Soviet agitation" and with plans to form an "anti-Soviet organization" (Articles 70 and 72 of the R.S.F.S.R. CC). Sentenced to 7 years in strict-regime camps. While in camp participated in several protest hunger strikes and signed appeals to Soviet authorities for recognition of the political prisoner status. Transferred to Vladimir Prison in Dec. 1974.

PENSON, BORIS (1946-   ): Jewish artist. After authorities repeatedly denied his family permission to emigrate to Israel, Penson in 1970 joined 11 others in a plan to hijack a plane for an escape to Sweden. The entire group, including Penson, was arrested June 15, 1970 before it could carry out the plan. Penson was charged with "treason," as were others, and sentenced to 10 years' strict-regime labor camp. Authorities also confiscated his property, including his paintings and sketches. Incarcerated in a camp in the Mordovian A.S.S.R. Has joined other political prisoners in hunger strikes and other forms of protest. Recognized as a talented artist, some of his works have been exhibited in, among other places, New York and Israel.

PLAKHOTNYUK, MYKOLA (1936-) : Ukrainian physician. Active participant in the cultural renaissance in Ukraine in the 1960's; helped organize literary evenings while at the Kiev medical institute; active in defense of arrested Ukrainian intellectuals, especially Valentyn Moroz. Dismissed as senior research worker at the Kiev medical institute for writing in 1969 an open letter to a Soviet Ukrainian newspaper in which he defended the repressed Ukrainian poet Ivan Sokulsky and others. Arrested in January 1972 and charged with complicity in the preparation and dissemination of Ukrainian samizdat materials, including the journal *The Ukrainian Herald*. Judged to suffer from "schizophrenia with a persecution mania and periods of irresponsibility" by Serbsky Institute. Sentenced in absentia in Nov. 1972 by a Kiev court to an "indefinite period of treatment" in a special psychiatric hospital. Subjected—according to testimony of former political prisoner and fellow-inmate Leonid Plyushch—to forced drug "treatment" resulting in dangerous deterioration of his physical and mental state. In August 1976 Plakhotnyuk, reportedly suffering from advanced tuberculosis, was transferred to another special prison-type mental hospital in Kazan, Russian S.F.S.R.

PLUMPA-PLYUIRAS, PETRAS (1939-) : Lithuanian activist. Arrested at the age of 18 in 1958 and charged with planning to "overthrow the Soviet regime by means of force" after a search of his apartment uncovered a knife and a grenade without a percussion cap. Sentenced to 7 years' strict-regime camps. Following release, again arrested on Nov. 19, 1973 for preparing and distributing prayer books and other religious literature. Held without trial until December 1974, then charged with "organizational activity directed to commission especially dangerous crimes against the state" and with participating in "anti-Soviet organizations." Sentenced to 8 years' strict-regime camps and sent to one of the Perm colonies.

PLYUSHCH, LEONID (1939-) : Ukrainian mathematician, cyberneticist. Active participant in the civil rights movement; member of the Initiative Group for Defense of Human Rights in the U.S.S.R. Expelled from the Cybernetics Institute, Academy of Sciences of the Ukr.S.S.R., in 1968 for open letter he wrote in defense of Russian dissident Alexander Ginzburg. Arrested in January 1972 for "anti-

Soviet agitation and propaganda"; tried in camera in January 1973, and sentenced, on the basis of psychiatric examinations at the Serbsky Institute in Moscow, to an indefinite term in a special psychiatric hospital for treatment of "schizophrenia with messianic and reformist tendencies." Held from July 15, 1973, in special prison-type psychiatric hospital in Dnipropetrovsk until January 8, 1976, when he was released and allowed to leave the U.S.S.R., as a direct result of widespread protests on his behalf in the West.

PONOMARYOV, ANATOLI (1933-): Russian engineer from Leningrad; graduate of the Institute of Military Engineering. Attempted to obtain foreign publications, criticized Soviet policy and spoke out against the invasion of Czechoslovakia prior to his arrest in October 1970. Charged under Art. 190-1 of the R.S.F.S.R. CC with "circulating fabrications which defame the Soviet system." Sent on Jan. 29, 1971 to the Leningrad Special Psychiatric Hospital for compulsory treatment. Discharged in autumn 1973; again confined to a psychiatric institution on April 15, 1974. Released in June of that year. Arrested in Sept. 1974 and taken to a psychiatric hospital. Released in July 1975 as a direct result of intercession on his behalf by British psychiatrists. Following his release, wrote several open letters to Soviet authorities and Western leaders regarding violations of his personal rights. Re-arrested and again incarcerated in a psychiatric hospital on Oct. 25, 1975.

RODE, GUNAR (1934-): Latvian human rights activist. Arrested for membership in the underground "Baltic Federation." Sentenced in 1963 to a 15-year term of imprisonment. While serving his sentence in Mordovia, actively demanded recognition of political prisoner status. As punishment was transferred several times to Vladimir Prison.

ROITBURD, LEV (1936-): Jewish activist from Odessa; engineer. Applied unsuccessfully in 1972 for an exit visa. Subsequently dismissed from his job. Arrested on July 2, 1975 while boarding a plane for Moscow at Odessa airport. Sentenced on Aug. 25, 1975 to 2 years' general-regime camps.

ROMANYUK, VASYL (1922-): Ukrainian Orthodox priest. First arrested in 1944 for "nationalist-religious activity"; sentenced to 10 years' labor camp; family deported to Siberia. Protested against arrests and trials of Ukrainian intellectuals in the 1960's; removed from his parish in the village of Kosmach after he sent a letter to the Supreme Court of the Ukr.S.S.R. in defense of Valentyn Moroz in 1970. Arrested in January 1972; tried in July and sentenced to 10 years' special-regime labor camp and 5 years' exile for "anti-Soviet agitation and propaganda." On August 1, 1975, in a labor camp in the Mordovian A.S.S.R., declared a hunger strike in support of his demand to be allowed to have a Bible and in protest against persecution of dissidents; in the summer of 1975, wrote appeal to Pope Paul VI and to the World Council of Churches, asking for their intervention on behalf of those imprisoned for their defense of civil rights and religious freedom.

RONKIN, VALERI (-   ): Russian engineer from Leningrad; leading member of Marxist "Union of Communards." Arrested in a crackdown on the "Union" in June 1965 and sentenced to 7 years' strict-regime camps and 3 years' exile. Took part in various camp protests against the violation of prisoners' rights, for which he was transferred in 1963 to Vladimir Prison. Returned to the Leningrad region in 1975 upon completion of sentence.

RUDENKO, MYKOLA (1920-   ): Ukrainian poet, writer; graduate of the Philosophy Department of Kiev University; WWII veteran; published author of numerous poetry and prose collections. Became active in the human rights movement in Ukraine in the early 1960's, and later joined the U.S.S.R. chapter of Amnesty International. Detained in April 1975—following the arrest of A. Tverdokhlebov, the A. I. chapter's secretary—but released after several days. Addressed open letter to Brezhnev on July 3, 1975; subsequently dismissed from the party and expelled from the Writers' Union of Ukraine. At about this time authored *Ekonomichni Monolohy* (Economic Monologues), an extensive work on the incompatibility of Marxist theory with the laws of Nature. Confined in early 1976 for 2 months in a psychiatric hospital in Kiev, where he wrote a poem entitled *Medical Case History (The Diary of a Candidate of Schizophrenia)*, which became popular in the samizdat. Founded in Nov. 1976 the Kiev-based Ukrainian Public Group to Promote the Implementation of the Helsinki Accords. Arrested, together with O. Tykhy, another Ukrainian Group member, on Feb. 5, 1977. Sentenced to 7 years' imprisonment and 5 years' exile on June 30, 1977.

SADUNAITE, NIJOLE (1938-   ): Lithuanian activist. Arrested Aug. 24, 1974 for copying and distributing the underground *Chronicle of the Lithuanian Catholic Church*. Refused to testify before and during her trial, arguing she had not committed any criminal offense. Threatened with confinement in a psychiatric hospital. Tried June 16-17, 1975 on charge of "anti-Soviet agitation and propaganda" (Art. 68 of the Lith.S.S.R. CC); sentenced to 3 years' strict-regime camps and 3 years' exile. Imprisoned in a Mordovian camp. Participated in numerous camp protests against violations of political prisoners' rights.

SAFRONOV, ALEKSEI (1952-   ): Soviet army soldier. In Nov. 1970, while stationed in East Germany, attempted to cross the border into the West. Arrested and indicted for "treason" under Art. 64 of the R.S.F.S.R. CC. Tried in East Berlin and sentenced to 12 years' imprisonment. Participated in hunger strikes and other forms of protest while in a Perm camp; transferred Aug. 4, 1974 to Vladimir Prison for a 3-year punishment period.

SHAKHVERDYAN, BAGART (1940-): Armenian. Arrested May 19, 1973 for nationalist activities and charged with "anti-Soviet agitation and propaganda" and with participation in "anti-Soviet organizations." Sentenced in November 1973 to 5 years' strict-regime camps and 2 years' exile. In camp his insistence on using the Armenian language in official complaints and statements led to increased censorship and virtual suspension of his correspondence to force him to write in Russian. Signed numerous appeals demanding that prisoners be given the right to profess their religion, and demanded compliance with the Helsinki accords and recognition of political prisoner status.

SHIKHANOVICH, YURI (-): Russian mathematician from Moscow; author of several works on mathematics. Arrested on Sept. 28, 1972 and charged with "anti-Soviet agitation," apparently for distributing *The Chronicle of Current Events*. Subjected to compulsory psychiatric examination and diagnosed to be mentally ill during the pre-trial period, which extended for more than year. Although many of his friends as well as foreign mathematicians, among them members of the U.S. National Academy of Sciences, spoke out in his defense and called for an open trial—in Paris an "International Committee of Mathematicians for the Defense of Shikhanovich and Plyushch" was set up—he was tried in absentia in Moscow on Nov. 26, 1973. Sentenced to compulsory treatment in a psychiatric hospital of the general type in Yakhroma, near Moscow, where he remained until his release in July 1974. Freedom House awarded him its Freedom Prize on Dec. 4, 1973.

SIMUTIS, LYUDVIKAS (1935-): Lithuanian activist; member of the underground organization "Movement for the Freedom of Lithuania." Arrested in 1955 while bedridden in a hospital suffering from tuberculosis of the spine. Tried for his nationalist activities and sentenced to be shot; sentence commuted to 25 years' special-regime camps. Although a medical commission in 1958 ruled his illness incurable and recommended his release, he continued his sentence and was forced to do hard labor. In 1970, after 15 years of imprisonment, Simutis personally appealed to the Supreme Soviet, stating that although he did not feel sympathy towards the authorities, he renounced his struggle in view of its fruitlessness and asked to be released because of his poor health. The Chief Procuracy of the U.S.S.R. answered that there were no grounds for reconsidering the case.

SHKOLNIK, ISAAK (1937-): Jewish activist from Vinnytsya, Ukraine; metal worker. Arrested in July, 1972 and charged with "slandering the Soviet state" after expressing desire to emigrate to

Israel. Also accused of "espionage" for England, charge later altered to espionage for Israel. Despite the total lack of evidence he was indicted under Art. 56 of the Ukr.S.S.R. CC for "treason" and "anti-Soviet propaganda," tried by a military tribunal between March 29-April 11, 1973, and sentenced to 10 years' imprisonment. Sentence later commuted to 7 years' strict-regime camps.

SINYAVSKY, ANDREI (1925-): Russian writer and literary critic; former senior member of the Gorky Institute of World Literature, U.S.S.R. Academy of Sciences. Author of numerous novels, short stories and critiques, published in the West under the pseudonym "Abram Tertz." Works include *The Trial Begins, The Makepeace Experiment, On Socialist Realism* and, most recently, *A Voice From the Choir.* Arrested in Sept. 1965 together with the poet Yuli Daniel. Charged under Art. 70 of the R.S.F.S.R. CC with pseudonymously publishing in the West works of an "anti-Soviet" character. Sentenced in Feb. 1966 to 7 years in strict-regime camps. The trial of Sinyavsky and Daniel is viewed as having played a decisive role in the emergence of the Russian Democratic Movement. Released from Mordovia on Jun 8, 1971 after various appeals on his behalf. Received invitation to lecture at the Sorbonne, and emigrated to France in Aug. 1973.

SLEPAK, VLADIMIR (1927-): Jewish activist from Moscow; engineer; activist in the movement of Soviet Jews for the right to emigrate; member of the Public Group to Promote Implementation of the Helsinki Accords in the U.S.S.R. Authored numerous letters to Soviet and world leaders describing the difficulties encountered by Soviet Jews who want to emigrate.

SLIPYJ, JOSEPH (1892-): Ukrainian Major-Archbishop and Metropolitan of the Kiev-Galician See; Cardinal of the Roman Church; Proto-Hierarch of the Ukrainian Catholic Church. A long-time prisoner of the Gulag Archipelago, a symbol for Ukrainians of the unconquered spirit of their church. Ordained to priesthood on Sept. 30, 1917. Received Doctor of Sacred Theology degree from the Canisianium in Innsbruck, Austria in 1918. Author of numerous theological treatises; authority on subjects dealing with the spiration of the Holy Trinity. Consecrated Archbishop on Dec. 22, 1939. Became Metropolitan of the Galician Province on Nov. 1, 1944 after death of Metropolitan Andrew Sheptytsky. Arrested by the NKVD on Apr. 11, 1945, together with all other bishops in Soviet-occupied territory and sentenced to 8 years' hard labor March 1946. Resentenced to an indefinite term in 1953 and in 1957 sentenced—for a third time—to 7 years in prison. Spent part of sentence in Mordovia. Released on Feb. 9, 1963 through the intercession of Pope John XXIII; settled in Rome. As a Major-Archbishop acquired rights equivalent to those of a patriarch; appointed Cardinal of the Church by Pope Paul VI on Feb. 22, 1965. Founded Ukrainian Catholic University in Rome.

SOLZHENITSYN, ALEXANDER (1918-): Russian writer; Nobel Prize laureate for literature. Completed his education in mathematics at the University of Rostov just a few days before war with Germany broke out. Served in the Soviet army until February 1945, when—by then a highly decorated commander of a reconnaissance artillery battery—he was arrested for making "disrespectful comments" about Stalin in a letter to a school friend. While serving his 8-year sentence in concentration camps Solzhenitsyn developed cancer, which, by the time he was released in March 1953, was threatening his life. Was sent for treatment to a clinic in Tashkent and in 1954 was cured; the experience became the basis for his novel *Cancer Ward*. By 1956 Solzhenitsyn had completed his 3-year term of exile and in 1962, with support from the liberal publisher A. Tvardovsky, succeeded in getting published the novel *One Day in The Life of Ivan Denisovich*, based on his experiences in Soviet labor camps. But initial acclaim soon turned to official condemnation; *Ivan Denisovich* was to be his first and last work to be published officially in his own country. His works, though, became very popular in the samizdat. In October 1970 was awarded the Nobel Prize for literature but was not permitted to attend the presentation ceremony. Government harassment and pressure on Solzhenitsyn increased after *The Gulag Archipelago* was published in the West in 1973. Arrested in February 1974, stripped of his Soviet citizenship and deported to West Germany. In 1976 he and his family settled in the United States. Solzhenitsyn used royalties from his works published in the West to set up a fund to assist families of Soviet political prisoners.

SOROKA, MYKHAYLO (1911-1971): Ukrainian revolutionary; architect. Prior to WWII, spent 7 years in Polish jails for participating in organized resistance to Polish rule in western Ukraine. In 1940, shortly after Soviet invasion of western Ukraine and during the wave of arrests and deportations of Ukrainians suspected of opposing Soviet rule, arrested as a member of the leadership of the Organization of Ukrainian Nationalists. Sentenced to 8 years in concentration camps, which he served mainly in Vorkuta in the Far North. Released in 1948; arrested again 4 years later in exile in the Krasnoyarsk territory in central Siberia. Sentenced to death (commuted to a 25-year term) for organizing self-defense organizations among political prisoners during his imprisonment in the Vorkuta camps. Died on June 16, 1971 following heart attack in Camp No. 17A of the Dubrovlag camp complex, the Mordovian A.S.S.R. Spent a total of 36 years in prisons and concentration camps.

STASIV-KALYNETS, IRYNA (1940-): Ukrainian poetess; along with her husband, poet Ihor Kalynets, an active member of the group of nationally conscious intellectuals in Lviv. After the 1965-66 arrests of Ukrainian cultural and civic activists, Ihor Kalynets among them, she could no longer publish. Protested against Russification policies and violations of civil rights in Ukraine, which led to her dismissal from Lviv's Polytechnical Institute in 1970; especially active in defense of Valentyn Moroz; attended his trial in 1970 and wrote several protests to Soviet authorities. Arrested in early 1972; tried in July in Lviv on a charge of "anti-Soviet agitation and propaganda"; sentenced to 6 years' labor camp, 3 years' exile. Detained in a labor camp in the Mordovian A.S.S.R., where, though in very poor health, she is an active participant in protests and hunger strikes; co-author of several appeals to the U.N. and the world community.

SUPERFIN, GABRIEL (1943-   ): Russian literary scholar; author of several research works published in the Soviet Union and abroad; editor of the memoirs of the Soviet statesman A. Mikoyan. Arrested in July 1973 on charges of "anti-Soviet agitation" and participation in "anti-Soviet organizations" for alleged complicity in the publication of the samizdat journal *Chronicle of Current Events*, and presumably for editing the prison diary of Edward Kuznetsov. Moved from a Moscow prison to a prison in Orel, where he was kept in isolation and not permitted to meet with relatives or legal counsel. A Committee in Defense of Superfin was formed in the U.S. in Dec. 1973. Despite appeals for his release by the Committee and other American organizations, as well as Soviet human rights activists, Superfin was sentenced in May 1974 to 5 years' imprisonment and 2 years' exile. Transferred from a Perm camp to Vladimir Prison in 1975.

SVERSTYUK, YEVHEN (1928-   ): Ukrainian literary critic, writer. Member of the Psychological Association of the U.S.S.R. One of the leading supporters of the literary renaissance of the 1960's. Author of the popular samizdat essay *Sobor u ryshtovanni* (Cathedral in Scaffolding, 1968), in which he held up Oles Honchar's novel *Sobor* (The Cathedral) as an example of what Ukrainian literature could achieve if allowed to grow without repression. Imprisoned briefly during the 1965 wave of arrests. Active defender of other repressed intellectuals, especially Valentyn Moroz and Vyacheslav Chornovil; Dismissed from the Institute of psychology, Academy of Sciences of the Ukr.S.S.R. in 1969; arrested in January 1972; tried in March 1973 and sentenced to 7 years' imprisonment, 5 years' exile, on a charge of "anti-Soviet agitation and propaganda." Detained in a labor camp in Perm Region, the R.S.F.S.R.

SVITLYCHNA, NADIYA (1925-   ): Ukrainian philologist; sister of Ivan Svitlychny. Actively defended repressed Ukrainian intellectuals, among them her brother and Vyacheslav Chornovil; pressed for a thorough investigation of the mysterious murder of her friend, the artist Alla Horska, despite strong indications that the KGB was behind the crime. Arrested in April 1972 for possession of samizdat literature; tried in March 1973 on a charge of "anti-Soviet agitation and propaganda"; sentenced to 4 years' labor camp, which she served in a camp for female political prisoners near Barashevo, the Mordovian A.S.S.R. While in camp, co-authored several appeals to the U.N. and the world community, and wrote protest statement to the procurator-general of the U.S.S.R. Released in May 1976, but not permitted to return to her home city Kiev.

SVITLYCHNY, IVAN (1929-   ): Ukrainian literary critic, publicist, translator. Strong supporter of the group of young poets and writers of the sixties, the *shestydesyatnyky*, which brought him into disfavor with the authorities. Dismissed in 1964 from the Institute of Philosophy, Academy of Sciences of the Ukr.S.S.R., for a public speech at an evening in honor of Vasyl Symonenko, a leading poet of the *shestydesyatnyky* group who died in 1963; dismissed in 1965 from a position at a publishing house for his criticism of influential academician Bilodid; imprisoned for 8 months during the 1965-66 arrests in Ukraine and forbidden to publish. Active defender of others repressed for political reasons, especially Valentyn Moroz. Arrested again in January 1972; tried in closed court in March 1973 on a charge of "anti-Soviet agitation and propaganda"; sentenced to 7 years' labor camp, 5 years' exile. Incarcerated in labor camp VS 389/35 in Perm Region, the R.S.F.S.R., where he has been an active participant in protests and hunger strikes by political prisoners; in 1974 took part in a samizdat-organized interview of political prisoners.

TALANTOV, BORIS (1903-1971): Defender of freedom of religion in the U.S.S.R. Born in Kostroma into the family of a priest. Graduate of the Physics and Mathematics Faculty of the Kirov Pedagogical Institute. Arrested in June 1969 on a charge of "defaming the Soviet state" (Art. 190-1 of the .S.F.S.R. CC) and sentenced to 3 years' imprisonment. Charge based on his works in which he expounded the true position of religion and believers in the Soviet Union, among them *On the Destruction of Churches of Architectural Values* (1963) and the *Letter from 12 Believers of the Kirov Region to Patriarch Aleksei* (1969). In camp Talantov's health deteriorated sharply; he died in the prison hospital in Kirov on Jan. 4, 1971.

TERELYA, YOSYP (1942-   ): Ukrainian activist; born in the Trans-Carpathian Region. Served prison term in Ukraine on an unknown charge; escaped, and lived underground for 2 years. Caught, tried on a political charge, and in early 1968 transferred to a labor camp in Mordovia. Tried again for allegedly preparing leaflets espousing "Ukrainian nationalist propaganda" and given an additional 8-year term. Transferred in summer 1969 to Vladimir Prison on suspicion of trying to organize an escape. Transferred in 1975 to a psychiatric hospital in Chelyabinsk; released from hospital in April

1976. Held in a psychiatric hospital in Vynnytsya throughout November 1976. According to the Ukrainian Public Group to Promote the Implementation of the Helsinki Accords, Terelya "has spent 14 of the 33 years of his life in camps, prisons, and special psychiatric hospitals for his religious and nationalistic convictions." Rearrested in June 1977.

TSITLENOK, BORIS (1944-   ): Jewish activist from Moscow; participant in the movement of Jews to obtain permission to emigrate to Israel. Subjected to KGB harassment for his activities; on several occasions was placed under administrative arrest for periods of up to 15 days. Arrested in 1975 for participating in a demonstration in defense of Soviet Jews' right to emigrate. Sent to Krasnoyarsky krai for a 5-year term of internal exile.

TURCHIN, VALENTIN (-   ): Doctor of Physical and Mathematical Sciences; author of 65 scientific works in the field of physics and cybernetics; well-known activist in the human rights movement in the US.S.R. Published in 1969 *The Inertia of Fear*, a samizdat brochure which probes the question of liberalization of Soviet society. Coauthored in 1970 the letter *To the Leaders of the Party and the Government*, which appeals for the democratization of Soviet society. Has spoken out in defense of numerous repressed human rights activists, among them Academician A. Sakharov, for which he was first demoted at his job at the Institute for Automized Systems in the Building Industry, then dismissed in July 1974. Founding member of the U.S.S.R. chapter of Amnesty International; has served as its chairman since its inception. Invited to lecture at Columbia University in New York. In September 1977 was issued an exit visa and in October of that year left the U.S.S.R.

TVERDOKHLEBOV, ANDREI (1940-   ): Moscow physicist; author of scientific articles on electro-dynamics and elementary particles; former editor of the journal *Abstracts and Theoretical Physics;* one of the most outspoken human rights activists in the U.S.S.R. Has written numerous articles analyzing discrepancies between Soviet legislation and international conventions ratified by the Soviet Union. Cofounder of several human rights organizations in the U.S.S.R., among them the Moscow Human Rights Committee; "Group-73," a group of human rights activists which helped political prisoners and their families; and the Soviet chapter of Amnesty International. Co-editor of the samizdat journal *International Amnesty*, first issued in 1973. Publicly spoke out in support of numerous repressed dissidents, among them Plyushch, Shikhanovich, Osipov, Kovalev, as well as persecuted Baptist believers. Subjected to several searches during the winter of 1974-75. Arrested in Moscow on April 18, 1975. Tried April 14-15, 1976 on a charge of "circulating fabrications which defame the Soviet state." Sentenced to 5 years of exile; sent to Yakutia.

VASHCHENKO, DANIIL (1955-): Pentecostal Christian from Nakhodka, Primorsky krai; son of Bishop Grigori Vashchenko. Called up for military service on May 7, 1974, but refused to comply on the basis of his religious convictions. Sentenced on Aug. 6, 1974 to 3 years' general-regime camp.

VASHCHENKO, GRIGORI (1927-): Bishop of the Pentecostal Church in Nakhodka, Primorsky krai, whose father was imprisoned for his beliefs in 1942 and died in prison. Baptized in 1948; since 1952 active in the religious movement. Attacked in the Soviet press and interrogated by the KGB for his activities in connection with the evangelical faith. Arrested in 1961 for organizing religious communities and sentenced to 10 years' imprisonment. Released in 1964 as a direct result of appeals on his behalf both in the Soviet Union and abroad. Has attempted to receive permission to emigrate from the U.S.S.R. since April 1973.

VINS, GEORGI (1928-): Baptist leader in Ukraine. Vins' father, also a Baptist minister, died in a Soviet prison while serving his third term for missionary activity; his mother was also imprisoned for religious activity. One of the leaders of a grass-roots movement among Baptists in the U.S.S.R., which accused the officially sanctioned All-Union Council of Evangelical Christians and Baptists of "submitting to an atheist government" and of discouraging evangelism, and which in 1965 broke off to form its own organization, the Initiative Baptists. Arrested in 1966, charged with violating laws on the separation of church and state, and sentenced to 3 years' corrective labor camps. Returned to his ministry after his release; arrested again in March 1974 after 2 years of underground religious activity. Tried in Kiev in January 1975 on charges of "defaming the Soviet state" and "infringing on the rights of citizens under the guise of performing religious ceremonies"; sentenced to 5 years' strict-regime labor camp and 5 years' exile, with confiscation of property.

VORONEL, ALEXANDER (-   ): Jewish physicist from Moscow; active participant in the Jewish movement for emigration to Israel; former editor of the samizdat journal *Jews in the U.S.S.R.*, published since 1972. Authored and supported various appeals on behalf of those persecuted for wanting to emigrate. In Nov. 1974 was among nine Soviet Jews who sent an open letter to President Ford describing the government's repressive measures against would-be emigrants from the U.S.S.R. Also participated in protest actions, including hunger strikes against the forcible retention of Jewish scientists in the Soviet Union. Barred from participating in professional activities; detained by the KGB on June 24, 1974, and subjected to other kinds of official harassment. Granted permission to emigrate to Israel on Dec. 27, 1974.

VUDKA, YURI (1947-): Jewish activist from Ukraine. Tried in 1970 in Ryazan, the R.S.F.S.R., on a charge of "anti-Soviet agitation and propaganda" and sentenced to 7 years' imprisonment. Transferred in 1973 from a Perm Region labor camp to Vladimir Prison for insisting on his right to practice Judaism. While in Vladimir, went on a hunger strike to protest against denial of right to correspondence; participated in other protest actions by political prisoners. Released from Vladimir Prison in 1976 and allowed to emigrate to Israel.

YAKIR, PYOTR (1923-): Historian and prominent civil rights activist; member of the Initiative Group for the Defense of Human Rights in the U.S.S.R. Arrested at the age of 14 in 1937 because he was the son of a Soviet general who was executed that same year. Rehabilitated in 1956. His experiences of childhood imprisonment are described in his memoirs *A Childhood In Prison*. Has taken part in many activities in defense of human rights, sharply attacking the revival of Stalinism in the U.S.S.R. Arrested on June 21, 1972 and charged under Art. 70 of the R.S.F.S.R. CC with "anti-Soviet agitation and propaganda." Kept in pre-trial detention for 14 months; brought to trial on Aug. 27, 1973 together with V. Krasin. While both pleaded guilty, Yakir stated that his actions stemmed from the conviction that Stalin's crimes must not be repeated. Sentenced on Sept. 1, 1973 to 3 years' imprisonment and 3 years' exile; sentence was later commuted to 16 months' imprisonment and 3 years of exile. Officially pardoned and released on Sept. 16, 1974.

YAKOBSON, ANATOLI (-): Poet, translator, literary critic; member of the Initiative Group for the Defense of Human Rights in the U.S.S.R. Arrested on Dec. 21, 1969 for participating in an anti-Stalinist demonstration in Moscow. Tried for "petty hooliganism" and fined for violating public order. Subjected to repressive measures, including official threats of arrest, because of his activities in connection with the human rights movement. Emigrated in September of 1973.

YAUGELIS, VIRGILIUS (1948-): Lithuanian activist. Arrested on April 4, 1974 for having prepared and distributed prayer books and other religious literature. Indicted in December 1974 under Art. 199-1 of the Lithuanian S.S.R. CC for "circulating fabrications which defame the Soviet state," and sentenced to 2 years' strict-regime camps. Severely beaten in camp by criminal inmates; contracted cancer, but refused to be operated on in camp and demanded transfer to a civil hospital. Went on a hunger strike on May 2, 1975 to stress his demands. Released and allowed to return home May 7, 1975 in view of his health. Arrested again Dec. 9, 1975 for attempting to attend the trial of S. Kovalev, but released on Dec. 12, 1975, again in view of his poor health.

YESENIN-VOLPIN, ALEXANDER (1924-): Mathematician, poet and legal expert from Moscow. Formerly employed at Moscow's All-Union Research Institute for Scientific and Technical Information. Since 1949, subjected several times to compulsory treatment in Soviet psychiatric hospitals (for example in 1959, after he sent abroad a philosophical treatise and a collection of his poems, entitled *A Leaf of Spring*). Participated in the Dec. 5, 1965 demonstration in Moscow's Pushkin Square against the arrests of Sinyavsky and Daniel. Arrested Feb. 8, 1968 following his protests on behalf of Galanskov and Ginzburg; again forcibly interned in a psychiatric hospital. Released after 3 months as a result of a protest against his forced confinement, signed by 95 mathematicians. In 1970 he became legal consultant to the Moscow Human Rights Committee. Emigrated from the U.S.S.R. to the United States in 1972.

ZAND, MIKHAIL (-   ): Jewish literary scholar, specialist on the history of Persian and Tadzhik literature. Employed at the U.S.-S.R. Academy of Sciences' Institute for the Peoples of Asia in Moscow; dismissed for his public statements in defense of civil rights. Arrested in March 1971 and detained for 15 days, which he spent on a hunger strike protesting his detention. Granted exit visa and emigrated to Israel on June 24, 1971.

ZARYTSKA, KATERYNA (1914-): Ukrainian revolutionary. First imprisoned in the late 1930's by Polish authorities for her part in an assassination attempt by Ukrainian nationalists on a Polish government official. Arrested again by Soviet authorities in 1939 following the Soviet occupation of western Ukraine. Gave birth to a son, Bohdan, while in a prison in Lviv. Her husband Mykhaylo Soroka was also arrested at that time, and later spent 29 years in Soviet prisons and labor camps for Ukrainian nationalism. Soroka died in a Mordovian camp in 1971. After her initial arrest by Soviet authorities, Zarytska was released and returned to underground activity. Helped organize the Red Cross for the Ukrainian Insurgent Army, which fought the Germans during the war and continued to oppose Soviet occupation of Ukraine after the war; also served as courier. Arrested in 1947 for her role in the Ukrainian underground and sentenced to death; sentence commuted to 25 years' imprisonment. Spent more than 20 years in Vladimir Prison; transferred in spring of 1969 to a labor camp in the Mordovian A.S.S.R. Released in 1972 upon completion of full term.

ZDOROVY, ANATOLIY (1938-): Ukrainian physicist from Kharkiv. Sentenced in 1972 to 7 years' imprisonment for "anti-Soviet agitation and propaganda." Term reduced to 4 years on appeal, but later reinstated in full following procurator's protest against reduction. Served part of sentence in Camp No. 36 in Perm Region, then transferred to Vladimir Prison as punishment for his continued protests, especially his demand to be given political prisoner status. Has joined other political prisoners at Vladimir in hunger strikes and other protests against prison conditions.